Advance praise for *Brothe*

There is a mysterious connection between the saints and us. We all have our favorite saints that we pray to often, and serve as models in our life. However, we don't pick our favorite saints. The saints in Heaven have chosen us. Melanie's book is an invitation to allow some saints that you might know such as St Damien of Molokai, but also saints that are less known such as Hyacinth of Poland. Let these friends of God open the door to you to learn about them, and be inspired by them. Let them choose you. We are surrounded by a great cloud of heavenly witnesses cheering us on.

—Father Stefan Starzynski, author, *Miracles: Healing for a Broken World*

Brotherhood of Saints is a great book. It highlights the lives of 365 of the over 10,000 Saints who came from many different backgrounds and life situations. This book verifies the biblical passage: "For the body does not consist of one member but of many" (1 Corinthians 12:14). What is neat about the book is that every person who reads it can identify with one or more saints. If you want to get inspired, this book of daily readings fits the bill.

—Phil Kiko, former lay director, Diocese of Arlington, Virginia Cursillo

I highly recommend *Brotherhood of Saints* for your daily inspiration. For the past several years, I have been using Melanie Rigney's *Sisterhood of Saints* which reminds me everyday of the gifts God gives all kinds of different people. I see *Brotherhood* as a great companion to that book. Every saint has a short one-page bio and a word of inspiration either from scripture or from the saint's own words. Each day has a challenge to grow. This is the perfect combination of contemplation and action. You will be blessed by following the saints each day.

—Father Horace "Tuck" Grinnell, Diocese of Arlington, Virginia

For many, if not most, of us the idea of achieving sainthood is a real stretch. Saints are very pious, very holy, good in every way. Or maybe not. In this book Melanie Rigney tells relatable stories of people who weren't always so different from us. She superbly connects each story to some brief words to ponder during your day and a meaningful challenge to help you on your own journey toward sainthood. *Brotherhood of Saints: Daily Guidance and Inspiration* is an enriching gem that you will turn to often.

—Vince Stricherz, Seattle, Wash.

Melanie Rigney serves up a delicious stew that really does provide guidance and inspiration. Scores of male saints, one for each day, are offered for our instruction and edification. Some of them are household names, others are not. But all are in Heaven, interceding for us close to the Most Holy Trinity and the Holy Family of Nazareth. The "Challenge" from every entry is just that: an inviting summons to answer, not unlike those embraced by the saints listed. Have at this tasty meal, and please help yourself to seconds.

—Monsignor Charles M. Mangan, Diocese of Sioux Falls, South Dakota

Catholics are familiar with saints like Apostles Peter and Paul and Francis of Assisi because many religious institutions are named for them. However, there are many saints unknown to most Catholics. In *Brotherhood of Saints*, as she did in *Sisterhood of Saints*, Melanie Rigney introduces lesser-known saints as well as familiar ones in three-part daily readings. The first part explains why they became saints, the second what inspired their saintly acts, and the third challenges readers to emulate them. For example, Maximillian Kolbe was a Franciscan priest killed August 14, 1941 at the Nazi concentration camp Auschwitz after volunteering to replace a married prisoner picked for execution. Under *Inspiration* is his quote: "A single act of love makes the soul return to life." The *Challenge* is "Set an example of sacrifice for Christ that will inspire others." The readings introduce interesting male saints along with daily doses of spirituality.

—Michael V. Uschan, author, *Pope Francis (People in the News)*

Saints have not always lived under halos or in stained-glass windows. Melanie Rigney's study of these "brothers" brings you inside their lives to encounter how they connect with each other and with us. You will learn that Jesuits Ignatius, John, and Francis Xavier counted John of Avila as a key influence on their lives. The same John of Avila was spiritual director to John of the Cross and Teresa of Ávila! Plus, Ignatius and Francis took on another saint-to-be as a roommate! Meet the Franciscans: Charles, Felipe, Egidio, Ludovico, and Amato Ronconi (only three when the canonization of Francis of Assisi inspired him). Mingle with Bernardino, Anthony of Padua, Junípero Serra, Bonaventure, and others to find on your own. Connect with the Benedictines—Wulfstan, Ildephonsus, Robert of Molesme, Thomas Aquinas, Boniface, and Benedict of Nursia—who also are "breathing, flawed vessels of humanity." *Brotherhood* inspires us with stories, quotes, and prayers to show how even the most pious and holy people started as human as you and me. Whether you read this cover-to-cover or take it as designed in day-by-day installments, you'll come away knowing those who inspired each other as they continue to inspire us today.

—Anthony DeCristofaro, Catholic blogger

Brotherhood of Saints

DAILY GUIDANCE
AND INSPIRATION

Melanie Rigney

franciscan
media®
Cincinnati, Ohio

Cover and book design by Mark Sullivan

Library of Congress Control Number: 2020943512

ISBN 978-1-63253-305-0

Published by Franciscan Media
28 W. Liberty St.
Cincinnati, OH 45202
www.FranciscanMedia.org

Printed in the United States of America.
Printed on acid-free paper.
20 21 22 23 24 25   5 4 3 2 1

For my uncles John T. and Craig Smith, whose examples of faith-filled living and love of their families have inspired me for as long as I can remember. In different ways, you showed and continue to show me what it means to be Catholic. Thank you! Bless you!

Every saint has a past, and every sinner has a future.

—Oscar Wilde

PREFACE

Quick, who do you think of when you think of the male saints? Joseph? Peter? Paul? Maximilian Kolbe? John XXIII? John Paul II? Patrick? Benedict? Francis of Assisi? One of the many, many Johns?

Oh, you'll find them in these pages: apostles, popes, desert fathers, order founders, martyrs, Doctors of the Church. But you'll also find the stories of quieter men. Men like Daniel Comboni, who burned to be a missionary to Africa, only to find out the way he thought it should be done, top down, wasn't going to work. Men like Nicholas of Flüe, who somehow managed to get his wife's buy-in and become a wandering pilgrim, even though the youngest of their ten children was only a few months old. Men like Filippo Smaldone, whose seminary tests suffered because he was already working with the deaf community in poverty-stricken areas of his hometown.

I've written several books on women saints, starting with this one's companion, *Sisterhood of Saints: Daily Guidance and Inspiration*. At one point as I was writing that book, I held a relic of St. Elizabeth Ann Seton, and she told me this: "Listen, and you will find your vocation."

Unlike the women, I found it took a whole lot of listening, months in some cases, for the quiet men to talk to me. Once they did, I heard stories that I hope will move and inspire you.

Behind those stoles and miters and vestments are men just like you and me. They lost parents when they were young. They had trouble at the office, whether that office was a cathedral or an abbey or a hospital. They suffered heartache and physical aches and pains, and not just the martyrs. For at least some of them, the pain was over relatively quickly. Some of the others, like us, lived with pain for years.

Consider this book a gateway drug—a positive one. My prayer is that you'll reconnect with your name saint or your confirmation saint or someone else who has inspired you along the way. But I also pray that you'll find a man you've never heard of and that this taste of his life will intrigue you enough to find out more. We're blessed to live in a time when many of these men's writings and contemporary or close to contemporary biographies are available online, and almost always translated.

Each day, you'll find a short synopsis of a saint's life as it might relate to you, today's reader; something from Scripture, his writings, or something else relevant; and a challenge item that won't cost you anything but time, talent, or maybe pride. Each reading shouldn't take you more than ten minutes, but I hope the story will stay with you all day.

Whenever possible, you'll find the saint on his feast day. In cases where several men shared a date, I tried to place them all close to the date, but that wasn't always possible.

Just as our spiritual journeys are greatly influenced by those we love,

canonized or otherwise, so were those of our saints. As a result, if another saint in this book is referenced in an entry, you'll find the date for his story in parentheses after his name.

Don't worry if you're not starting on January 1, or if life intervenes and you miss a day or a week. Just open to a random page—and listen.

—Melanie Rigney

Zygmunt Gorazdowski

November 1, 1845–January 1, 1920

Zygmunt didn't have to travel far to be a missionary of Christ. Born in what is now Poland, he went to law school about a hundred miles away, and after two years, determined he had a vocation as a male religious. After serving as a vicar and administrator in a few other parishes, he returned to the city where he had gone to law school, Lviv. Zygmunt remained at the parish of St. Nicholas for forty years until three years before his death, establishing homes for the poor and single mothers and their children, a school, soup kitchen, and more. He also wrote a number of catechetical works, and established a community of women religious.

People in our own backyards need our help, and while financial contributions are wonderful, coins and e-currency are no substitute for a smile at the intake desk or across the serving table. Let's endeavor to remember that we may be Christ's face to neighbors whose names we will never know.

⌦ Inspiration

Every creature loves its like,
  and every person the neighbor. (Sirach 13:15)

⌦ Challenge

Spend in-person time with someone who needs it.

Basil the Great

Circa 329–379

Basil was surrounded by a cloud of saints from birth. Both of his parents, Basil the Elder and Emmelia, are regarded as saints. So are his maternal grandmother, Macrina the Elder, with whom he spent much time as a child; a sister; and three brothers. Indeed, his brother Gregory (of Nyssa) (*January 10*) and their friend Gregory Nazianzen (*January 3*) and Basil are known as the Cappadocian Fathers; all three are Doctors of the Church. Basil's body of writings is vast, from sermons to doctrine to prayers.

Imagine what meals and prayer time must have been like in this family! While not all of us may go on to be formally canonized, we can build a domestic church with those we love.

Inspiration

There would be neither rich nor poor if everyone, after taking from his wealth enough for his personal needs, gave to others what they lacked. (St. Basil the Great)

Challenge

Devote conversation at one meal this week to sharing the favorite prayers of all those at the table.

Gregory Nazianzen

Circa 329–389

Gregory Nazianzen is called "The Theologian" for his writings on topics such as Jesus's divinity and the doctrine of the Holy Trinity. He is known for his clear, concise summations. But some of Gregory Nazianzen's most beautiful writings come not in theological treatises, but in eulogies and other works that touch on his family. You see, his mother, Nonna, was responsible for the conversion of her husband, and raised their three children as Christians. All five are saints.

Sometimes, we do our work for Christ in our very own homes. Let's learn from the model that Nonna and her husband (Gregory the Elder) set for their children, and the gratitude and love that Gregory Nazianzen expressed for them.

✒ Inspiration

For the most excellent of men and of women were so united that their marriage was a union of virtue rather than of bodies…because in virtue they were quite equally matched. (St. Gregory Nazianzen)

✒ Challenge

Consider who in your family (or someone who's like family) most influenced your religious path in the past year. Write that person a thank you note or better still, spend an afternoon with him or her if that is possible.

Charles of Mount Argus

December 11, 1821–January 5, 1893

He was a stranger in a strange land nearly all his adult life. Charles went into the military at nineteen, but didn't fit in there. He did, however, learn of the Passionist community of priests, and determined he had a vocation. Just about a year after his ordination, he was sent to England, and would never return to the Netherlands, where he had grown up. In 1857, he was assigned to the new Mount Argus monastery in Dublin. Charles never completely mastered the English language, but his kindly ways, compassion in the confessional, and ability to cure the sick more than made up for that.

We all feel out of place from time to time: We move to a new city, switch schools or jobs, adjust to new ministries. When we show compassion and vulnerability and trust in the Lord's plan, we often find our new "home" as welcoming as Ireland became for Charles.

❧ Inspiration

Therefore, live in the fear of the Lord and flee from anything that would give the slightest offense to God; he is the Most Holy One, and he sees everything. (St. Charles of Mount Argus)

❧ Challenge

Welcome a stranger—the new person at work or in the neighborhood—as Christ does.

John Neumann

March 28, 1811–January 5, 1860

John knew he was called to be a priest. But he could not have had any idea how rich—and busy—his twenty-four years of vocation would be. He left what is now the Czech Republic for New York in 1836 because there was a surplus of priests at home and no more were being ordained. Three weeks after his arrival, he was ordained and sent to upstate New York. He found the work isolating, and a few years later became a Redemptorist, working primarily among German Catholics in the Mid-Atlantic. John was just forty-one and had been a priest for sixteen years when he was consecrated as bishop of Philadelphia. His seven years as bishop saw construction of dozens of churches, hospitals, and orphanages. In 1977, he became the first U.S. Catholic bishop and male U.S. citizen to be canonized.

John's accomplishments included the first diocesan school system in the United States. He mastered a number of languages to better communicate with immigrants under his spiritual care. He shows us the importance of engaging people in Christ's name, rather than solely sitting behind a desk.

Inspiration

My God, possess me that I may become a fit instrument of your graces and mercies to the souls you have confided to my care. (St. John Neumann)

Challenge

What souls are confided to your care: your family? Your employees? Your friends? Ask one of them how you can be more helpful.

André Bessette

August 9, 1845–January 6, 1937

It's not surprising that André (born Alfred) had a special devotion to St. Joseph *(March 19)*. Both his parents had died by the time he was twelve. The boy was adopted by an uncle, who worked him hard as a farmhand. When he was twenty-five, André entered the Congregation of the Holy Cross. He kept a statue of St. Joseph on his windowsill and frequently was found in prayer there at night. His congregation had long wanted to buy land on Montreal's Mount Royal, but the owner wouldn't budge until after André and others planted St. Joseph medals there. André saved up about two hundred dollars and built a small chapel where the St. Joseph Oratory Basilica now stands. He met with people in the chapel or went to their homes to pray with them, and many healings were reported. In August 1924 when the basilica's cornerstone was blessed, Brother André celebrated the fiftieth anniversary of his perpetual vows.

Losing a parent is hard at any age, and some of us had or have less than loving relationships with our living relatives. André's story reminds us that St. Joseph and the Blessed Virgin yearn to fill those voids and protect and love us.

Inspiration

Then Joseph got up, took the child and his mother, and went to the land of Israel. (Matthew 2:21)

Challenge

Take a problem you're not comfortable sharing with anyone to St. Joseph.

Raymond of Peñafort

Circa 1175-January 6, 1275

He was sixty-five, and he thought that was old enough to retire. Indeed, Raymond had written into his revision of the Dominican constitution that sixty-five was the age when master generals would step down. He'd held the office for two years, and earlier was a noted philosopher, canon law expert, and confessor to the pope. But it turned out Raymond was nowhere near retirement. He continued his work to convert Muslims to Christianity for another thirty-five years!

People often tell us we're too old or too young or too something to carry out a particular ministry. Their advice may or may not be well founded. It's important to hear them out, but ultimately, we look to God for guidance in our decisions.

Inspiration

"Blessed is that slave whom his master will find at work when he arrives." (Luke 12:43)

Challenge

Attempt not to judge someone's ability based on physical aspects.

Apollinaris the Apologist

Died circa 180

It had been an amazing victory by Roman Emperor Marcus Aurelius's forces over a Germanic tribe. But Apollinaris, a bishop in what is now Turkey, took the opportunity to advance the cause of Christianity. It was not merely the soldiers' bravery and tactics that won the day, he argued; it was also the fact that a particularly brave unit was made up primarily of Christians, who prayed beforehand. Apollinaris also credited a rainstorm that blinded the enemy and provided water to the Roman forces. The bishop is considered one of the first Christian apologists, those who defend the faith verbally and in writing.

Apologists are always prepared to explain the faith to those who deny Christ or, charitably, perhaps don't understand him. As Christians, it's part of our responsibility to be prepared to discuss our faith intelligently, as Apollinaris did. That means diving into scripture and Sacred Tradition and other tools.

Inspiration

We destroy arguments and every proud obstacle raised up against the knowledge of God, and we take every thought captive to obey Christ. (2 Corinthians 10:4-5)

Challenge

In addition to some of the great saint apologists and apologetics, consider delving into the work of their modern counterparts such as Peter Kreeft, G.K. Chesterton, or Scott Hahn to prepare yourself for battle.

Charles of Sezze

October 19, 1613–January 6, 1670

His Italian parents had a plan for Charles: He would become a priest. They prayed for this when he was but a child, dressing him in a habit of sorts. But while Charles became a Franciscan friar, he never was ordained. Instead, he chose what he saw was the humbler life, which included serving as a porter, sacristan, beggar, and gardener. Charles was subjected to a number of trials, including once setting a kitchen on fire, and receiving the stigmata—but his time was also filled with blessings such as counsel from a number of saints. Though his formal education was limited, he wrote numerous works, including a treatise on meditation and contemplation, and an autobiography that still makes for lively reading today.

Of course we should listen to our loved ones' hopes and dreams for us. But ultimately, it's best to heed God's desire for us, even if it conflicts with what we, our parents, or others think would be best.

Inspiration

The blessed God does not command us to live dressed in hair-shirts and chains, or to chastise our flesh with scourges, but to love him above all things and our neighbor as ourselves. (St. Charles of Sezze)

Challenge

Say yes to a small thing—maybe a new ministry opportunity, or a different prayer style—that those around you don't understand.

Gregory of Nyssa

Circa 330–395

To have been among the youngest children in this deep-thinking, holy Turkish family must have been difficult at times. Gregory started his adult life as a teacher of rhetoric, but was convinced by others to enter religious life. (Gregory; his older brother Basil *(January 2)*; and their friend Gregory Nazianzen *(January 3)* are known as the Cappadocian Fathers for their writings in the early Church.) Gregory lacked the administrative and oratory skills of the other two, and actually was removed from his bishopric for two years. Not long after Gregory returned home, Basil and an older sister died within a year of each other. At that time, Gregory seems to have come into his own as a theologian. He is known for his study of the Holy Trinity and his writings on God's limitless nature.

It's hard when you have siblings or parents who possess a particular skill or charism, and everyone expects your gifts to be the same. With time, Gregory found the way God desired him to serve. May we all find the same patience and listen to what God wants and not attempt to turn ourselves into cookie cutters of those we admire.

✺ Inspiration

I praise you, for I am fearfully and wonderfully made. (Proverbs 139:14)

✺ Challenge

Don't compare yourself, positively or negatively, with anyone today.

Tommaso da Cori

June 4, 1655–January 11, 1729

The life of a hermit spoke to Tommaso, but so did the life of a shepherd. After all, that was how he had spent his early years, helping his parents tend their sheep. (They died when he was fourteen, and he sold off the sheep to raise money for his two sisters' dowries before he entered the Order of Friars Minor.) Not long after his ordination, Tommaso heard his community was beginning a hermitage in a nearby Italian town, and he requested assignment there. He spent most of the rest of his years there, but in a way that sounds to us rather unusual for a hermit. While he lived in his small cottage, he did not stay there all the time. Indeed, Tommaso became known for his commonsense preaching style throughout the small villages in the area.

The idea of being a hermit appeals to many of us—in theory. Oh, to get away from the world and devote oneself exclusively to prayer and contemplation! But for most of us, ministry also involves active evangelization. Tommaso's story shows us a balance can be struck regardless of our core spirituality (and personality).

Inspiration

He said to them, "Come away to a deserted place all by yourselves and rest a while." (Mark 6:31)

Challenge

You likely can't spend an entire day in solitude. But try unplugging from social media for an hour before you go to Mass the next time. Consider whether your focus on the Eucharist is richer.

Antonio Maria Pucci

April 16, 1819–January 12, 1892

This saint's father was a parish sacristan, but he fought his son's desire to become a priest. Maybe it was because the family was impoverished, and the father needed help in the fields. Maybe the father just didn't think his son had a vocation or was not cut out for the priestly life. In any event, he was wrong. Antonio was ordained as a Servite priest when he was twenty-four, and was pastor of the same parish for more than forty years. Known as "the little parish priest" for his physical size, his heart and soul were huge in the way he ministered for the poor, the elderly, the young, and the sick.

Antonio's father likely rejoiced that he was wrong about God's plans for his son. In the same way, may we be careful in judging the choices of those younger than us. Perhaps they understand the Lord's desires better than we do.

✎ Inspiration

Beloved, let us love one another, because love is from God; everyone who loves is born of God and knows God. (1 John 4:7)

✎ Challenge

Listen to a young person's dreams about the future without attempting to provide a reality check.

Hilary of Poitiers

Circa 315–367

It just didn't make sense. Hilary had been raised in a wealthy pagan family, had a wife and a daughter, Abra, whom he loved deeply. But life just didn't make sense without a greater purpose. Eventually, Hilary turned to the Old and New Testaments, and found his answer, in particular when he read the exchange in Exodus 3 when God tells Moses, "I am who I am." Hilary and his family were baptized when he was about thirty-five, and three years later, he became bishop of his hometown in France. (Priestly celibacy was not a requirement at that time.) Hilary used his intellect and convert's fire to fight with words those who disagreed with Church teachings in particular on the Holy Trinity, and was named a Doctor of the Church in 1852. Abra, who died before her father, also is regarded as a saint.

As Catholics, we know that conversion is not a once-in-a-lifetime event. Many events and encounters offer the opportunity to deepen our belief and reliance on the Lord. It's a special joy when, like Hilary, we find that those moments also are experienced by those we love.

✒ Inspiration

I know, O Lord God Almighty, that I owe you, as the chief duty of my life, the devotion of all my words and thoughts to yourself. (St. Hilary of Poitiers)

✒ Challenge

Journal about conversion moments you've had in the past few months.

Paul the Hermit

Circa 229–342

Initially, the Egyptian desert was a place of escape for Paul; the twenty-two-year-old's brother-in-law was going to report him as a Christian so as to gain more of the family estate. But Paul found the solitary life brought him closer to God, and so he stayed for more than ninety years. What we know about Paul, believed to be the first Christian hermit, comes from St. Jerome *(September 30)*, who wrote about an encounter between Paul and St. Anthony of Egypt *(January 17)*.

Escape. Sometimes, our desire to get away from situations isn't avoidance, but Spirit-inspired for our own physical or spiritual safety. Like Paul, it may be that living in a way that others find puzzling—few possessions, service to those less fortunate than us, hours of contemplation—is exactly what's desired of us.

Inspiration

He sustained him in a desert land,
in a howling wilderness waste;
he shielded him, cared for him,
guarded him as the apple of his eye. (Deuteronomy 32:10)

Challenge

Identify your desert, and consider why God has placed you there.

Joseph Cafasso

January 15, 1811–June 23, 1860

Joseph was a firm believer in the power of penance—and reconciliation. The Italian was known as the priest of the gallows because of his ministry to the condemned. In at least one case, more than five dozen men whose confessions Joseph had heard offered their impending executions as their penance; the priest assured them this would win them places in heaven. Joseph is also known for his lifelong friendship with St. John Bosco *(January 31)*; Joseph was just four years older, and served as John's spiritual director for nineteen years.

Do you really believe your sins are washed away after you finish your penance? Remember, that's why it's called the sacrament of penance and reconciliation. If Joseph's condemned men could believe it, surely, we can embrace this gift as well.

✒ Inspiration

"For if you forgive others their trespasses, your heavenly Father will also forgive you…" (Matthew 6:14)

✒ Challenge

Go to confession. Give thanks for God's forgiveness.

Joseph Vaz

April 21, 1651–January 16, 1711

When Indian-born Joseph arrived in what is now Sri Lanka in 1686, he found a place where Catholics had been gathering for decades without a priest. The island was controlled by the Dutch government, and Calvinism was the only religion allowed. But Joseph had known that going in, and relished his assignment to serve Catholics and evangelize, even though he had to begin in secret. Three years later, he relocated to an independent kingdom in the middle of the island, which was more tolerant of Catholics, especially after 1696 when the area was hit by a drought that ended when Joseph prayed publicly for rain. By the time of his death, it's estimated Sri Lankan Catholics numbered seventy thousand.

God's plans for us sometimes seem daunting, and we can't see any way we can be successful. Joseph's example shows us that if we trust him, miraculous things (including rain storms!) can happen.

Inspiration

The priest replied, "Go in peace. The mission you are on is under the eye of the Lord." (Judges 18:6)

Challenge

Pray for God to show you how to best use the tools provided to you.

Anthony of Egypt

251–356

It was a Mass like any other Mass for the young Egyptian who had come into a great deal of wealth after his parents' death. But then Anthony heard Jesus's words to sell his possessions and follow for what seemed to be the first time. Unlike the young man who encountered Jesus and went away sorrowful, Anthony embraced the challenge. He rid himself of his wealth and went to live in solitude. Eventually, he would organize the first Christian monastery, where the monks saw each other only at worship. Anthony occasionally re-entered society to battle Christian persecutions and heresies. We also know him for his writings about his fights with the devil.

A lifelong Christian, Anthony had heard Matthew 19:21 dozens or hundreds of times. But one day, he not only heard but listened to the words, and his life was changed forever. May we also open our hearts and souls to scripture and other sacred teachings, regardless of how familiar we think we are with them.

✎ Inspiration

Jesus said to him, "If you wish to be perfect, go, sell your possessions, and give the money to the poor, and you will have treasure in heaven; then come, follow me." (Matthew 19:21)

✎ Challenge

Spend your prayer time today with a New Testament verse you can recite by heart.

Wulfstan

Circa 1008–1095

In 1066, the Norman Conquest of England was complete. William the Conqueror had no use for English-born bishops—except one. That was Wulfstan, a Benedictine priest and bishop of the diocese of Worchester for four years. Tradition is that the bishop put his crozier into the tomb of King Edward and said since he had been appointed by Edward, only Edward could remove him. No one but Wulfstan could extract the crozier. He and William went on to have a cordial relationship.

Wulfstan stood his ground, but in a way that demonstrated his faith rather than confronting William over whether or not he had the right to remove him. Let's remember that being combative isn't the only way to go about showing our confidence in God.

Inspiration

"See, I am sending you out like sheep into the midst of wolves; so be as wise as serpents and innocent as doves." (Matthew 10:16)

Challenge

Show innocence and wisdom today as you navigate a difficult conversation.

Fabian

Circa 200–January 20, 250

We don't know why Fabian, a Roman countryman of little note, came into town to watch the election of a pope to succeed Anterus, who had died after just forty days in office. But when a dove landed on Fabian's head, it was seen as a sign from the Holy Spirit, and the election quickly concluded. Fabian served for fourteen years before being martyred in the Decian persecutions.

It's probably happened to all of us—we show up for a meeting or other gathering, and all of a sudden, we're in charge of something. (Or, we're put in charge of something because we didn't attend the meeting.) That old saying is true: God doesn't always call the qualified, but he qualifies the called.

❧ Inspiration

"Before I formed you in the womb I knew you,
and before you were born I consecrated you;
I appointed you a prophet to the nations." (Jeremiah 1:5)

❧ Challenge

Refrain from complaining about a commission you feel unqualified to take on.

Sebastian

Died circa 288

Put aside the legend that Sebastian survived being shot with a round of arrows and left for dead, and faced down Emperor Diocletian and was killed sometime soon after that. Put aside the legend that he entered the Roman army in hopes of converting soldiers to Christianity. Whether those stories are true does not diminish his martyrdom—or the inspiration millions have received over the centuries from artwork depicting his persecution.

We all have a way of embellishing stories—how far we walked to school in the snow, how big that fish we caught was. The same happens with some stories of the saints. But behind the fanciful tales typically is a big truth: Sebastian was martyred for the faith. That's a fact that should resonate regardless of the details.

Inspiration

I gave my back to those who struck me,
  and my cheeks to those who pulled out the beard;
I did not hide my face
  from insult and spitting. (Isaiah 50:6)

Challenge

Turn the other cheek today.

Arnold Janssen

November 5, 1837–January 15, 1909

Arnold became a priest at twenty-three, and initially found his vocation as a science and math teacher, then as his diocese's prayer director. But he kept hearing a need to reach people beyond his German home, and started up a monthly magazine about missionary work. Arnold became a missionary of sorts himself when Germany's anti-Catholic Kulturkampf policies took him to a nearby city in the Netherlands, where he established what would become the Divine Missionaries community. Within three and a half years, the first two "graduates" left for China. Arnold also was involved in a congregation of women missionaries and a cloistered community focused on adoration and praying for missionaries.

Imagine being forced out of your homeland due to government persecution. While we who live in the United States are unlikely to experience that in our lifetimes, government policies threaten Catholic beliefs about the value of life. Like Arnold, may we forge on, undiscouraged, doing God's work.

❧ Inspiration

May the holy Triune God live in our hearts and in the hearts of all people. (Arnold Janssen)

❧ Challenge

Pray for today's missionaries around the world.

Vincent Pallotti

April 21, 1795–January 22, 1850

Vincent was a priest who thought building up the Church involved everyone, not just clerics. It was a somewhat novel point of view for the time, that the laity had critical roles in the body of Christ beyond receiving the sacraments. This Italian priest helped to bring all facets of the Church together through the foundation of the Society of the Catholic Apostolate, as well as by establishing workers' guilds, trade schools, and more. He also worked to bring the Eastern and Latin churches together and for the return of the Church of England.

Scandals within the Church can tempt us to turn away from an active role. But the imperfections of the ordained make it all the more important that the laity raise our voices and hands in the Church's future.

Inspiration

Finally, all of you, have unity of spirit, sympathy, love for one another, a tender heart, and a humble mind. (1 Peter 3:8)

Challenge

Do one thing this week to build up your parish.

Ildephonsus

Circa 607–January 23, 667

You may not have heard of this saint, but he is well known to Spanish Catholics. Ildephonsus had a harmonious life as a Benedictine monk, including close to ten years as Toledo's bishop. In Spain, he is known for his devotion to the Blessed Virgin—legend has it that she gave him a chasuble unlike any ever seen before to thank him for his devotion. He also wrote numerous documents about her, including *On the Perpetual Virginity of Holy Mary.*

Mary wants nothing more than to bring us closer to her son. Our model for humility and surrender, we can learn much from conversations with her and from the devotion of those such as Ildephonsus.

✒ Inspiration

His mother said to the servants, "Do whatever he tells you." (John 2:5)

✒ Challenge

Have a twenty-minute talk with Mama Mary today. Offer up a rosary.

Francis de Sales

August 21, 1567–December 28, 1622

Francis was well educated, trained as a lawyer and prepped for his father's dream that his son would be a diplomat. It's not the background one expects for a priest known for his gentle outreach to common laypeople, but that is precisely where Francis found his life's work. Early in his priesthood, he spent three years traveling Calvinist Switzerland, offering religious tracts and friendship and converting thousands as a result. Francis was among the first of his time to advocate for spiritual direction and formation for laypeople as well as the ordained and consecrated religious.

Like Francis, we don't have to flaunt our knowledge in our efforts to bring souls to the kingdom. Evangelization can start with a simple conversation among friends.

✏ Inspiration

Remember what St. Augustine says of his mother Monica, of her determination to serve God in her married life and in her widowhood; and St. Jerome and his beloved daughter St. Paula amid so many changes and chances. What may we not achieve with such patterns before our eyes? (St. Francis de Sales)

✏ Challenge

Is there someone in your family or circle of friends for whom you pray because he or she seems so far from God? Consider starting a conversation about faith with stories from your life. Leave the scripture chapter and verse citations for another time.

Robert of Molesme

Circa 1029-April 17, 1111

People just wouldn't behave. Robert knew what a good Benedictine monk did—after all, he became one when he was just fifteen—but his efforts to reform one abbey went so poorly that the pope sent him to lead some hermits instead. Things went well after he moved the group to Molesme, France, at least for a while. But the community's austere life became so appealing that it drew many men, including some unsuited to it. Robert and two others then were sent to Cîteaux to establish what would become the Cistercians. After just a year or so, the chastened Molesme monks promised to do better, and Robert returned. He spent the rest of his life there.

If you're a parent or have been in a supervisory position at work or in ministry, you know the frustration that can occur when your best efforts are ignored. Robert must have been tempted to levy retribution when he returned to Molesme but instead, he kicked his emotions to the curb and was an effective administrator. May we show that same ability to forgive and love.

☞ Inspiration

For we ourselves were once foolish, disobedient, led astray, slaves to various passions and pleasures, passing our days in malice and envy, despicable, hating one another. (Titus 3:3)

☞ Challenge

Pray for someone whose disobedience injured you.

Timothy

Died circa 97

That Timothy was of great support to St. Paul, we are confident. After all, two of Paul's letters in the New Testament are addressed to Timothy, who evangelized at Bera, Thessalonica, Corinth, and beyond. But while Paul's conversion on the road to Damascus was big and bold, Timothy was schooled in the faith in a more common way: through his mother, Eunice, a Jewish convert, and his grandmother Lois. Tradition tell us that the man inferred to be shy and timid became the first bishop of Ephesus and was martyred for opposing a pagan festival.

We likely all have priests, women religious, and teachers who played and continue to play key roles in our formation. But let's not forget the Loises and Eunices in our own lives, the parents, the grandparents, the aunts and uncles, who teach us how to love the Lord in words and deeds.

Inspiration

I am reminded of your sincere faith, a faith that lived first in your grandmother Lois and your mother Eunice and now, I am sure, lives in you. (2 Timothy 1:5)

Challenge

Offer up your prayers today for a parent or grandparent.

Henry de Ossó y Cervelló

October 16, 1840–January 27, 1896

Young Henry was struggling. His father wanted him to work in the textile business; his mother thought his future lay in the priesthood; and Henry himself wanted to be a teacher. As this dispute went on, he was introduced to the works of St. Teresa of Ávila by a relative. You might say Henry fell in love. He was ordained a few weeks before his twenty-third birthday, and from then on, Teresa was his focus in ministry. He established the Teresian Apostolic Movement for young people, and later, what is now the Teresian Sisters community. Like Teresa, Henry was a prolific writer; much of his work seeks to advance the spiritual education of girls and women.

It's inspiring to learn about saints who were so influenced by other saints. It reminds us that we all are called to holiness, and that those who went before us are eager to help us join them.

Inspiration

My Jesus and my all. Let me love you or die, rather, to live and die loving you above everything else. (St. Henry de Ossó y Cervelló)

Challenge

You picked your confirmation saint for a reason, however dim that memory may be. Read some of his or her writings and renew or deepen your relationship.

Thomas Aquinas

1225–March 7, 1274

You may associate his name with the *Summa Theologica,* one of western Christianity's most important documents. It includes Aquinas's five arguments for the existence of God. But all that brainpower and deep thought started with a simple question that he like many five-year-olds asked: "What is God?" There was a very human side to this great mind. He frequently shed tears at Mass and during prayer. He tolerated being called a dumb ox by his classmates. He became a Dominican despite his family's higher aspirations for his future, and was held captive by well-meaning relatives for fifteen months before they relented.

We tend to think about our saints as perfect, almost untouchable examples of heroic virtue. It's both challenging and encouraging to learn about them as breathing, flawed vessels of humanity who did their best to be obedient and surrender their fears and wills to God. For, if they did it, so can we.

✹Inspiration

For just as it is better to illuminate than to shine, so it is greater to pass on the fruits of contemplation to others than just to contemplate. (St. Thomas Aquinas)

✹Challenge

Work on illuminating your world today.

Joseph Freinademetz

April 15, 1852–January 28, 1908

It would have been a daunting task for any missionary, let alone a brand-new one. However, Joseph relished the challenge of going to an eastern Chinese province with 12 million people—and fewer than two hundred Christians. He threw himself into his work, dressing and eating as those to whom he was talking about Jesus. The Lord's love was Joseph's main message, and beatings and persecution could never keep him for long from sharing those words with people who wanted to hear them. He contracted typhus while tending to the sick. After his death, it was estimated he was responsible for the conversions of 45,000 people.

We don't have to go abroad to share the Good News with those who don't know Jesus; some of them live next door to us or work with us. May we, like Joseph, reflect Jesus to all those we encounter.

✐ Inspiration

Missionary work is useless if one does not love and is not loved. (St. Joseph Freinademetz)

✐ Challenge

Humble yourself and do a kind deed or give a kind word to a non-believer.

Mutien-Marie Wiaux

March 20, 1841–January 30, 1917

It must have seemed to him that he would never be good at anything. Louis Wiaux wasn't much of a blacksmith, unlike his father. He thought about becoming a Jesuit like his brother, but that didn't seem right either. His pastor suggested he go to the new Brothers of the Christian Schools school that was opening in a nearby town. He entered the novitiate, and when he was sixteen, became Brother Mutien-Marie. His initial two years of elementary school teaching went so poorly—he couldn't control disruptive students—that the community considered dismissing him. But a sympathetic brother stepped in and provided guidance and direction. Mutien-Marie would go on to teach, primarily art and music, for the next fifty-eight years, until his death.

A couple of people—the pastor and a confrere—helped guide Mutien-Marie to find his way and develop his skills. Instead of criticizing people we might consider unqualified or incompetent, let's do what we can to assist them.

✒ Inspiration

May my teaching drop like the rain,
 my speech condense like the dew;
like gentle rain on grass,
 like showers on new growth. (Deuteronomy 32:2)

✒ Challenge

Offer support, even if it's only for a few minutes, to someone who is struggling.

John Bosco

August 16, 1815–January 31, 1888

John's father died when he was just two years old, and his mother didn't have much material wealth to share with him and his two brothers. She did, however, shower them with love. John had a dream or vision as a child of being in the midst of a group of fighting children and being counseled to treat them gently. That dream and his mother's example would serve him well. John was ordained in 1841, a time when the northern Italy city of Turin was experiencing rapid industrial growth. Young factory workers lacked positive influences; other boys were living on the streets. John reached out to them, finding apprenticeships and providing education, catechesis, and places to live. At the time of his death, his Society of St. Francis de Sales (commonly known today as the Salesians of Don Bosco) was making a difference in the lives of more than 100,000 boys in 250 houses.

Children often mimic what they experience. The loving care John's mother lavished on her sons was a strong example in his work with young people. It's something to think about with our own children and those in our neighborhoods and parishes.

Inspiration

Try to gain love before inspiring fear. (St. John Bosco)

Challenge

Look at photos of your parents or a favorite sibling, aunt, uncle, or teacher. How do their kindnesses toward you inform your interactions with young people today?

Jaime Hilario Barbal

January 2, 1898–January 18, 1937

Jaime's poor hearing had been an impediment all along. The young Spaniard initially had to leave the seminary for this reason. Then he became a De La Salle brother, and was an effective Latin teacher for more than a dozen years. His disability forced him to leave teaching behind, however, and he became a gardener at an associated college. Jaime's hearing challenges could have saved his life: after his arrest during the Spanish Civil War, his attorneys encouraged him to testify that he was a gardener, not a religious brother. He refused to do so, and was executed by a firing squad.

It wouldn't have been a lie for Jaime to tell the court he was a gardener. But it wouldn't have been the whole truth either. When we are in situations where shading the truth about our faith would save us aggravation and ridicule, may we remember his example and leave our pride and comfort at the altar.

❧ Inspiration

My friends, to die for Christ is to reign. (St. Jaime Hilario Barbal)

❧ Challenge

Come out as a practicing Catholic to someone in your neighborhood or at work.

Lawrence of Canterbury

Died 619

Lawrence was discouraged. He was part of a group of Italian monks who arrived in England in 597, and initially, things had gone well. It appears that's why the Kentish king, Ethelbert, converted to Christianity, and a few years later, Lawrence was named archbishop of Canterbury. But trouble came when Ethelbert died in 616, and his son not only married his stepmother but encouraged a return to pagan traditions. Lawrence thought about going back home, only to be scolded in a dream or vision by St. Peter *(June 28)*. The king converted after Lawrence told him about what had happened.

Don't give up. That's the lesson we learn from Lawrence. Even when our prayers and ministry don't seem to be bearing fruit, it's important to remember that God, not we or the world, will determine success.

Inspiration

Whoever obeys a command will meet no harm, and the wise mind will know the time and way. (Ecclesiastes 8:5)

Challenge

Try not to second-guess God today.

Blaise

Died 316

Tradition has it that Blaise was a healer of humans and animals, and may have been a physician before becoming the bishop for an area in what is now Turkey. In that role, he was an obvious target for the Roman emperor's persecution of Christians. We are told that even as he was being led away to prison, Blaise healed a boy who was choking to death on a fishbone.

Whether or not it's completely factual, the story of Blaise's healing of the boy offers us food for thought. Blaise knew his own death was imminent, yet he was able to minister to someone else. Perhaps it was because Blaise was confident in his hope for eternal life, and so could remain in the moment. In the same way, we can help others even when our own problems seem overwhelming.

Inspiration

"And now, Lord, look at their threats, and grant to your servants to speak your word with all boldness, while you stretch out your hand to heal, and signs and wonders are performed through the name of your holy servant Jesus." (Acts 4:29-30)

Challenge

We all have very real physical and emotional aches and pains. Look for a way in which you can ease someone else's suffering today by not focusing on your own.

Alfonso Maria Fusco

March 23, 1839–February 6, 1910

For Alfonso, divine intervention came even before his conception. His Italian parents, childless after four years of marriage, prayed before relics of St. Alphonsus Liguori *(August 1)* for a child. A priest told them they would have a son and name him in honor of the great saint. So, it's perhaps no surprise that Alfonso first expressed a desire to be a priest when he was eleven. While still in seminary, he had a dream that he was called to found an orphanage as well as a community of sisters to care for the children. The Congregation of the Sisters of St. John the Baptist got off to a somewhat rocky start, with Alfonso being advised to leave as their leader at one point, but he persevered. The women continue to do good works today in Europe, the Americas, Africa, and Asia.

Alfonso obviously felt a special relationship with Alphonsus Liguori, who had died about fifty years before Alfonso's birth. That's the beautiful thing about our saints. The bond can come before birth; when our parents name us; when we are confirmed; or when we are in need of a special friend. Praying with saints doesn't diminish our dependence on God; it helps to deepen and enhance it.

❧ Inspiration

I wish that even my shadow could do good. (Alfonso Maria Fusco)

❧ Challenge

Spend some time today with a saint who's special to you.

Felipe of Jesus

1572–February 5, 1597

Life as a Franciscan hadn't worked out initially for Felipe, so the young Mexico City native had entered into business in the Philippines, doing very well for himself. He still felt called to religious life and later re-professed as a Franciscan. Because the Philippines bishopric was vacant at that time Felipe went home to Mexico City to be ordained. But the ship taking him back to the Philippines as a priest ended up in Japan due to a series of typhoons. After landing in Japan, twenty-five-year-old Felipe and his companions were taken into custody, then released. A few months later, the Franciscan friars were all arrested at their community in Kyoto. Felipe and Japanese Jesuit priest Paul Miki (February 6) were among the twenty-six crucified in Nagasaki. Felipe was the first to die.

Storms come through all our lives. We may not get out of the storm in the same state we went in. But as Felipe knew, God is always there to guide and comfort us.

☙ Inspiration

And he said to them, "Why are you afraid, you of little faith?" Then he got up and rebuked the winds and the sea; and there was a dead calm. (Matthew 8:26)

☙ Challenge

Go back and look at your journal or photos from a tumultuous time. Think about how God carried you through it, even though you didn't see that at the time.

Paul Miki

1562–February 5, 1597

Francis Xavier's *(December 3)* missionary work among the Japanese had borne fruit—by some accounts, some two hundred thousand Japanese, including Paul and his parents, had become Catholics. The emperor became concerned, and ordered out all Catholics in 1587. By this time, however, Paul had discerned a vocation and was studying to be a Jesuit priest. He would become the best known of the crucified Martyrs of Japan canonized in 1862. The others included seventeen laypeople as well as Franciscan and Jesuit religious. On his cross, Paul prayed for his executioners.

The world's evil has a way of making it appear God's plans for us were in error, or that we didn't understand what was wanted. Paul's example reminds us to hold fast to our faith, even when others wonder why we do.

Inspiration

After Christ's example, I forgive my persecutors. I do not hate them. I ask God to have pity on all, and I hope my blood will fall on my fellow men as a fruitful rain. (St. Paul Miki)

Challenge

Think of a situation where well-meaning people are trying to take you off course. Maybe they tell you volunteering at a homeless shelter is dangerous, or that praying outside an abortion clinic would scare them. Say thank you for their concern… and soldier on.

Francesco Spinelli

April 14, 1853–February 6, 1913

It must have seemed like a good idea at the time. Francesco had fulfilled an eight-year dream with the cofounding of the Sacramentine Sisters, a community devoted to the Eucharist and Adoration. The congregation had grown to five houses in just three years. Now, he decided to set up a chain to create vestments and sacramentals, including farms and textile manufacturing. However, the funding source he had been promised withdrew, and the operation had to file for bankruptcy. He had to leave the community; fortunately for him, a bishop in a neighboring diocese invited him in. There, Francesco went on to found a similar community, known as the Sister Adorers of the Blessed Sacrament.

Francesco learned that while he was fulfilling God's call to set up the Sacramentine Sisters, he may have overreached by getting into business dealings about which he knew little. He understood that unwise decisions didn't deprive him of God's love. His story reminds us that though we might disagree with people's actions, we're called to love, not judge.

Inspiration

Consider my affliction and my trouble, and forgive all my sins. (Psalm 25:18)

Challenge

Forgive someone who made a choice that affected you negatively.

Egidio Maria of St. Joseph

November 16, 1729–February 7, 1812

It was a quiet and simple life. The saint known as Egidio Maria of St. Joseph had little education, and not much of anything tangible in his early life. That lack of learning kept him from becoming a priest, so he instead became a Franciscan brother. Egidio spent fifty-plus years at a community in Naples, where his primary responsibility was to beg for the poor. He brought joy to those he served despite numerous physical ailments, including sciatica and asthma.

We know we're all called to holiness, but sometimes answering that call seems impossible with the personal crosses we bear. Egidio reminds us that serving the Lord doesn't have to involve big, showy actions. It can be as simple—and as challenging—as putting aside our aches and pains and excuses, and being kind to someone.

Inspiration

The law of the Lord is perfect,
  reviving the soul;
the degrees of the Lord are sure,
  making wise the simple... (Psalm 19:7)

Challenge

What excuse are you making not to say yes to God? How can you set that excuse aside?

Miguel Febres Cordero

November 7, 1854–February 9, 1910

It's easy to understand why this saint's father, Francisco, opposed his son's plan to become a LaSalle Christian Brother. The boy was born with a congenital foot abnormality, and couldn't stand until he was five. Miguel's mother died when the child was nine. And while Miguel was a standout at the Christian Brothers' school in their tiny town in Ecuador's mountains, Francisco also knew that joining the community would mean his son would have to move nearly three hundred miles away to Quito. He wanted Miguel to attend the nearby diocesan seminary. Reluctantly, Francisco eventually acquiesced. Miguel went on to become a brilliant educator and writer, with many of his textbooks adopted for use throughout Ecuador.

We want to protect those we love; it can be harder to see a child face illness or other challenges than to suffer them ourselves. Yet these precious beings also have special work to do. Miguel's story reminds us that our role is to love and protect others where we can, not to seek to control them.

🐦 Inspiration

And pointing to his disciples, he said, "Here are my mother and my brothers! For whoever does the will of my Father in heaven is my brother and sister and mother." (Matthew 12:49-50)

🐦 Challenge

Resolve not to stand in the way of a loved one's God-given journey, even if it will take him or her away from you.

José Sánchez del Río

March 28, 1913–February 10, 1928

Like many youngsters, José wanted to be like his older brothers. They had joined the Cristero rebels fighting the Mexican government's perceived anti-Catholic policies, and now the teenager wanted to join them. José's desire initially met with opposition from his mother, but it was not long before she relented and he became a flag bearer. He was captured by government forces on February 5, 1928, and was tortured and forced to watch a hanging. José still refused to renounce his faith. He was marched to a cemetery, where he shouted, "Long live Christ the King!" one last time and was shot.

If José had a child's faith, may we all be children! Sometimes, adults make things more complicated than they have to be. If we love God, we are called to bear witness to him regardless of the cost.

Inspiration

He called a child, whom he put among them, and said, "Truly I tell you, unless you change and become like children, you will never enter the kingdom of heaven." (Matthew 18:2–3)

Challenge

Ask a child (with the parents' permission, if you are not the parent) to describe Jesus to you.

Jerome Emiliani

1486–February 8, 1537

Jerome was in chains in more ways than one. He was one of only four soldiers who survived a 1511 battle in what was known as the Italian Wars and was captured and imprisoned. It wasn't that Jerome was an atheist; he just hadn't made much room for religion. That all changed when after a month, he escaped, giving total credit to the Blessed Virgin Mary's assistance. The story drew such attention that Jerome ended up being mayor of the town for a while. But by 1518, he was ordained and began working tirelessly to help orphans and others. His efforts included the founding of what today is the Somascan Fathers and Brothers. Jerome died from the plague, which he caught while assisting other victims.

We all have earthly responsibilities—family, jobs, house and car payments, and the like. Sometimes, we don't even realize how much those responsibilities may become false gods. Jerome's encounter with Mary made him re-examine his priorities—and reminds us to take a look at our own.

Inspiration

If you remain steadfast in faith, especially during temptations, the Lord will console you in this world, will lead you out of temptations and will give you peace and tranquility in this world. (St. Jerome Emiliani)

Challenge

With the Blessed Virgin's help, identify your chains.

Desiderius

Died 607

Parts of the story sound like the martyrdom of John the Baptist *(December 27)*. Desiderius was the bishop of a diocese in eastern France, and was not shy about criticizing wayward priests or rulers, especially the Frankish queen Brunhild. Desiderius called her out so often for her lack of adherence to Catholic tenets that she saw to it that he was exiled for four years. Time away, however, did not temper Desiderius's truth speaking; Brunhild eventually had him assassinated.

Speaking truth was hard in the seventh century, and it's hard today. While those we call out may not have us killed physically, they can cost us our reputation. Desiderius reminds us some truths are worth that, because we answer ultimately not to those with earthly power, but to God.

Inspiration

For Herod himself had sent men who arrested John, bound him, and put him in prison on account of Herodias, his brother Philip's wife, because Herod had married her. (Mark 6:17)

Challenge

Speak God's truth to power today—directly, or in an email, phone call, or letter.

Methodius

Circa 815–884

Who better than a pair of Slavic brothers to win the hearts and souls of non-Christian Slavs in the late ninth century? And what a pair of brothers they were. Cyril (circa 827–869) had prior missionary experience; Methodius was a Greek monastery's abbot when the call came. They were both sensitive to the need to share Jesus with the Slavs in their own language, despite the disapproval of German church authorities who had tried and failed to make headway in what is now part of the Czech Republic. The brothers developed an alphabet that is still the basis of some Slavic languages, then translated the Bible and liturgy. After Cyril's death, Methodius went on to become the archbishop of the Slavic region and persevered against more unfounded charges of heresy.

Celebration of the liturgy in a tongue other than Latin is commonplace to us today, but it was controversial in Methodius's and Cyril's time. Yet they were committed to meeting people where they were. It's a good reminder to us if we're tempted to judge others when their form of practicing Catholicism is different from ours.

Inspiration

"Whoever does the will of God is my brother and sister and mother." (Mark 3:35)

Challenge

Find out more about the roots of a Catholic rite or practice that interests you.

Valentine

Died circa 270

There's confusion and debate over whether there were one, two, or even three Valentines; it appears that the two most likely candidates were in fact the same person, one a Roman priest, one a bishop. Regardless, we know the man we celebrate today was devoted to his flock and for God; he died for his faith.

It may seem odd that this day full of flowers and candy and professions of romantic love has its roots in someone who was martyred. But isn't that the ultimate sign of love and faith, to die rather than renounce that which we hold dearest?

☙ Inspiration

If I speak in the tongues of mortals and of angels, but do not have love, I am a noisy gong or a clanging cymbal. (1 Corinthians 13:1)

☙ Challenge

Write a Valentine's Day love note to Jesus.

Claude de la Colombière

February 2, 1641–February 15, 1682

You're likely aware of the Catholic devotion to the Sacred Heart of Jesus and of the French nun, Margaret Mary Alacoque, who carried the message of the devotion in the seventeenth century. But you may not know about Claude, a Jesuit priest who served as Margaret Mary's spiritual director during the time that her mother superior and others scoffed at her visions. Claude believed, and developed a devotion to the Sacred Heart himself. It likely brought him comfort when he ended up in London about a year later as the confessor to a duchess and wrongly accused in a plot to assassinate the English king. After being imprisoned for five weeks, Claude was banished, and returned to France for the final two years of his life.

Jesus sent Claude to Margaret Mary to sustain her during a difficult time. She in turn was with Claude when he was persecuted. Let's remember the small roles we have in the lives of others may not seem like much to us, but are exactly where God wants us.

Inspiration

God sought me out when I fled from him; he will not abandon me now that I seek him, or at least do not flee from him anymore. (Claude de la Colombière)

Challenge

Do something small for a family member or friend today.

Sigfrid of Sweden

Died circa 1045

It's hard to imagine the tragedy. Sigfrid, two other bishops, and his three nephews—all priests or deacons—had been called as missionaries from England to Scandinavia. Sigfrid apparently was in Denmark when a group of Swedish pagans murdered his nephews. The bodies were buried in a forest; the heads, placed in a box at the bottom of a lake near the church. When Sigfrid found out, he retrieved the heads and said they spoke to him. Needless to say, this shook the pagans. The murderers were found, and the king ordered them put to death. But Sigfrid's opposition saved their lives. He also refused to take a cent of the resulting fine levied against them. All of this resulted in even more Christian conversions. For his missionary efforts, Sigfrid is known as the Apostle of Sweden.

What would you have done if you were Sigfrid? Left for the comfort of England? Privately rejoiced in the executions of those who killed your loved ones? His story reminds us that something good can come out of any tragedy.

✿ Inspiration

Put away from you all bitterness and wrath and anger and wrangling and slander, together with all malice, and be kind to one another, tender-hearted, forgiving one another, as God in Christ has forgiven you. (Ephesians 4:31-32)

✿ Challenge

Forgive someone who has grievously wronged you or a loved one.

Alexis Falconieri

Circa 1200–1310

Alexis was one of seven young Italian noblemen, devoted to the Blessed Virgin, who gathered regularly to pray. On Assumption Day in 1233, they received a visit from Mary, who encouraged them to leave their homes and come together in prayer and quiet. The Servants of Mary, or Servites, were established in 1244. Alexis was the only one among the group who never was ordained. He lived to the ripe old age of 110, and in his seventies was involved in the rearing of his niece Juliana, whose father had died. Juliana founded a corresponding Servite community for women, and was canonized in 1731.

Alexis could have joined his friends in becoming priests, but the humble man said he was not worthy of that. His involvement in his niece's life might have been more difficult had he been ordained. His example reminds us to say no to the world's expectations, and yes to God's.

☙Inspiration

He sat down, called the twelve, and said to them, "Whoever wants to be first must be last of all and servant of all." (Mark 9:35)

☙Challenge

Say no to something the world asks of you today in favor of something God desires.

Kuriakose Elias Chavara

February 10, 1805–January 3, 1871

The first male saint of Indian origin felt called to the priesthood at an early age. Kuriakose was only thirteen when he entered a seminary fifty miles from home. He had not been there long when word came that his parents and only brother were victims of a smallpox epidemic. Kuriakose didn't find out in time to attend their funerals. Most extended family members insisted that as the only heir, he return home. Only one relative supported the boy—and that person was so persuasive that Kuriakose remained in seminary. He founded India's first indigenous community of male religious, the Congregation of the Mother of Carmel, and a sister community for women. Kuriakose was known for his zeal in empowering and educating women.

Kuriakose's family members likely weren't evil people; they just had strong opinions on the right thing to do and that did not involve him becoming a priest. Other people may not always understand God's plan for us. As his children, we must follow his plan, not theirs.

✒ Inspiration

For surely I know the plans I have for you, says the Lord, plans for your welfare and not for harm, to give you a future with hope. (Jeremiah 29:11)

✒ Challenge

Listen to the dreams of someone—child or adult—today. Refrain from weighing in on what you see as the unlikelihood the dream will be realized.

Odran

Died circa 452

Was Odran in the wrong place at the wrong time? Tradition has it that he was St. Patrick's *(March 17)* chariot driver, taking Patrick hither and yon across Ireland as he evangelized. This of course did not sit well with pagan-worshipping Irish chieftains. Odran may or may not have heard about a plot to kill Patrick, of which in any event his boss was unaware. Odran pleaded fatigue to trade places in the chariot, and was killed by a spear meant for Patrick. The result was forty-one more years of ministry for Patrick.

We've all heard of St. Patrick, but Odran's story is an obscure one. Still, his sacrifice opened the way for Patrick to do more good. Let's remember that our small sacrifices also may yield great fruit through others.

Inspiration

I appeal to you therefore, brothers and sisters, by the mercies of God, to present your bodies as a living sacrifice, holy and acceptable to God, which is your spiritual worship. (Romans 12:1)

Challenge

Think of ways you can be a living sacrifice today.

Francisco Marto

June 11, 1908–April 4, 1919

He was just a little boy, one who liked to look at the stars and the sky and to play his flute. But Francisco's life was turned inside out when he was eight, and he, his younger sister, and a cousin saw the beautiful lady while they were minding their families' sheep. The authorities and some of the neighbors scoffed, and ridiculed the children's reports of what the lady wore and said. But all three remained steadfast. Francisco was the first to die, a few weeks shy of his eleventh birthday. in an influenza epidemic.

It can be tempting to discount the spiritual experiences of others, especially children. But the Fatima trio show us that the Lord has plans beyond our understanding to gather souls, and that messengers are sometimes sent to those we might be inclined to doubt.

Inspiration

I don't want to be anything. I just want to die and go to heaven. (St. Francisco Marto)

Challenge

Talk with a child about his or her thoughts about heaven. Or, revisit photos of your own First Communion or Confirmation. How did you feel that day?

Peter Damian

Circa 1007–1072

Call it the story of the bad brother. Peter was the youngest child in a large family. After his parents died, Peter ended up living with an older brother who put him to work as a swineherd and begrudged him life's basic necessities. Peter eventually was taken in by another brother, a male religious, who saw potential in the lad and made sure he received an education. In gratitude, Peter added that brother's name, Damian, to his own. Peter Damian grew up to be a brilliant rhetoric teacher before becoming a Benedictine monk known for his battles against clerical excesses and for Church reform. His prolific writings include thoughts on God's omnipotence. He was designated a Doctor of the Church in 1828.

Think about this saint's brother Damian. His own life was going well, but he saw that his little brother needed assistance, and made sure he got it. Peter Damian's writings have been praised by many, including Pope Benedict XVI. The saint's story shows us that a little help at the right time can change the world.

Inspiration

Let the simplicity of Christ instruct me, and the true humility of the wise loose me from the chains of doubt. (St. Peter Damian)

Challenge

Give someone a helping hand. It doesn't need to cost you anything but time or effort.

Alexander Akimetes

Died circa 403

Akimetes means "does not rest," and it was a fitting moniker. This saint, who likely was born in Greece and educated in Istanbul, began adult life as a soldier. He had a conversion experience and spent several years in Syria as a hermit. (Tradition has it that upon his emergence, he burned a pagan temple, then converted his jailers and other authorities.) Alexander founded several monasteries, including one that had no permanent home. He established a tradition when he divided one community into six choirs, enabling the singing of the Divine Office 24/7.

We all feel restless from time to time. We tire of the same home, the same town, the same job, maybe even the same family and friends. When we do, let's be like Alexander and allow our souls to rest in God even if our bodies must wander.

Inspiration

What should I do then? I will pray with the spirit, but I will pray with the mind also; I will sing praise with the spirit, but I will sing praise with the mind also. (1 Corinthians 14:15)

Challenge

Sing the prayers of at least one of the Divine Office hours. It's fine to do it in the privacy of your own home.

Polycarp

Circa 59–155

Polycarp was old—at least eighty-six—and revered by those in the early Church as possibly the only remaining disciple of John the Apostle *(December 27)*. He had defended the faith against false teachings. Yet, after he returned home to Smyrna from a trip to Rome, government authorities came to arrest him. He offered them a meal and asked them to wait while he prayed. Two hours later, he accompanied them to appear before the proconsul where he refused to renounce his faith. When an attempt to burn him alive failed, he was stabbed to death.

Polycarp's hospitality to his persecutors sounds like the stuff of legends, but his is one of the oldest authentic stories of post-New Testament martyrdom. His actions challenge us to offer grace to those who seek to harm us.

Inspiration

You threaten the fire that burns for an hour and in a little while is quenched; for you do not know the fire of the future judgment and of eternal punishment, the fire reserved for the wicked. (St. Polycarp)

Challenge

Pray for someone who threatens to take you away from God with his or her actions and words.

Leo of Catania

Died 789

It's said that Leo, a hermit, ended up as the bishop of Catania, Italy, because all the residents had a dream that a hermit should fill the post. Leo was reluctant, but eventually said yes. It wasn't the easiest of times to be a Church leader; a movement to destroy religious icons (they were seen by some as violating Mosaic law against graven images) was picking up strength. Leo became such a force of opposition to iconoclasm that he had to leave the city for his own safety. He lived as a nomad for a time, including dwelling in a cave he created with his own hands. Eventually, he was reinstated as bishop and continued to battle the iconoclasts.

Challenging tradition isn't always a bad thing; sometimes, we find out that what we thought was tradition is personal bias or a misinterpretation of doctrine or dogma. But destroying tradition for the sake of destroying it is harmful. May we, like Leo, stand up for acceptance of practices that are within Church teachings and that bring people closer to God.

❧ Inspiration

"Be strong and bold; have no fear or dread of them, because it is the Lord your God who goes with you; he will not fail you or forsake you." (Deuteronomy 31:6)

❧ Challenge

Learn about a Catholic tradition that seems outdated to you but might be more relevant than you think.

Tarasius

Died 806

Tarasius's connections and humble nature had helped him do well for himself. Indeed, he was named patriarch of Constantinople even before being ordained, thanks to a good relationship with the young king and his mother. But all that changed ten years later when the king, now grown, wanted to divorce his wife and marry one of her servants. Tarasius understood the backstory, that the king's mother had forced the first marriage. Tarasius took a middle road, refusing to celebrate over the new marriage, but also refusing to excommunicate the king. Amid all the political intrigue, Tarasius continued to live a simple, monk-like life as patriarch for twenty-one years, and devoted much of his time to assisting the poor.

Everything, it seems, is political in our world today, and many of us try to navigate life without getting into arguments about what's going on with our nation's leaders. Tarasius's story shows us that there is often a middle ground, the one God wants us to walk, to be found without compromising our integrity.

✍Inspiration

As a father has compassion for his children,

so the Lord has compassion for those who fear him. (Psalm 103:13)

✍Challenge

Propose a path of compromise on something where family members or friends are on opposite sides.

Porphyry of Gaza

Circa 347–420

Five years as a monk in Skete, Egypt. Five years as a hermit. Perhaps it was all that quiet time with God that made Porphyry so insistent on providing a safe place for Christians in Gaza. He was ordained at forty, and named bishop a few years later. Gaza was a hotbed of pagan activity, and the emperor was initially reluctant to do much about it because that community represented a reliable source of tax revenue. Porphyry's repeated pleas finally took root, initially with destroying the pagan temple where much of the Christian persecution was being fomented. As the destruction of other temples ensued, the bishop's life was threatened. Ultimately, the Christians prevailed, and Porphyry built a church where the main pagan temple had been.

Complain, complain, complain. Many times, it's pointless; we're called to take action, not merely speak the same words over and over again. But Porphyry eventually found the words that changed the emperor's mind…or made it easier to destroy the pagan temples than to keep listening to the bishop! From him, we learn to be persistent in Christ's name.

Inspiration

Proclaim the message; be persistent whether the time is favorable or unfavorable; convince, rebuke, and encourage, with the utmost patience in teaching. (2 Timothy 4:2)

Challenge

Pray for new words to share in what seems to be a deadlocked situation.

Gregory of Narek

Circa 950–1005

Gregory had been a monk since his mid-twenties. He taught at his Armenian community's monastic school, and had drawn some attention for a commissioned analysis of the Old Testament's Song of Songs. But now, he was in his fifties, and may have been suffering from a terminal illness. His *Book of Lamentations,* an offering of ninety-five deeply personal prayers on God's grace and his own unworthiness, continues to speak to people more than a thousand years later. In 2015, Pope Francis named Gregory as a Doctor of the Church.

Physical limitations can drive us away from God. We can feel that what we or those we love are enduring is just unfair. Or, like Gregory, we can turn that sorrow into a deeper definition of worship. The choice is ours.

Inspiration

The soul's every movement is a reminder of God... (St. Gregory of Narek)

Challenge

Consider writing a four-line poem praising the Almighty's goodness. It doesn't have to rhyme or follow any type of form. It doesn't even have to be very good. Just write from the heart.

Gabriel Possenti

March 1, 1838–February 27, 1862

God kept knocking—and Francesco heard him. Really, he did. But so many other attractive things—including girls—kept getting in the way. The popular young Italian was known for his dancing skills and his engaging personality. Twice—once, when he was very ill, and the second time, when he managed to dodge a stray bullet—Francesco felt called to religious life. But it wasn't until he was attending a procession in honor of the Blessed Virgin and heard a voice asking why he remained in the lay world that Francesco took action. Despite initial objections from his father and other relatives, the eighteen-year-old entered the Passionist congregation and took the name Gabriel. He proved to be a sharp student, but died of tuberculosis before his ordination.

Like this saint, we can find many things to distract us from prayer and worship. May we, like him, send aside those worldly temptations, as harmless as they may seem, if they take us away from time with him.

Inspiration

"Whoever listens to you listens to me, and whoever rejects you rejects me, and whoever rejects me rejects the one who sent me." (Luke 10:16)

Challenge

Say no to an attractive distraction this week. Spend the time at adoration or in the study of scripture or other spiritual work.

Alexander of Alexandria

Died circa 328

As the bishop of Alexandria, Alexander wasn't looking for a fight. But one of his priests, Arius, seemed intent on getting him into one. Arius's theological positions included many counter to Church teachings, especially about Jesus's eternal role as part of the Holy Trinity and whether he was capable of sin. Alexander tried dialogue and minor censures for eight years, but Arius's heresy continued to gain supporters. Finally, in 321, Alexander excommunicated Arias, an action his council of bishops confirmed.

None of us wants to be the bad guy. We try to find common ground with those who think differently from us, to understand their position. But as with Alexander, a time may come when the views of someone else are so antithetical to what we believe that we need to cut them out of our lives, lest they take us away from what we believe.

☙Inspiration

For it is incumbent on us who are Christians, to turn away from all those who speak or entertain a thought against Christ, as from those who are resisting God, and are destroyers of the souls of men… (St. Alexander of Alexandria)

☙Challenge

Make a list of beliefs or practices other Catholics embrace that you question. Talk with a priest about your struggle. Don't give evil an opening.

David of Wales

Died 589

The facts about this saint are limited. We know that he did exist, was born in Wales, became a bishop, and founded a number of monasteries. Beyond that, the unreliable legends are of a pious, austerely living man: It's said those at his monasteries were total vegetarians who drank nothing but water and a bit of milk, and who plowed their fields themselves, without animals. They prayed for three hours each night before bedtime. David also was known as a preacher, divinely inspired; a dove once came to his shoulder as he was speaking.

Legends are part of the fabric of our lives. We likely have stories about a grandparent or great-grandparent that aren't provable, but that fit with the type of person he or she was. Those stories inspire us in weathering storms; stories of the saints, reliable or not, can do the same for us.

Inspiration

Be joyful, keep the faith, and do the little things that you have heard and seen me do. (St. David of Wales)

Challenge

Write down a favorite story about a family member. Share it with someone in the next generation.

Rudesind

907-977

Perhaps Rudesind never really wanted the responsibility of being a bishop anyway. The son of a Spanish count, he was named a bishop at eighteen, and shortly thereafter was moved to the Compostela bishopric to replace one of his cousins, who had a reputation for corruption. Rudesind also had a good military mind, successfully leading troops when Compostela was threatened from the north and east. The king who was Rudesind's champion died in 967, and the wayward cousin escaped from prison and demanded the return of the bishopric. Rudesind gave it to him, and spent his remaining years founding more monasteries.

God sometimes calls us to positions for which we might not feel suited: marriage, parenthood, caregiving, the big corner office at work. Only he knows how long our tenure will be. Like Rudesind, let's spend the time we have in those positions glorifying him.

⌦ Inspiration

I give thanks to you, O Lord my God, with my whole heart,
   and I will glorify your name forever. (Psalm 86:12)

⌦ Challenge

Surely, there's some task or responsibility you're doing only because no one else will. Offer up the difficulties related to it today.

Anselm of Nonantola

Died circa 803

Anselm was connected. His sister had married a Lombardy king, and that meant special treatment for the soldier turned Benedictine monk. Times were good; his brother-in-law even gave him a property in northern Italy known as Nonantola, at which Anselm eventually was leading more than a thousand monks as abbot. But things changed when his brother-in-law died. The new ruler in essence banished Anselm to another monastery more than three hundred miles away. Charlemagne became the area's ruler seven years later, and Anselm was able to come back to Nonantola, where he died.

Anselm learned that the only connection that matters is our connection to God. Let's keep that in mind the next time we're tempted to use our friendships and associations for our own advancement rather than working together to bring souls to the kingdom.

☞ Inspiration

Do not boast about tomorrow,

for you do not know what a day may bring. (Proverbs 27:1)

☞ Challenge

Examine whether you are remaining in relationships solely because you get something tangible out of them. What can you do to change that?

Casimir

1458-1484

Plans—his father, the king of Poland, had plans for young Casimir. His parents had thirteen children, and when the Hungarian nobility expressed displeasure with their king, Casimir's father saw it as an opportunity to put his thirteen-year-old son on the throne. However, the effort failed as troops deserted. The Polish king's perception was that his pious son had not fully embraced the effort, and so he imprisoned him for a time. Eventually, the father relented, and Casimir, who was increasingly known for his piety and simple lifestyle, was the titular head of Poland for a few years. He died at sixteen, apparently of tuberculosis.

Sometimes, people try to rope us into plans for their own good, not ours. Casimir's story shows us that the best plans are the ones God has for us—and to discern when other people's agendas would take us off course.

✍ Inspiration

He stands by you for a while,

but if you falter, he will not be there. (Sirach 12:15)

✍ Challenge

Pray for the faith to say no to someone who wants you to advance his or her plans, not God's.

Giovanni Antonio Farina

January 11, 1803–March 4, 1888

They called him the bishop of the poor, and he was criticized by people who didn't think he should be doing what he was doing. But Giovanni didn't much care. The Italian bishop established a free school for girls, the first in his diocese, and followed that up with something else unheard of in the area at that time, the foundation of a community of teaching women religious. He pushed the boundaries further by expanding the sisters' work into hospitals. Giovani also set up groups in each of his parishes to help those in need.

Not everyone can see the need God puts before us, and even if others see something should be done, they may have a different plan. While we should listen attentively to others' views—after all, God loves them too—like Giovanni, we must be true to what's been placed on our hearts.

☙Inspiration

His prosperity will be established,

and the assembly will proclaim his acts of charity. (Sirach 31:11)

☙Challenge

Say yes to that unusual request God is making of you, whether it's something about a family member, a work situation, or another ministry.

Stephen of Obazine

Died 1154

When this French priest was newly ordained, he and a confrere went into the countryside on Good Friday, and found the hermit lifestyle suited them. So, Stephen divested himself of his possessions, and the pair began living in crude structures they built in the forest. Other people heard about what they were doing, and after a year, the local bishop allowed them to found a monastery. About eight years later, Stephen joined a nearby Cistercian community; within five years, all those living in Stephen's original monastery and a convent he had founded joined him with the Cistercians. He served as abbot for a time before his death.

God's plans sometimes confound us. Stephen and his confrere knew in their souls that it was the right thing to become hermits. They didn't know then that the life would so appeal to others that they would end up in more public positions, leading flocks. Like them, may we embrace the changes and turns of our paths.

Inspiration

God is our refuge and strength,

a very present help in trouble.

Therefore we will not fear, though the earth should change…

(Psalm 46:1-2)

Challenge

Say yes rather than why to a change God has put on your soul.

Paul the Simple

Died circa 339

It couldn't have been much simpler for Paul: After the sixty-year-old Egyptian found his wife with another man, he left her and decided it was time for him to become a monk. So, he went into the desert to inform the man we know as St. Anthony of Egypt *(January 17)* of his decision. Anthony was, however, less than convinced of Paul's vocation, due in no small part to his age. But every test Anthony gave him, Paul passed, whether it was fasting, praying, or working. As a monk, Paul also became known for his healing powers. He became known as "the simple," because of his childlike innocence.

Sometimes, we make life harder than it needs to be. Paul could have come up with all kinds of reasons not to go into the desert. He could have argued with Anthony about why the tests were necessary. But instead, he just said yes. And we can do the same.

Inspiration

The unfolding of your words gives light;

it imparts understanding to the simple. (Psalm 119:130)

Challenge

Be simple today. Trust in God.

John of God

March 8, 1495-March 8, 1550

Small wonder that the man we know as John of God got knocked off his moorings when he heard John of Ávila *(May 7)*. His life had been a series of mistakes and resets, with time as a soldier, a shepherd, a seller of religious images. John, who was nearly forty-two when he heard the priest's preaching, ended up in a mental institution when he realized the enormity of his errors. He found healing when John of Ávila came to him and said the best way to redeem himself would be to help others. And so he did, establishing services and homes for the sick and poor that became the Hospitaller Order of St. John of God.

Do you ever feel overwhelmed by your sins, afraid that God cannot forgive you? As John of God's story shows us, sometimes, the answer is getting out of our own despondency and helping others. Give it a try.

Inspiration

If we consider how great the mercy of God is, we would never stop doing good while we could... (St. John of God)

Challenge

Just for today, turn off your inner critic. When it starts to rear its head, do something for someone else—a quick supportive text or email, a phone call, or something else.

Abraham Kidunaia

Died circa 360

Abraham failed at facing up to his first big decision. His wealthy parents had arranged a marriage for him, and he was reluctant to tell them or his bride-to-be that he had decided to be celibate. In fact, he waited until the wedding was over and the seven-day feast was underway to share that news. But any fear of confrontation Abraham had went away after ten years in a sealed cabin. The local bishop, impressed by his holiness, asked Abraham to go out among the people and convert them from paganism. So Abraham did, for three years, despite numerous attempts on his life. Finally, impressed by his persistence and faith, the populace began asking to be baptized. After another year, Abraham went back into his cell for the remainder of his life.

We understand Abraham's reluctance to talk with his parents and fiancée; difficult conversations are, well, difficult. Through his story, we learn that we too can leave behind our fear of confrontation and other shortcomings to help bring souls to the kingdom.

Inspiration

But overhearing what they said, Jesus said to the leader of the synagogue, "Do not fear, only believe." (Mark 5:36)

Challenge

Do something dangerous for Jesus. Ask him to hold your hand while you have that conversation or take on that service.

John Ogilvie

Circa 1579–March 10, 1615

John, a newly ordained Jesuit priest, knew that leaving continental Europe to return to his native Scotland would likely be a death sentence. He'd spent the first thirteen years of his life there, the son of a Calvinist noble. But after two and a half years of pleas, his request was granted. He spent ten months as an undercover priest, traveling between Edinburgh and Glasgow before he was betrayed. Despite five months of torture, John refused to provide names of any other Scots Catholics or to pledge allegiance to Scotland's king. Legend has it that he threw his rosary into the crowd just before his execution, resulting in the conversion of one of his enemies.

John embraced danger in Jesus's name. We're called to show the same fearlessness in sharing our beliefs in a world that sometimes disparages Catholics and other Christians.

☙ Inspiration

Those who forsake the law praise the wicked,

but those who keep the law struggle against them. (Proverbs 28:4)

☙ Challenge

Talk about your faith with a friend or family member who has rejected God.

Manuel González García

February 25, 1877–January 4, 1940

It was one of the young priest's first assignments: to preach a mission. He envisioned a lively, Spirit-filled congregation. But that was not what Manuel found. The church was in general disrepair, the people's faith lukewarm at best, the tabernacle dusty. Manuel had a vision of Jesus, saddened by the state of things. This, he realized, is what happens to people who abandon the True Presence. Manuel vowed that from that moment on, he would be devoted to the Eucharist, and to bring others to that devotion. He was as good as his word, focusing on the Eucharist as bishop of Spanish dioceses and as the founder of the Eucharistic Missionaries of Nazareth and two other communities.

If we have learned nothing else through the isolations of the coronavirus pandemic, it is that we are a Eucharistic people, and not even the best livestreamed Mass can replace it. Like Manuel, let's resolve to bring the food that never fails to nourish to others.

✿ Inspiration

I ask to be buried next to a tabernacle, so that my bones, after death, like my tongue and my pen in life, always will be saying to those who pass by: There is Jesus! There he is! Do not leave him abandoned! (St. Manuel González García)

✿ Challenge

Say thank you. Spend an hour at adoration.

Cuthbert

Circa 634–March 20, 687

It may sound odd to us today, but not all Catholics have always celebrated Easter on the same date. In 664, a synod determined what is now northern England and southeast Scotland would adopt the Roman church's method of calculating the date rather than that of Celtic missionaries. Knowing this would be a tough sell at the Lindisfarne priory, Church authorities sent in Cuthbert. He was considered the ideal prior because of his reputation and the fact that he had accepted the change. Cuthbert had some success, then in 676 began nine years as a hermit. He was called back to active ministry as a bishop in Lindisfarne, and spent the final two years of his life ministering to his flock, including those struck by a plague.

Cuthbert was a peacemaker, helping the Lindisfarne faithful accept what for them must have been a difficult change. His example can help us minister compassionately to family members and friends whose lives change suddenly due to illness and other issues beyond their control.

Inspiration

For my thoughts are not your thoughts,

nor are your ways my ways, says the Lord. (Isaiah 55:8)

Challenge

Spend some time with someone who is struggling to find grace.

Berthold

Died circa 1195

French-born Berthold may have been a priest when he accompanied a relative on the Crusades. What he saw during the siege of Antioch was carnage. In the aftermath, he had a vision of the soldiers being denounced by Jesus and the dead Christians being transported to heaven by angels. Berthold determined his personal response would be to put battles behind him and live a hermit's life at Mount Carmel, where the prophet Elijah dealt with Baal's false prophets as described in 1 Kings 18. While Berthold is not regarded as a founder of the Carmelites as we know them, it is believed he organized the region's first community of hermits.

Like Berthold, what we see firsthand or in the news or on social media can sicken us. May we have the strength he showed to break with the world's evils, and find a way to rebuild our spirits and those of others.

Inspiration

When all the people saw it, they fell on their faces and said, "The Lord indeed is God; the Lord indeed is God." (1 Kings 18:39)

Challenge

What can you do to take a break from the drumbeat of evil and find a place of peace for yourself?

Clement Mary Hofbauer

December 26, 1751-March 16, 1820

Life was never easy for the man known in religious life as Clement Mary Hofbauer. The ninth of a dozen children born into a poor family in what is now the Czech Republic, there simply wasn't enough money for him to study for the priesthood. So, the apprentice baker did the next best thing, going to work in a monastery bakery. Finally, thanks to the kindness of two women he barely knew, when he was twenty-nine he and a friend entered the University of Vienna. They were ordained four years later as Redemptorist priests, and sent to expand the community north of the Alps. They settled in Warsaw in February 1787, a time of upheaval and conquest for Poland, and the foreign-born Redemptorists were viewed with skepticism. Eventually, they gained the people's trust by their work among the poor. But then in 1808, they were expelled. After four weeks in prison, Clement Mary returned to Vienna, where he lived until his death.

Clement Mary encountered many financial and political obstacles. But he persevered on the course God had set for him. His example reminds us that what God asks of us may be difficult, but never impossible.

Inspiration

Human success is in the hand of the Lord,
and it is he who confers honor on the lawgiver. (Sirach 10:5)

Challenge

Pray for the strength and faith to persevere.

Daniel Comboni

March 15, 1831–October 10, 1881

From an early age, Daniel believed he was called to missionary work in Africa. And indeed, within three years of his ordination at age twenty-two, Daniel and five other missionaries were in Sudan. There, his dream collided with reality. The climate was far different from that of his native Italy. The Sudanese were leery of the men, regarding them in the same light as slave traders. The work was hard with little fruit. Daniel returned home in 1859 and spent a few years teaching and rethinking his missionary strategy. He then was inspired to refocus on creating disciples within Central Africa. At that time, it was a novel approach. He called the effort "Save Africa Through Africa." Daniel founded communities of men and women religious to support Christian disciple-building that continue to do good work today. He died in Sudan.

Sometimes, we're on the path the Lord desires, but we're not using the right vehicle. Daniel's example shows us the importance of embracing humility and exploring options when we feel stuck, rather than giving up.

Inspiration

The thought that one sweats and dies for the love of Jesus Christ and the salvation of the most abandoned souls in the world is far too sweet for us to desist from this great enterprise. (St. Daniel Comboni)

Challenge

Where do you feel stuck, spiritually or in ministry? Talk with a priest or trusted friend about ways you could change that.

José Gabriel del Rosario Brochero

March 16, 1840-January 26, 1914

For the man they called "the gaucho priest" or "the cowboy priest," life was all about connections. José was twenty-nine with three years of priesthood under his belt when he was assigned to the San Alberto parish in Argentina's highlands. The parish of eighty square miles had about ten thousand people… and in many cases, no easy way to get to them. So José rode mile after mile on his mule, prayer book and Mass kit always with him, getting to know the residents. He was personally involved in the construction of roadways and aqueducts to connect people physically. To see to their spiritual needs, he saw that retreat houses and schools for girls were built. Along the way, José contracted Hansen's disease, then known as leprosy, and eventually retired from his ministry.

Some of us might have stayed in the rectory rather than travel via mule and get our hands dirty helping to build roads the way the gaucho priest did. But then, that wouldn't have been doing the work the Lord desired. May we approach our ministries by rolling up our sleeves and diving in, not rolling down the shades so we don't see the needs in front of us.

☛Inspiration

Woe if the devil is going to rob a soul from me. (St. José Gabriel del Rosario Brochero)

☛Challenge

Don't let the devil rob a soul today. Have a conversation with someone who's hurting.

Patrick

Circa 389–circa 461

Much of what we think we know about Patrick—the use of the shamrock to explain the Holy Trinity, the driving of snakes out of Ireland—is uncertain, and doesn't really matter. The key to Patrick's life comes in his initial years in Ireland. (He may have been kidnapped by pirates, as he wrote, or he may have been the prodigal son, going into indentured servitude to avoid obligations at home in England.) When he left England, his belief was lukewarm, much to the dismay of his faithful family. It was in Ireland, when he wasn't busy herding animals, that Patrick experienced his conversion. Having found spiritual freedom in physical captivity in Ireland, it's not surprising that Patrick embraced the opportunity to return and offer the same freedom after becoming a priest.

When life is going along as we think it should, it's easy to take credit for what we have—good family, good home, enough to eat. Adversity offers us the gift of a reset, to rededicate ourselves to the Great Provider.

Inspiration

Then the nations in the whole world will all be converted and worship God in truth. (Tobit 14:6)

Challenge

Journal about, or share with a friend, how a hard time increased your reliance on God.

Cyril of Jerusalem

Circa 315–386

No good deed goes unpunished. Cyril sometimes ran into trouble about what he did or didn't say, and what he did or didn't do. In one case the bishop of Jerusalem was exiled because he had sold Church property and refused to appear before a synod of bishops to defend himself. It appears Cyril was suspicious about the makeup of the panel, and from today's vantage point, if the sale had been made, it was likely to raise funds to feed famine-ravaged families. Cyril also is noteworthy for his writing skills; his twenty-three homilies targeting those preparing for baptism or having recently been baptized resulted in his naming as a Doctor of the Church.

Have you ever done something for the right reasons, only to be second guessed? Think of Jesus at his trial, or Cyril's refusal to defend himself. Remember that God is fully aware of our actions and motivations. Attempting to justify them to others can be a fool's errand.

✎ Inspiration

God has called you, and you have your calling. (St. Cyril of Jerusalem)

✎ Challenge

Pray for the grace to choose your words wisely today.

Joseph

Died 1st century

He may have descended from royalty, but the outer trappings of status were long gone; Joseph was a carpenter with a servant's heart. He listened to God and his messengers, and said yes, even though those in his community likely were whispering about him. But Joseph knew whispers don't matter in this world unless they come from above. He said yes to those whispers: to taking Mary as his wife; to naming her baby Jesus; and to taking his family to Egypt to protect him. After Jesus disappears in Jerusalem at age twelve and is found again, we hear nothing further about Joseph. But our hearts and souls tell us that Jesus learned more than carpentry from this man.

Consider how much easier life would have been for Joseph if he had put Mary aside quietly, and found another wife. The visits from angels likely would have stopped. Sometimes, we think life would be easier if we could turn off God's guidance for us. Joseph's example reminds us that easier isn't always better—or right.

Inspiration

When Joseph awoke from sleep, he did as the angel of the Lord commanded him; he took her as his wife, but had no marital relations with her until she had borne a son; and he named him Jesus. (Matthew 1:24-25)

Challenge

Pray with Joseph about a decision you're struggling to commit to, even though you know what God desires.

Józef Bilczewski

April 26, 1860–March 20, 1923

Józef was the oldest of nine children born to Polish peasants. His quick mind led him to a doctorate in theology (from the same university where John Paul II *(October 22)* later studied) and a professorship in dogmatics. When he was forty, Józef was named archbishop of Lviv, a sprawling diocese in what is now western Ukraine. His twenty years in that post encompassed World War I and the Polish-Ukrainian War, both of which resulted an influx of refugees and displaced people (and, in the case of World War I, the deaths of more than one hundred of his priests). Józef was an advocate for solving challenges by helping people, not by wars, and was known to wear a simple habit as he traveled among the people. At his request, he was buried in Lviv's paupers' cemetery.

With Christ's help, we can all rise above the "lowest" of circumstances. If we do, may we emulate Józef and never forget to use our hands to serve those on society's margins.

Inspiration

"Do not turn your face away from anyone who is poor, and the face of God will not be turned away from you." (Tobit 4:7)

Challenge

Give a helping hand—or smile—to someone who needs it.

Nicholas of Flüe

1417–March 21, 1487

Nicholas had struggled for some time with being obedient to his call to become a hermit. While he'd talked with his spiritual director, he hadn't yet said anything to his wife of twenty years. Finally, he began the conversation one evening just after Dorothea finished nursing the youngest of their ten children, only a few months old. After several days of talking and more than a few tears, Nicholas struck out for his new life, first as a wandering pilgrim of sorts, then as a recluse about a day's walk from his family. The simple yet profound spirituality of the man some called Brother Klaus attracted people from all over Europe. He is credited with offering the advice that may have prevented civil war within the Swiss confederation.

God has a way of beckoning us toward new paths just when the current one is getting comfortable. Regardless of the love and joy we find in the familiar, may we learn from Nicholas's example and say yes to where we are led.

Inspiration

Peace is always in God as God is peace and peace may not be broken but conflict must be eradicated. (St. Nicholas of Flüe)

Challenge

Summon up the courage to listen to the Lord, and to be obedient.

Nicholas Owen

1562–circa March 2, 1606

Some called him Little John because of his stature, but surely not because he was small in faith or bravery. During Elizabeth I's reign, this stone mason and carpenter became expert at designing and building small places for priests to hide. Nicholas also managed to help two Jesuit priests escape from the Tower of London. This lay brother spent about twenty years at this work. He was arrested, tortured, and ransomed, and went right back to what he'd been doing. In 1606, he was arrested again; this time, the torture was so severe that it resulted in his death.

Nicholas's design skills could have earned him a great deal of money had he renounced his faith or lived it quietly and put his talent to work for other purposes. But he put God first. When we are put to the test in less physically threatening situations, may we have the courage to do the same.

Inspiration

"I hereby command you: Be strong and courageous; do not be frightened or dismayed, for the Lord your God is with you wherever you go." (Joshua 1:9)

Challenge

Be disruptive. Stand up for someone who is experiencing discrimination.

Turibius de Mogrovejo

November 16, 1538–March 23, 1606

Some men and women hear the call to religious life when they are children. Turibius was not among them. In fact, Lima, Peru's second archbishop wasn't even a priest when he was named to the post, but an attorney who was the chief judge of the Spanish Inquisition at Granada. Turibius protested to the king about this unusual appointment, but to no avail. He was ordained in 1578 and two years later consecrated as archbishop and headed to Lima. Turibius remained in that role until his death twenty-five years later, and is sometimes called the Charles Borromeo *(November 4)* of Peru; he fought against clerical excesses and advocated for humane treatment of the indigenous people. Two future saints—Rose of Lima and Martin de Porres *(November 3)*—were among those he baptized.

Sometimes, God's plans for us seem so ridiculous, we just laugh. Seriously, how does an attorney get tapped to be an archbishop six thousand miles away? Like Turibius, at some point we need to stop laughing...and surrender.

❧ Inspiration

Do you not know that if you present yourselves to anyone as obedient slaves, you are slaves of the one whom you obey, either of sin, which leads to death, or of obedience, which leads to righteousness? (Romans 6:16)

❧ Challenge

Surrender to a plan of God's that you find ridiculous.

Óscar Romero

August 15, 1917–March 24, 1980

He was seen as a safe choice for a very unsafe time. Óscar had been a priest for almost thirty-five years before he was named archbishop of San Salvador in 1977. El Salvador was on the precipice of civil war, and many regarded him as conservative or traditional. But less than a month after his appointment, a Jesuit priest who was a good friend of Óscar's was gunned down. The tragedy was a conversion moment for Óscar. In the three years before the 1979 Nobel Peace Prize nominee was assassinated while offering Mass at a Carmelite sisters' hospital, he spoke out loudly and boldly on behalf of the poor and others persecuted by the ruling junta.

Some people regarded Óscar as dangerous. Some people regarded Jesus as dangerous. Being a Christian is a risky, sometimes fatal thing. While few of us living in the United States are called to give up our lives for Christ, we all are called to work for justice in our families, our neighborhoods, and our world.

Inspiration

Our Christian faith requires that we submerge ourselves in this world. (St. Óscar Romero)

Challenge

Write a letter. Make a donation. Have a conversation. Give a smile. Do something risky for Christ today.

Dismas (The Good Thief)

Died circa 33

He's commonly known as Dismas, the thief who was crucified next to Jesus who took ownership of his crimes—and asked Jesus for forgiveness. Scripture indicates that both he and the other man being crucified that day initially mocked Jesus but that Dismas had a conversion moment on his cross. Jesus didn't condemn him, didn't remind him of his previous words. Instead, Jesus told Dismas they would be together in paradise that very day.

Jesus showed mercy almost up to his very last breath, forgiving Dismas and offering him hope. And if Jesus would do that for a man like Dismas, we must have faith that we too may join him in paradise.

✿ Inspiration

Then he said, "Jesus, remember me when you come into your kingdom." (Luke 23:42)

✿ Challenge

Avail yourself of the Sacrament of Penance and Reconciliation. Believe that with a contrite heart, you can be forgiven

Stephen of Mar Saba

Circa 725–794

For eight years, Stephen had done the usual public-facing duties at Palestine's Mar Saba monastery. He'd worked in the pharmacy, as a cantor, and so on. What he really wanted to do, he told the abbot, was to leave to become a hermit. But the abbot had another idea for the nephew of St. John Damascene *(December 4)*. Stephen could have five days each week as a hermit if he made himself available to the community on weekends. And so they reached an agreement, though as time went on, Stephen made himself more and more available to the others. Overall, the arrangement worked for nearly forty years, until Stephen's death.

Stephen's story shows us that what we want and what God desires of us aren't always so very far apart as it seems. Just as he gave up some privacy, we can give up some unnecessary spending and activity to serve God and our family and friends.

☙ Inspiration

There is nothing of value in life except the soul's gain, but the soul's gain is to be found only in the love of God. (St. Stephen of Mar Saba)

☙ Challenge

Offer a compromise in a situation that seems hopelessly deadlocked.

John Climacus

Circa 570–649

John was the closest to spiritual perfection, it seems, when he was alone. He was just sixteen when he became part of a group of monks on Mount Sinai. He lived as a hermit for thirty years before being pressed to serve as the community's abbot. He was at least seventy at the time, and after four years in leadership, returned to his hermitage. But all that quiet time led to *The Ladder of Divine Ascent,* a thirty-step manual of sorts for monks that also offers much food for those living in the world.

The spiritual life of a hermit or monk, it turns out, is not very different from that of the rest of us. *The Ladder of Divine Ascent* offers lessons in how to grow closer to God, with topics ranging from renouncing the world to living our lives in love. Some crosses and gifts are universal.

✒ Inspiration

Obedience is a renunciation of discrimination in a treasure of discernment. (St. John Climacus)

✒ Challenge

Compose a list of three ways in which you can grow in spiritual perfection.

Leonardo Murialdo

October 28, 1828–March 30, 1900

Some might say Leonardo moved down in the world as life went on. The thing is, that's just how he wanted it. He grew up in a moderately wealthy Italian family and didn't think about the priesthood as a boy, but an unspecified personal crisis in his mid-teens eventually drove him into Christ's arms, with a desire to show others the mercy he had received. After Leonardo's ordination, he began working with poor children in the Turin area; he went on to a position at a trade school. About that same time, he organized the Catholic Workers Union in the area as well as a community of priests commonly known as the Murialdines. His support system included two other priests who would go on to become saints, John Bosco *(January 31)* and Joseph Cafasso *(January 15)*.

We all have crises. When we beg God to help us weather them, the outcome can not only inspire others, it can also galvanize us to share his mercy. Let's put our gratitude into action.

☙ Inspiration

You came back into possession of a soul destined to be your temple, but which for a long time had been only a dwelling of demons. Oh! How sensitive your infinite mercy became to me then! (St. Leonardo Murialdo)

☙ Challenge

Pray in gratitude for a time God showered mercy on you, even though you felt so unworthy you didn't even ask for it.

Gwynllyw

450–600

It was a life so different from most saints, including a friendship with King Arthur. Gwynllyw was a king himself, of a Welsh tribe, but that did not stop him from resorting to robbery and plunder and getting his men to do the same. He fell in love with the beautiful Gwladys, whose father was determined the match would not occur. What followed was the stuff of legends—three hundred of Gwynllyw's men spiriting away the willing Gwladys. When Arthur met her, he wanted her for himself, but he was dissuaded from that course when he learned of Gwynllyw's passion. The pair married and carried on their merry, thieving ways. Eventually, they were converted by their oldest son, whom we know as St. Cadoc, and became hermits.

The story of Gwynllyw and Gwladys shows us that no one is beyond redemption. We just have to say yes when he asks.

Inspiration

"Just so, I tell you, there will be more joy in heaven over one sinner who repents than over ninety-nine righteous persons who need no repentance." (Luke 15:7)

Challenge

Talk about the difference God has made in your life with someone who may have given up on the Almighty.

Ludovico of Casoria

March 11, 1814–March 30, 1885

Ludovico was thirty-three years old. He'd already been a Franciscan priest for ten years, serving as a philosophy and mathematics teacher. But then, something happened one day when he was at adoration. He felt called to refocus his energies on helping Naples' neediest people. The ways in which he delivered on this call included establishment of a school for African children formerly enslaved and a center to help those unable to see, hear, or speak. Ludovico also founded communities of men and women religious to support his work.

We can be happy and fulfilled in what we're doing, only to find one day that, bam! God desires us to take on something different and outside our comfort zone. If that happens, may we follow Ludovico's example and embrace that new direction with gusto.

✒ Inspiration

The love of Christ wounded my heart. (St. Ludovico of Casoria)

✒ Challenge

In your prayers today, ask God if there's something different you need to do for others. Listen carefully.

Lodovico Pavoni

September 11, 1784–April 1, 1849

He was the oldest son of a well-respected, wealthy northern Italian family, and stood to inherit much in terms of money and responsibility. But Lodovico had seen his parents' example of philanthropy, and started engaging with children in poorer neighborhoods. Small wonder that when he was ordained at twenty-six, one of his first assignments was with youth centers. There, he realized the boys who stopped by weren't coming to Mass, and their employers often were exploiting them. So, Lodovico came up with an alternative. He set up a vocational school where trades could be learned, including Italy's first printing school and a publishing house that still exists today. A week before his death, rebellion threatened the town where they lived. Lodovico managed to get his charges to safety.

Lodovico could have easily turned his back on the young men who were coming by the center but not attending Mass. Instead, he met them where they were: in need of better job situations and of mentorship. God desires us to do no less.

Inspiration

Rigorism keeps heaven empty. (Lodovico Pavoni)

Challenge

Give someone the benefit of the doubt today.

Nuno Álvares Pereira

June 24, 1360–November 1, 1431

While his parents were not married when he was born (legend has it that his father sired twenty-three children), Nuno still received an education befitting a knight, and joined the military at thirteen. Three years later, he married a wealthy widow. Portugal was in turmoil in 1383 when the king died without an heir, and Nuno was named supreme military commander to the man who became John I of Portugal. (The two would be lifelong friends, with Nuno's daughter marrying the king's son.) John's rule was cemented by Nuno's win in a major battle in 1385. While some call him the fighting saint, Nuno also was known for his charity to the people of his opponents and his devotion to the Blessed Virgin. After his wife died, Nuno lived his last eight or so years as a Carmelite friar.

Ever feel like there's too much drama and conflict in your life? May we, like Nuno, remember to pray, love, and tithe, regardless of the degree of fame we achieve.

Inspiration

For the love of God is this, that we obey his commandments. And his commandments are not burdensome, for whatever is born of God conquers the world. And this is the victory that conquers the world, our faith. (1 John 5:3-4)

Challenge

Pray for help in accepting or coping with drama in your life beyond your control.

Pedro Calungsod

July 21, 1654–April 2, 1672

Pedro was young—and fast. Exactly what drew the Filipino teenager to go to Guam with Spanish Jesuit missionaries is unclear. A sense of adventure? A blooming vocation? Regardless, it was Pedro who was with the Jesuit superior when the priest was called to baptize the newborn daughter of a non-Christian chieftain. Things got confusing, and the little girl was baptized with the approval of her Christian mother. This enraged the chieftain, and both Pedro and the priest were attacked. It's believed Pedro likely could have escaped as the spears flew, but instead, he chose to remain with the priest and be martyred.

Standing with a friend or family member when others have turned against that person puts us at risk. And yet, if we believe in them, that's what we're called to do. Remember how Jesus laid down his life for us, even though we did nothing to deserve it.

Inspiration

"No one has greater love than this, to lay down one's life for one's friends." (John 15:13)

Challenge

Lay down some pride or prestige to support someone.

Francis of Paola

March 27, 1416–April 2, 1507

From a young age, Francis wanted a stripped-down life, one focused on worship and sacrifice. He began living as a hermit on his parents' property in his mid-teens, and soon was joined by like-minded young men. He was only twenty when what would become the Minim Friars was founded, requiring abstinence from meat or other animal products in addition to vows of poverty, chastity, and obedience. But then a funny thing happened. The Italian's adherence to the contemplative life put him into public ministry at high levels. The French king called Francis to come to him when the king was very ill; Francis did so reluctantly but at the pope's urging. The king died in Francis's arms, and the king's son built a monastery for the Minims so Francis would stay nearby. Francis was canonized just twelve years after his death.

It's a struggle, isn't it, when we feel called to a particular means of service that seems so suited to our personality, only to find God tugging us in a different direction? Like Francis, may we humble ourselves and offer our obedience when the Father pulls us out of our comfort zone.

Inspiration

Be lovers of peace, the most precious treasure that anyone can desire. (St. Francis of Paola)

Challenge

Think about where you could find peace in a family or ministry situation that would mean a big change.

Benedict the African

1526-April 4, 1589

Benedict was a natural leader. But the way he exercised his leadership was different from the way we might expect. The son of enslaved Africans brought to Italy, Benedict was freed (either at birth or at age eighteen) and found work as a shepherd or day laborer. He was invited to join a nearby group of hermits, and spent time as their leader. When the group was forced to align more closely with the Franciscans, Benedict became a friar and relocated to Palermo, where he served as the community's cook. His confreres had so much respect for his spirituality and temperament that they selected him as their superior even though he was not a priest. After one term, Benedict asked to return to the kitchen, where he ministered not only through food but through private counsel and healing for his community and other visitors.

Benedict likely found the responsibilities of formal leadership to be soul-sucking, and knew his call was to lead by example and love. We can lead from his example, and not accept promotions and titles simply because they're offered.

Inspiration

"For who is greater, the one who is at the table or the one who serves? Is it not the one at the table? But I am among you as the one who serves." (Luke 22:27)

Challenge

Say no to the offer of a new responsibility that would be all about you and your ego and not about service.

Isidore of Seville

Circa 560–April 4, 636

Isidore's list of accomplishments is long and impressive: archbishop of Seville for more than three decades; leader of Catholicism in Spain at a time when Arianism had divided the country; founder of numerous schools and seminaries. But he's best known for his response to a friend's request for what we would today call an encyclopedia. Isidore compiled *Etymologies* amid all his other responsibilities. The compilation included not only the origins of words or Christian views but also topics including animals, music, and more. It featured the works of more than two hundred authors and ran to twenty volumes. The compilation was used for nine centuries and was name-checked by the likes of Dante and Chaucer. Isidore was named a Doctor of the Church in 1722 for this and his other writings.

Isidore was brilliant, but even a brilliant man would have found the task of compiling the world's knowledge daunting! God's requests to us may seem just as overwhelming, whether it's being a parent, a cantor, a civic leader, or a volunteer at a homeless shelter. Just as Isidore did by incorporating and crediting others' works in *Etymologies,* let's remember we don't have to do everything on our own. We have Spirit-filled help.

☙ Inspiration

Faith should come by persuasion, not by extortion. (St. Isidore of Seville)

☙ Challenge

Swallow your pride. Let your control go. Ask someone to help you with a big project.

Vincent Ferrer

January 23, 1350–April 5, 1419

Vincent, a Spanish Dominican, had a mentor: Cardinal Peter de Luna. In 1378, de Luna and other cardinals decided the election of Pope Urban VI was invalid, beginning the schism of the Avignon antipopes. De Luna became antipope Benedict XIII, and Vincent's ties with him continued; he was the antipope's personal theologian and confessor. As time went on, Vincent tried to convince his friend to reconcile with Rome, but instead, things went in the opposite direction, with a third claimant surfacing by 1409. Vincent pleaded with Castilian King Ferdinand to withdraw his support of de Luna. The king did, and the schism ended in 1417. Vincent died less than three years later.

Mentors give us wise counsel and sometimes understand better than we do ourselves how to use our skills and how to address our shortcomings. But they're people, just like we are, and sometimes they need friendly correction. May we find the courage to tell those we admire when they go down a wrong path.

Inspiration

"If another member of the church sins against you, go and point out the fault when the two of you are alone. If the member listens to you, you have regained that one." (Matthew 18:15)

Challenge

Pray for the words to provide gentle correction to someone whom you greatly respect, but who needs to hear from you.

John Baptist de La Salle

April 30, 1651–April 7, 1719

Later, John would say that if he had known all the trials and all the good that would come through founding the LaSalle Brothers, he probably wouldn't have been brave enough to do it. John came from a wealthy French family, and had experience with educating his younger siblings following the deaths of both parents in less than a year. However, when he agreed to help a friend set up a school for the poor in his hometown of Rheims, he was disgusted by not only the students but the teachers. They were in very different social classes than his family. But John took a deep breath, and started taking the teachers into his home to educate them. It wasn't long until, over his family's objections, he'd bought a home in a poorer area of town, moved in with the teachers and resigned as canon of the local cathedral. In May 1694, John and a dozen other men took perpetual vows in the new community.

Let's be honest. Sometimes, people disgust us. They don't have good hygiene, they don't speak well, their clothes leave much to desired. And yet, as John learned with his teachers, there's one sure antidote to disgust—providing assistance to people who don't even know it in a way that shows we are equals.

Inspiration

Your faith must be a light that guides you in all things and a shining beacon to lead to heaven those you instruct. (St. John Baptist de La Salle)

Challenge

Have a conversation, even a brief one, with someone who disgusts you.

Zeno of Verona

Died 371

That Zeno started life in Africa, we are sure. Experts say that his ninety-plus surviving letters and homilies, including his thoughts on the Trinity, the Blessed Virgin Mary, and the sacraments, have a cadence and style found among African writers of the day. He may have made the move to Verona, Italy, about 340 due to his father's work or because he was a follower of Athanasius of Alexandria *(May 2)*. Regardless of the reason, the city became his spiritual home; he served as bishop for nine years despite persecution by rulers who supported Arianism.

We're told to bloom where we are planted, and Zeno is a great example of that truism. He likely didn't look or sound like most Veronese Catholics, but his devotion to God paved the way for his acceptance. It can do the same for us in unfamiliar situations.

✍Inspiration

You shall also love the stranger, for you were strangers in the land of Egypt. (Deuteronomy 10:19)

✍Challenge

Share a smile, a conversation, or a meal with someone who doesn't look like you.

Acacius of Amida

Died 425

As the bishop of Amida (now in Turkey), Acacius surely had much to do: care for his flock, see to the formation of his priests. But he was troubled by the lack of basic human care for seven thousand Persians who were being held in his city. The Roman captors had plenty of other priorities for the funds they had, and the Persians were starving. Acacius sold the church's gold and silver dishes and cups to ransom the captives, restore them to good health, and provide passage back home. It's said that this gesture prompted the Persian emperor to end Christian persecutions in his domain.

We all see suffering and injustice every day, but turn our eyes away. Acacius's action reminds us that we have more power and resources than we are willing to admit to alleviate someone else's suffering.

❧ Inspiration

Our God, my brethren, needs neither dishes nor cups; for he neither eats nor drinks, nor is in want of anything. (St. Acacius of Amida)

❧ Challenge

You don't have to sell all your possessions to connect with someone being treated unjustly. Maybe sharing time is all that's necessary. Ask.

Michael de Sanctis

September 29, 1591–April 10, 1625

It was a short life, a quiet life, but one lived in obedience. Michael was only eleven when his father died. The child already was feeling he had a vocation, and had begun practicing personal austerities. His mother was understandably less than excited about losing her son so soon after her husband, but she agreed to his entry into a Trinitarian seminary in Barcelona when he was twelve. Michael took his final vows just before his sixteenth birthday. Eventually, he learned of the Discalced Trinitarians, whose simple lifestyle resonated with him. Michael moved to their community, and served two terms as superior at the Valladolid monastery before his death.

Not all of our saints lived "big" lives as martyrs, writers, preachers, and so on. But we can learn just as much from those like Michael whose worship and obedience were done in quieter ways.

✒Inspiration

But I have calmed and quieted my soul,
  like a weaned child with its mother;
    my soul is like the weaned child that is with me. (Psalm 131:2)

✒Challenge

Spend some quiet time with God today.

Stanisław of Szczepanów

July 26, 1030-April 11, 1079

Stanisław had been bishop of Kraków for seven years, and his relationship with the Polish king, Bolesław, had gone from bad to worse. There are two sides to the story, of course; there always are. Some say Bolesław was cruel and immoral; some say Stanisław conspired with the king's brother to have Bolesław removed or his powers reduced. Things came to a head when the bishop excommunicated the king, and refused to continue Mass at Kraków cathedral when Bolesław entered. It was not long after that that Bolesław himself killed Stanisław as he was celebrating Mass at a chapel outside the city.

Stanisław must have felt he had no choice but to bar the king from the Eucharist. The result of this dispute shows us that stories don't always have happy endings on earth, and reminds us of the need to put on our spiritual armor when we do battle with those who oppose our beliefs.

✍ Inspiration

Therefore take up the whole armor of God, so that you may be able to withstand on that evil day, and having done everything, to stand firm. (Ephesians 6:13)

✍ Challenge

Stand firm—compassionately, gently, but firm—in the face of evil.

David Uribe Velasco

December 29, 1889–April 12, 1927

It was a time of uneasy relations between the Catholic Church and successive Mexican governments. Between 1911 and David's ordination two years later, Mexico had three presidents, with the last being assassinated. When he was fourteen, David had told his father that he was well aware of the persecution he was likely to face. The Cristero War began in 1926 and prompted Mexico's bishops to end public worship. Like many priests, David continued to offer Mass in private even though he had already been arrested once and released on his parishioners' petition. When he was taken into custody the final time on April 7, 1927, he was offered the option to be bishop of a state-run church. He rejected the offer, and was shot in the back of the neck a few days later.

Think how weary David must have felt at times, wondering when the next bad thing was going to happen. His strength reminds us that regardless of how much despair we feel, with God, we can endure anything that comes our way.

Inspiration

What happiness to die in defense of the rights of God! (St. David Uribe Velasco)

Challenge

How can you burnish your spiritual armor in a difficult situation?

Martin I

June 21 598–September 16, 655

Martin's short papacy—he served only six years—was marked by rancor, and by faith and bravery on his part. He knew how political the Holy See could be, as he had been the nuncio to Constantinople for his immediate predecessor, Theodore I. Martin faced the big challenge of the day head on by calling the Lateran Council, which confirmed Jesus had both fully (perfect) human and fully divine natures. Monothelitics, including several emperors and the bishop of Constantinople, believed Jesus had only a divine nature while he was on earth. Martin's refusal to back down caused him to be arrested, held for more than a year, and convicted of treason. It was only his poor physical health that spared him being put to death; instead, he was exiled to Crimea, where he died four months later. Martin is regarded as the last papal martyr.

Martin didn't take the easy way out of the argument with the Monothelitics. He knew what the Church taught, and stood by it. His example can bolster us as we navigate a world that does not value life in all forms and that disregards other Church teachings.

Inspiration

So Jesus asked the twelve, "Do you also wish to go away?" Simon Peter answered him, "Lord, to whom can we go? You have the words of eternal life." (John 6:67-68)

Challenge

Spend some time researching a Church doctrine you find hard to understand.

Peter González

1190–April 15, 1246

He was riding into the city of Astorga in northwest Spain, but it proved to be Peter's road to Damascus. He was young and quite full of himself, prideful about accepting a church official position that he was receiving only because the bishop happened to be his uncle. But then God intervened: Peter ended up in the mud and other street gunk when his horse stumbled. People laughed. But the incident broke Peter's self-satisfaction. He changed his ways and became a Dominican. He developed a reputation as a powerful preacher at the Spanish court and elsewhere, and spent his final years ministering to sailors.

Peter's comeuppance changed him spiritually. We all have the same opportunities when misfortune or embarrassment befalls us. If we don't learn from it, we can be almost certain God will provide another opportunity.

Inspiration
"While I was on my way and approaching Damascus, about noon a great light from heaven suddenly shone about me." (Acts 22:6)

Challenge
Think about what God is trying to teach you through some recent stumbles.

Michael Garicoïts

April 15, 1797–May 14, 1863

Michael, the oldest son of French Basque peasants, was far from a perfect child. He got into his share of mischief, including some minor thievery. Things changed after his First Communion, and he told his parents he believed he was meant to be a priest. This seemed far beyond the realm of possibility given the family's finances. His grandmother, however, knew a priest at a parish about ten miles away; the priest may have been sheltered by the extended family during the French Revolution. Together, they worked out a plan for Michael to further his education by working for the priest. He went on to found the Congregation of the Sacred Heart of Jesus of Bétharram, a teaching and missionary community.

Michael might have never become a priest if it hadn't been for his grandmother and her priest friend, whose name appears to be lost to time, coming together to help him. He then paid their kindnesses forward through his community. This story shows us the flame that can result from the smallest spark from us.

✺ Inspiration

"And the king will answer them, 'Truly I tell you, just as you did it to one of the least of these who are members of my family, you did it to me.'" (Matthew 25:40)

✺ Challenge

Help a family member or friend come closer to Christ by making a personal sacrifice.

Drogo

March 14, 1105-circa 1186

One couldn't have blamed Drogo for questioning God's love for him. Both his parents were dead before he came of age; indeed, it's possible his nobleman father died before he was born, and his mother died at his birth. After time as a shepherd, Drogo began making pilgrimages from his home country of France to Rome, and it was during one of those journeys that he contracted a disease that left him with ugly body sores, so ugly that there was a move to put him in a cell so that he wouldn't scare passersby. But Drogo didn't give up faith as a result of all this. Rather, he submitted to his enclosure with grace and humility. For the last forty years of his life, his only human contact came when the Eucharist was offered to him through a small window.

People close us off metaphorically today, sometimes because we don't look like them, other times because we don't share their worldly beliefs. Drogo's example reminds us to draw all the closer to God when things we can't understand happen.

Inspiration

"Blessed are you when people revile you and persecute you and utter all kinds of evil against you falsely on my account." (Matthew 5:11)

Challenge

Offer your morning prayers for someone who seeks to exclude you.

Benedict Joseph Labre

March 25, 1748–April 16, 1783

No religious community, it seemed, wanted him. Benedict Joseph was interested in the priesthood, mostly likely due to the influence of an uncle who was a priest and who was responsible for much of the boy's upbringing. But in turn, the Trappists, Carthusians, and Cistercians all rejected him for one reason or another. Given that, Benedict Joseph pursued a religious life in his own way. He became a nomadic pilgrim, carrying little with him beyond a coat, two rosaries, a crucifix, and beloved books including *Imitation of Christ*. His home until he died was a spot in the ruins of Rome's Colosseum.

People say no, or not now, to us often. It might be someone we love very much who doesn't feel the same way about us, or an employer who gives someone else that big promotion we so desired. Benedict Joseph's story reminds us to take our direction from God, who will never reject us.

❧ Inspiration

I never studied divinity. I am only a poor ignorant beggar. (St. Benedict Joseph Labre)

❧ Challenge

Offer your evening prayers for someone who hurt your ego with a rejection, large or small.

Hermenegild

Died 585

Hermenegild's royal Spanish parents raised him as an Arian—those who do not believe in Jesus's equal divinity with God the Father. But when Hermenegild married the young daughter of a ruler of part of France, she refused to convert from Catholicism. Hermenegild's father sent him to reign over a part of the kingdom that included Seville. There, the couple came under the influence of a Catholic monk, and Hermenegild converted. The relationship with his father worsened, and military action ensued. The father was the victor, and when he ordered Hermenegild to re-convert, Hermenegild refused and was executed.

Emotions can run high in families with religious differences. We want those we love to have the hope of eternal life, and we can't imagine being in heaven, if we get there, without them. Seeing us live a consistent, Christ-centered life is far more likely to influence a conversion than cutting them off would.

☙ Inspiration

As for you, always be sober, endure suffering, do the work of an evangelist, carry out your ministry fully. (2 Timothy 4:5)

☙ Challenge

Listen to a family member whose strong views on religion, politics, or anything else you find difficult to stomach.

Leo IX

June 21, 1002–April 19, 1054

It sounds novel to us almost a thousand years later. We'd think anyone selected as pope would be humbled and say yes immediately. But that's not what this saint did. Instead, he told Henry III, the Holy Roman emperor, he wouldn't take the position unless the people and clergy of Rome agreed with the nomination. They did, and Leo IX embarked on vigorous efforts to stop the sale of religious offices and to ferret out cases where priests were not observing their vow of celibacy. He traveled so much he became known as "the apostolic pilgrim." But those good works are not what Leo is most remembered for. Rather, he's known for agreeing to participate in an ill-fated expedition against the Normans in southern Italy that ended with the Great Schism between the Roman Catholic and Eastern Orthodox Churches.

It's not hard to work up some sympathy for Leo—and to see lessons for ourselves. Regardless of how much good we might do during our lives, we may be remembered for our missteps and sins by some. History may judge us harshly or fairly or not at all. But that doesn't matter. What matters is what God will say when he reviews what we did in his name.

✾ Inspiration

For all of us must appear before the judgment seat of Christ, so that each may receive recompense for what has been done in the body, whether good or evil. (2 Corinthians 5:10)

✾ Challenge

Consider what God loves about someone you find beyond redemption.

Cædwalla

Died 689

Today, we might call Cædwalla a brawler. As a young man, he'd been exiled from Wessex, but used the time to put together alliances and took over Sussex and then England's Isle of Wight, the latter in a particularly violent way, wiping out the pagan inhabitants. Cædwalla himself may or may not have been a Christian, but he hadn't gotten around to being baptized. It may have taken battle injuries in 688 (and some convincing by St. Wilfrid, whom he knew well) to get Cædwalla to Rome, where on April 10, 689, he was baptized by the pope. Tradition has it that Cædwalla was still wearing his baptismal robes when he fell gravely ill and died less than two weeks later.

Cædwalla waited until he was in distress to fully turn his heart and soul to God, and it's easy for us to do the same. When life is on track, let's remember to offer our adoration and gratitude, rather than only commune with the Father when we are in despair.

Inspiration

But we have this treasure in clay jars, so that it may be clear that this extraordinary power belongs to God and does not come from us. (2 Corinthians 4:7)

Challenge

Offer adoration and gratitude, not petitions, in your prayer time today.

Anselm of Canterbury

1033–1109

Anselm and his father seemed often to be in conflict, including when the father refused to give his consent for the fifteen-year-old son to enter a monastery. This helped precipitate Anselm's three years of wandering about, finally landing at the Bec Abbey in Normandy at age twenty-six. There, Anselm found the teacher he needed, the abbot Lanfranc. Anselm eventually became abbot himself, and it was during this period that he did much of the writing about God's existence that centuries later would lead to his naming as a Doctor of the Church. He also followed in Lanfranc's footsteps as archbishop of Canterbury, beginning thirty years of disputes with secular rulers, including two periods of exile.

One likes to think of the intellectual discourses Lanfranc and Anselm must have had at Bec. Perhaps they helped the young monk deepen his beliefs and develop his fortitude, which would be sorely needed in the final third of his life as archbishop. Mentors continue to influence us long after we're parted by miles or by death.

☙ Inspiration

For I do not seek to understand that I may believe, but I believe in order to understand. (St. Anselm of Canterbury)

☙ Challenge

Identify the most helpful non-family mentor you've had. What lessons did you learn that you use in your faith life today? Maybe it's patience or persistence or acceptance, or something else.

Conrad of Parzham

December 22, 1818–April 21, 1894

He loved being outside and doing the fieldwork at his parents' farm in southern Germany. It provided him with quiet time with God, time he would need after losing both his parents in two years. The man we know as Conrad of Parzham spent eight years as a secular Franciscan, but he felt he was being called to something different. At thirty-one, he entered a Capuchin friary and became a lay brother. For more than forty years, he was the doorkeeper, which provided the opportunity to interact with not only the friars but also visitors to a nearby shrine and those in the need in the area. Conrad was known for his devotion to the Blessed Mother, and for his patience.

Conrad by nature preferred quiet time, but his assignment as doorkeeper involved anything but quiet. He still managed, however, to find time for adoration and prayer. Let's remember his example when we think we're too busy to pray. The time—and God—are always there, if our priorities are in order.

Inspiration

The crucifix is my book. (St. Conrad of Parzham)

Challenge

Turn off your social media accounts (or better yet, your phone or computer) and sit in silence with God for ten minutes today. Try for fifteen minutes tomorrow.

George

Died circa 303

Did he kill a dragon after the townspeople agreed to become Christians? Did he save a princess? Did he marry a princess? Legends tend to obscure what we really know about George. Yes, he really existed. He may have been a soldier. We know that he sacrificed his life in what is now the Lod, Israel, area, by refusing to renounce his faith.

We love to tell stories, and they tend to get a little bigger each time we or someone else tells them. In the case of George, what matters is not the legends that have grown up around him, but his martyrdom. Let's remember that next time we're tempted to embellish a bit—or understate a bit—when we're talking with God about our accomplishments or shortcomings.

Inspiration

Birds roost with their own kind, so honesty comes home to those who practice it. (Sirach 27:9)

Challenge

Speak truth about yourself. Go to confession.

Benedict Menni

March 11, 1841–April 24, 1914

Benedict had been ordained for only a year when he was sent to reinvigorate his community, the Hospitallers of Saint John of God *(March 8)*, in Spain. The congregation had all but died out there after being banned in 1836. Never mind the Italian's relative youth (he was twenty-six) or the fact that he spoke no Spanish; that was his assignment. And Benedict succeeded in almost every way possible. Within months of arriving, he established the congregation's first hospital for children. He joined with two women who wanted to provide psychiatric care for women to found a corresponding community of women religious. By the time Benedict died, nearly two dozen Hospitaller facilities were in operation.

Benedict took very seriously his mission to rebuild his congregation in Spain. He didn't protest about obstacles or figure good enough was good enough after opening one hospital. His story encourages us to follow God's plan with excitement, enthusiasm, and faith.

Inspiration

Nothing fills my heart except love for my Jesus. (St. Benedict Menni)

Challenge

This week, tackle your work with the same enthusiasm Benedict would.

April 24

Mark

5–circa 68

The Gospel writer may or may not have ever heard Jesus himself. But the breakneck pace of his sixteen chapters—the shortest of the four Gospels—paints a picture of Christ as a man on the move, an almost restless savior intent on connecting with the people he had come to save. How did Mark get that sense of Jesus if they never met? While Mark traveled with his cousin Barnabas *(June 11)* and had a complicated relationship with Paul *(June 29)*, it just may be that he learned the most about Jesus through Peter *(June 28)*. Both Mark and his mother were Peter's friends.

Peter lived the years with Jesus. He preached his faith and would be martyred for it and was the rock on which the Church was founded. But Mark's role in sharing Jesus' story through writing was essential as well. We all are called to preach the Good News, through speaking, writing, or direct ministry to our families, colleagues, and communities.

✆Inspiration

"And the good news must first be proclaimed to all nations." (Mark 13:10)

✆Challenge

Think about what you are doing today to preach the gospel to all the "nations" you touch.

Rafael Arnáiz Barón

April 9, 1911–April 26, 1938

Rafael's life plan was in motion. He'd earned his bachelor's degree in 1930, and had been accepted at a Spanish architecture school. But before school started, he visited relatives who introduced him to the nearby San Isidoro de Dueñas Trappist monastery. Always a spiritual person, Rafael fell in love—with the monastery, with the community prayers, and with the silent time with God. He finished his studies and became a Trappist postulant. Shortly thereafter, Rafael developed diabetes, and he became so ill he had to leave the monastery to convalesce at home three times. His health put full profession as a monk out of reach, and so he became an oblate. He chose to spend his final months at the monastery, where he is buried.

Rafael was blessed to find a "thin place" where God felt particularly near. Those places abound—at monasteries, at adoration, in a park, in a room in our own homes. We just have to open our eyes and souls to seeing them.

Inspiration

What little I know I have learned from the cross. (St. Rafael Arnáiz Barón)

Challenge

Spend time in a thin place.

Giovanni Battista Piamarta

November 26, 1841–April 25, 1913

Giovanni knew better than to give up on poverty-stricken Italian youth—he'd been one himself. His mother died when he was nine, and he received little attention from his father. His formal education was lacking. But someone—a grandparent or someone to whom he was an apprentice—connected him with the opportunity to go to seminary. Giovanni was ordained at twenty-four, and spent the rest of his life helping boys and young men gain valuable life skills along with an introduction to Christ. The Artigianelli Institute he co-founded today offers training in electronics, computers, and more. Giovanni also founded the Congregation of the Holy Family of Nazareth and a community for women, the Humble Servants of the Lord.

It doesn't take much for a young person to get off track if he or she lacks family support. It also doesn't take much to be the adult who helps that young person to find faith and hope. Giovanni's story shows us the enduring value of lending a helping hand.

❧Inspiration

But Jesus said, "Let the little children come to me, and do not stop them; for it is to such as these that the kingdom of heaven belongs." (Matthew 19:14)

❧Challenge

Identify a way in which you can help a child you know draw closer to God—or, a way in which you can help at-risk children in your community.

Louis de Montfort

January 31, 1673–April 28, 1716

These days, it's hard to think of Marian devotion without thinking of Louis de Montfort and the numerous books and videos related to his two works, *True Devotion to the Blessed Virgin* and *The Secret of the Rosary.* But that was not always the case. During his lifetime, Louis spent much time studying Marian devotion throughout the ages, but he was primarily known for his gifted preaching, especially encouraging parish missions in France at a time when the political climate toward Catholics was chilly. *True Devotion* was lost for more than a hundred years after his death. It was finally published in 1853.

Do you ever wonder if doing what God desires is worth it? Maybe like Louis you're a writer whose work doesn't get the attention you think it deserves, or maybe your family doesn't seem to appreciate all you do. While affirmation from people can be gratifying, none of them can match God's "well done, good and faithful servant."

✒ Inspiration

Jesus gave more glory to God his Father by submitting to his Mother for thirty years than he would have given him had he converted the whole world by working the greatest miracles. (St. Louis de Montfort)

✒ Challenge

Spend some time with Mary today. Tell her Louis sent you.

Hugh of Cluny

May 13, 1024–April 28, 1109

His French nobleman father wanted him to be a knight; his mother, a priest. Perhaps navigating that discord between his parents helped Hugh in his sixty years as abbot of Cluny monastery. Hugh served as a counselor to nine popes, and was among the time's leading voices for reforms to end the selling of clerical offices and to foster clerical discipline. His diplomatic efforts fell short, however, in seeking long-term peace between his friend Pope Gregory VII *(May 27)* and King Henry IV, whose godfather happened to be Hugh.

Diplomacy—Hugh seems to have had a natural gift for it. Knowing how to bring differing viewpoints together to achieve a common good can be difficult, especially when we have personal experience with treachery or dishonesty by another. Like Hugh, may we acquire the wisdom to attune our ears to God's words in such situations.

❧ Inspiration

"Everyone then who hears these words of mine and acts on them will be like a wise man who built his house on rock." (Matthew 7:24)

❧ Challenge

Identify a situation in your family or at work or among your friends where God is calling you to be the peacemaker. Pray to receive the words they need to hear.

Pius V

January 17, 1504–May 1, 1572

Pius V was pope for just six years, but they were a whirlwind six years. He declared England's Elizabeth I a heretic and excommunicated her. He seemed to have been influenced by his friend Charles Borromeo *(November 4)*, saying the money that would have been spent on banquets celebrating his election should go to the poor instead. The missal that he made a Mass requirement remained in place until Vatican II. His actions were not all positive, however; some of his policies were anti-Semitic, and many say he overused Inquisition powers.

Pius V was a man of action and a disruptive leader, but underneath many of his actions was a desire to keep opponents of Catholicism at bay. In his mind, he was defending the truth. The stories of his excesses show us that when we turn to self-interest or fear, we can lose sight of the eternal truth.

✒ Inspiration

"Some even from your own group will come distorting the truth in order to entice the disciples to follow them." (Acts 20:30)

✒ Challenge

Be discerning in what you believe from people who say God has given them all the answers.

Peregrine Laziosi

Circa 1260–May 1, 1345

To begin with, Peregrine was a bit of a thug. A wealthy, politically connected thug, but a thug. Philip Benizi *(August 23)* of the Servite Order had been dispatched by the pope to Peregrine's hometown in hopes of reuniting faithful Catholics and those who opposed the papacy. (Peregrine was in the latter group.) One day, while Philip was speaking, Peregrine struck down the priest, hitting him in the face. Philip's response? A smile. Peregrine had a conversion moment, and asked Philip to forgive him. It was the first step to Peregrine becoming a Servite himself; he spent more than sixty years in service to the sick and the poor.

Meeting violence—physical, verbal, or on social media—with love is challenging. Where appropriate, restraining ourselves from retaliating in kind may be the first step to conversion for our persecutors.

☞Inspiration

Then Jesus said to him, "Put your sword back into its place, for all who take the sword will perish by the sword." (Matthew 26:52)

☞Challenge

Respond with a smile if someone criticizes the way you're raising your children, doing your job, driving, or carrying out another activity or practice.

Athanasius of Alexandria

Circa 296–373

Christianity wasn't for sissies in the early days. Athanasius became bishop of Alexandria when he was about thirty, and held the position for close to forty-seven years. But seventeen of those years were spent in five separate exiles by four different emperors. However, Athanasius wasn't one to lay low. His writings opposed Arianism, the belief that Jesus, while great, was not as great as God the Father. They were responsible for him being named the first Doctor of the Church. He is known as the Father of Orthodoxy.

Christianity isn't for sissies today either. Defending and explaining the Church's beliefs on the Trinity and the Holy Eucharist in particular can be difficult for most of us. But it's part of our job to be able to communicate what we believe in a clear, simple way. It's a great evangelization tool.

Inspiration

For the Son of God became man so that we might become God. (St. Athanasius)

Challenge

Pray the Nicene or Apostle's Creed out loud. Do you truly believe and understand each of the words you are saying? If not, consider consulting with a priest or trusted source.

Philip the Apostle

Died 80

Philip didn't exactly answer Jesus's question. When the Lord asked where bread could be bought for the large crowd that was approaching, Philip's answer was about how much such an endeavor would cost, the implication being there was no way the band of disciples had the financial resources. We know how the story ends: With just five barley loaves and two fish, thousands were satisfied, with plenty of leftovers.

Sometimes, we don't answer Jesus's questions either. When he invites us to spend time with him or his people, we don't say no exactly. But we come up with a list of reasons why this isn't a good time. We know God the Father, the Son, and the Holy Spirit are capable of anything without our help. We grow when we open our hearts and souls and answer their invitation, straightforwardly with love and confidence.

✒ Inspiration

Philip answered him, "Six months' wages would not buy enough bread for each of them to get a little." (John 6:7)

✒ Challenge

Answer Jesus's question for you, the one he is asking, not the one you're comfortable answering.

Riccardo Pampuri

August 2, 1897–May 1, 1930

The young Italian, named Erminio, felt called to a medical career, but his studies were interrupted by World War I. While he started out as a sergeant, he was reassigned to the medical corps. It's easy to imagine the tender care he gave his fellow soldiers; among the items he had taken with him were the Gospels and St. Paul's *(June 29)* letters. When the war was done, he finished his medical studies, then, in 1928, became a professed member of the Hospitaller Order of St. John of God *(March 8)*, serving as director of the brothers' dental clinic. As Brother Riccardo, he was known for his generosity of time, talent, and treasure.

Riccardo had wanted to be a missionary abroad, but his fragile health foreclosed that option. So, he made his mission the care of working-class Italians. Like Riccardo, let's keep our eyes and hearts open to service wherever we are led, not where we think we want to be.

☞ Inspiration

Now there are varieties of gifts, but the same Spirit; and there are varieties of services, but the same Lord... (1 Corinthians 12:4-5)

☞ Challenge

Think about a dream you had as a child, perhaps of becoming a parent or teacher or artist. How can you put that dream to work today to bring glory to God?

Nunzio Sulprizio

April 13, 1817–May 5, 1836

There were not a lot of what we would consider easy days in Nunzio's short life. Both his parents died by the time he was six; a beloved grandmother, who had provided him with spiritual instruction, followed three years later. That left the boy's upbringing to an uncle, who was a blacksmith and worked Nicholas hard despite serious health issues. Finally, after he underwent treatment for a gangrenous leg, Nicholas met people who understood him and his emerging desire to become a priest. But his health had deteriorated too much, and he died less than a month after turning nineteen. Despite all this, those who knew Nunzio remembered him for his gentleness and his piety.

Sometimes our struggles are visible, like Nunzio's medical issues. Other times, people can't see we're having a problem and don't cut us much slack. Fortunately, God is always aware of our challenges and is there to support us and love us.

✒Inspiration

Jesus suffered a lot for me. Why should I not suffer for Him? (St. Nunzio Sulprizio)

✒Challenge

Pray for the strength to shrug off the opinions of those who judge you harshly despite not knowing your story.

François de Laval

April 30, 1623–May 6, 1708

There were things the first bishop of North America's French colonies would compromise on, and there were things he would not. Liquor sales to the indigenous people definitely fell into the latter category for François. He found the practice immoral on the part of the French traders, and loathed the alcohol dependence that grew among the native peoples. François did more than preach from the ambo and wring his hands. When excommunication of the traders failed to curb the practice, he returned to France and successfully demanded the removal of the colonial governor. François also is known for his role in establishing a seminary in the colonies that also served as a home for aged priests and a financial center for parishes.

François' crusading against the alcohol trade didn't win him a lot of friends, but he believed his battle was a moral imperative. His example reminds us to speak up against practices today that conflict with our belief in the sanctity of life from conception to natural death, regardless of what society sees as private choices.

✒ Inspiration

We must not have another center than the pleasing of Our Lord. (St. François de Laval)

✒ Challenge

Write a letter, send an email, say a rosary to battle against the earthly laws, practices, and forces that would end or devalue human lives.

John of Ávila

January 6, 1499–May 10, 1569

His bold statements against wealth and immorality landed this priest in front of the Spanish Inquisition—and in prison for a year. John spent the year studying St. Paul's *(June 29)* letters, and when he was exonerated, spoke all the more strongly. John also walked the walk; his ordination feast had poor men rather than friends as the guests. That he was not named a Doctor of the Church until 2012 seems surprising; he was the spiritual director for both John of the Cross *(December 14)* and Teresa of Ávila, and influenced the journeys of numerous other saints, including John of God *(March 8)*, Francis Xavier *(December 3)*, and Ignatius of Loyola *(July 31)*.

When he was unjustly accused, John turned to the Bible for spiritual strength. It's a good reminder to us that when we are confined by illness, caregiving, or other situations that there are better remedies than turning to alcohol, overspending, or overeating to reduce our stress levels.

Inspiration

The proof of perfect love of our Lord is seen in the perfect love of our neighbor. (St. John of Ávila)

Challenge

The next time you feel your blood pressure rising over a personal injustice, say a Glory Be before answering.

Amato Ronconi

1225–May 8, 1292

Amato felt a special link to Francis of Assisi *(October 4)*. He was three when Francis was canonized, and his hometown was less than a hundred miles from Assisi. Francis's example led Amato to become a secular Franciscan, and to make several pilgrimages, including four to Santiago de Compostela, the tomb of St. James *(July 25)*. The home Amato shared with his sister Chiara was along a popular route for pilgrims headed for Rome, and they welcomed in travelers in need of a meal, a bed, or just some time to rest. Today, a nursing home named for Amato is on that site.

Amato's life wasn't always easy and included some scurrilous, unfounded rumors made against him by a sister-in-law. But instead of dwelling on this injustice, he focused on helping the pilgrims. In the same way, may we have the faith to continue in our service regardless of the opinions of others.

Inspiration

A highway shall be there,
and it shall be called the Holy Way;
the unclean shall not travel on it,
but it shall be for God's people;
no traveler, not even fools, shall go astray. (Isaiah 35:8)

Challenge

Learn more about the travels of your confirmation saint, or another saint whose story speaks to you. Are there aspects you can incorporate into your life without leaving home?

George Preca

February 12, 1880–July 26, 1962

George was concerned about the young men he saw in his Maltese town, the sailors and others whom "proper" society avoided. He knew they needed God even though they didn't know that, and came up with a then-novel approach to bring him to them: through lay ministry. In 1907, he established the Society of Christian Doctrine, known locally as M.U.S.E.U.M., wherein lay volunteers led Bible studies and other catechetical activities. Some objected to this effort, saying catechism should be led only by the ordained, and certainly not offered to the type of people George was trying to help. Ultimately, his efforts were approved, and the society continues its work today.

Do you ever privately wonder if there are people God has given up on? Maybe it's the grumpy barista with all the tattoos and piercings, or that person in the office who kisses up to the leadership but leaves you with all the real work. Guess what... God hasn't given up on any of them, and he's looking to you to begin their conversion experience.

✒ Inspiration

Now all the tax collectors and sinners were coming near to listen to him. And the Pharisees and the scribes were grumbling and saying, "This fellow welcomes sinners and eats with them." (Luke 15:1-3)

✒ Challenge

Reach out with kindness to someone whom you find off-putting. Consider asking how you can pray for him or her.

Damien of Molokai

January 3, 1840–April 15, 1889

We can imagine the feeling in the pit of Father Damien's stomach. For eleven years, he'd worked and lived among a Hawaiian community of people afflicted with Hansen's disease, then known as leprosy. He'd helped to improve the quality of food, water, and housing for hundreds of people, typically with little if any help. He'd established two orphanages for the children of those who had died. But eleven years of experience told him that the day in 1885 when he put his foot in scalding water and felt nothing was his death sentence. Nonetheless, he continued his work until he died four years later. His caregivers in his final few months included Marianne Cope, who was canonized three years after Damien.

Many priests refused to serve with Damien because of concerns for their own health. (It was not known then that Hansen's is only mildly contagious when good hygiene is vigilantly practiced.) Damien's example reminds us that Jesus did his ministry in "unsafe" ways—engaging with the disciples as friends, not as distasteful people for whom he had little love or respect.

Inspiration

I make myself a leper among lepers to gain all for Jesus Christ. (St. Damien of Molokai)

Challenge

Take a chance for Christ today. Connect, even if it's just saying hello, with someone who is an outcast because of his or her physical, emotional, or mental condition.

Gengulphus of Burgundy

Died 760

Gengulphus was the type of man you'd expect people to envy, or try to emulate. He was born into the noble class, but also was known for his good deeds among the poor and his piety. He served in the court of Pepin the Short (whose sons included Charlemagne) and was so trusted by the ruler that they traveled at each other's side and took meals together. Admiration of this man's good deals did not, however, extend to his wife. She was known to take lovers—possibly even a priest—and act inappropriately in other ways. When she failed a test of innocence, Gengulphus was grieved, but chose not to exact revenge. Instead, he retired to a solitary life at one of his residences. That was not enough for his wife and one of her lovers, who proceeded to kill Gengulphus in his own bed. It is said he forgave his killer and accomplice before he died.

Betrayal sends a shockwave to our system. But rather than stew in the injustice of our situation, Gengulphus's example reminds us to forgive, even if at a distance, and trust in the Lord to redeem our betrayer.

✒ Inspiration

"…but if you do not forgive others, neither will your Father forgive your trespasses." (Matthew 6:15)

✒ Challenge

Offer up your prayers this evening for someone you are quite sure doesn't deserve them.

Leopold Mandić

May 12, 1866–July 30, 1942

He had a grand vision, the boy born Bogdan Mandić did: to reunite Eastern Orthodox Christians and the Roman Catholic Church. Growing up in what is now Montenegro, many of his friends were non-Catholic. So he went to a Capuchin seminary in Italy, taking the name Leopold and hoping to emulate St. Francis of Assisi's *(October 4)* example. But his short stature and health problems proved to be impediments to doing that work back in his hometown. Leopold ended up offering reconciliation in a different way—forty-eight years of hearing confessions, including from a young seminarian who would become Pope John Paul I. It's said he listened to confessions for as many as eighteen hours a day, and was known for his lenient penances.

We don't have to go far away to offer forgiveness. The opportunities abound in our homes, our parishes, our neighborhoods, and our workplaces. We never know when our act will spark a conversion in the hardest of hearts.

Inspiration

Have faith! Everything will be all right. Faith, Faith! (St. Leopold Mandić)

Challenge

Forgive someone against whom you have harbored bitterness or resentment for some time. If you can do it safely, let him or her know.

André-Hubert Fournet

December 6, 1752-May 13, 1834

The priesthood was not something that appealed to André-Hubert as a young man growing up in France. So many other things did, to the despair of his mother! He tried studying the law, but that didn't work out. He tried joining the military. Finally, he spent time with one of his uncles, a parish priest, and he heard the call his mother had always known was in him. André-Hubert was ordained at twenty-three. While he was forced to relocate to Spain for five years during the French Revolution, when he returned, he connected with Jeanne-Élisabeth Bichier des Âges and together they founded the Sisters of the Cross, who continue to serve the sick and poor in nine countries today.

Nagging works with some people, but not many. André-Hubert found his way to his vocation by being around his priest uncle. May we remember that showing how we live in Jesus, not just telling people they should, is more powerful than we realize.

Inspiration

"Therefore, my brothers, let us set an example for our kindred, for their lives depend upon us, and the sanctuary—both the temple and the altar—rests upon us." (Judith 8:24)

Challenge

Take a young person with you to work or a day of ministry work. Don't preach; just show.

Anthony of St. Anne Galvaõ

May 13, 1739–December 23, 1822

The first Brazilian-born saint listened carefully to Sister Helena Maria of the Holy Spirit, a member of a community where he served as confessor. She said Jesus wanted her to form a new congregation for women. After much study and consultation, he and others believed this was in fact the Lord's desire, and so the Franciscan priest known as Frei Galvaõ worked with the nun to found the community, now part of the Order of the Immaculate Conception. However, Sister Helena Maria died suddenly just a year later. Frei Galvaõ then spent nearly thirty years helping to raise money for a convent and church and assisting with the community's formation. He is also known for his practice of writing short prayers on paper and rolling them into balls some think look like pills. The sisters in São Paulo still distribute them today.

It had to have been hard for Frei Galvaõ; he thought he was a partner in saying yes to Jesus, but instead, he ended up being the primary leader for realizing Sister Helena Maria's vision. The same thing happens to us; a spouse or friend with whom we made big plans is taken from us. May we follow his example, and keep doing the Lord's work.

Inspiration

Through the testing of this ministry you glorify God by your obedience to the confession of the gospel of Christ...(2 Corinthians 9:13)

Challenge

Create a dozen "prayer pills" of your own today. Leave them in places where you can be anonymous.

Isidore the Farmer

Circa 1080–May 15, 1130

Legend has it that Isidore was less than popular among the other laborers. He was never on time! For some reason, he thought going to daily Mass was more important than getting to work promptly. Finally, they complained so loudly that the property owner went to Isidore to discuss the matter. What he learned, however, was that Isidore's productivity was amazing—because angels were tending his plow while he was at Mass.

We can get prideful about our value at the office, and look with scorn at the people who still have tasks remaining when they leave for the day. But when we do that, we value output more than people—and God. Let's resolve to learn from Isidore's example, and get our priorities in order. The work will always be there.

✒ Inspiration

Render service with enthusiasm, as to the Lord, and not to men and women, knowing that whatever good we do, we will receive the same again from the Lord, whether we are slaves or free. (Ephesians 6:7-8)

✒ Challenge

Whatever your work is, at home or away from home, make time to attend daily Mass once this week. You may find, like Isidore, that tasks go faster.

Brendan of Clonfert

Circa 484–577

Nowhere, it seems, was too far for this Irish saint to travel to win souls for Christ. He most certainly existed, and was the founder of Clonfert monastery around 560, where upwards of three thousand monks lived. Legend has it that Brendan traveled the seas beyond Ireland to Scotland, Wales, northern France, possibly even North America, in his missionary activities.

How far are you willing to travel to introduce people to Jesus? You don't have to embark on journeys of thousands of miles and days to be a missionary. It can start right in your own home or workplace.

✒ Inspiration

And he said to them, "Follow me, and I will make you fish for people." (Matthew 4:19)

✒ Challenge

Cast your net today.

Simon Stock

Circa 1165–May 16, 1265

July 16, 1251 may have started out much like any other day for this English Carmelite. That was the day the Blessed Virgin appeared and offered him a brown scapular. She told him that those who died wearing it would receive her protection. Simon is remembered for this gift more than the work he did prior to that date to revise the Carmelite rule and expand the order's presence in England and beyond.

Scapulars, large or small, have been embraced by laypeople and religious communities alike. They are a prayer of sorts, a reminder of our dedication to Christ or a particular way of life. While the brown scapular is likely the best known, more than a dozen other devotional ones are recognized by the Church.

Inspiration

Put on the whole armor of God, so that you may be able to stand against the wiles of the devil. (Ephesians 6:11)

Challenge

Read about the different recognized scapulars. Journal about the one that most speaks to you.

Felix of Cantalice

1515–May 18, 1587

Felix must have wondered, at least for a second, what the Capuchin leadership was thinking. He had grown up in the central Italian countryside, working as a farmhand and shepherd, with no formal education. His decision to enter into religious life had been inspired in no small part by stories of the desert fathers, and he had considered becoming a hermit. Now, four years after becoming a lay brother, he was being sent to Rome! To come face to face with people as a beggar of alms! But the work suited Felix to a tee. He spent forty years in this way raising funds for the community's activities for the poor and needy. Felix became known as Brother Deo Gratias, because "thanks be to God" was his constant greeting.

God always knows what's best for us, even though it may make us uncomfortable. Growth is, sometimes. Felix's story shows us the blessings that can come from obedience and surrender. Thanks be to God, indeed.

Inspiration

Deo Gratias! (St. Felix of Cantalice)

Challenge

Make a list of five things that have happened to you in the past five years that made you squirm but that you now see as blessings.

Celestine V

1215-May 19, 1296

Celestine's name may sound familiar; he was the only pope in history other than Benedict XVI to voluntarily resign. Though both men were eighty-five at the time, the situations were totally different. Celestine, born Peter di Morone, was a total outsider who had spent a good share of his life as a hermit and for the past twenty years had been abbot of his own order of monks. But in 1294, the papacy had been vacant for two years because the cardinals were deadlocked. They turned to Celestine after he sent them a message that their delay was angering God. His five months as pope were disastrous as he knew nothing of the politics of the position. His successor, Boniface VIII, imprisoned Celestine. The reluctant pope died ten months later.

It was courageous of Celestine to acknowledge he was in over his head and to resign. Perhaps in those ten months in captivity, he wondered whether he had correctly heard God's warning to the cardinals. It's a cautionary tale, one that reminds us to gird ourselves for any outcome when we are the Lord's messenger.

❧ Inspiration

"Choose for each of your tribes individuals who are wise, discerning, and reputable to be your leaders." (Deuteronomy 1:13)

❧ Challenge

Consider whether a new role you covet is your plan, or God's.

Bernardino of Siena

September 8, 1380–May 20, 1444

Bernardino was the kind of person who threw himself wholeheartedly into what he did. He was barely twenty when he and friends took over operation of a hospital to help plague victims in his hometown. After being ordained as a Franciscan priest, he went into solitude for not a day or a month, but twelve years. When he emerged, Bernardino, who had been considered to have a weak voice, became one of the most influential preachers of his time. He crisscrossed Italy with his sermons that showed how Biblical themes applied to everyday life, though some of his beliefs we would find harsh today. Bernardino also encouraged the devotion to the Holy Name of Jesus, with signs bearing "IHS," and successfully fought charges that the devotion was heresy.

Bernardino lived his life with gusto! The man just would not quit, preaching several times a day for days on end. He shows us that regardless of how much we think we've done to please God, there's always another opportunity to evangelize, with words or otherwise.

Inspiration

If thou pray only with thy lips, it will avail thee naught. (St. Bernardino of Siena)

Challenge

Pray today with action, whether it's a volunteer ministry or helping a family member or friend.

Constantine the Great

Circa 280–337

We know him as the first Roman emperor to profess Christianity, even though his own baptism didn't occur until he was on his deathbed. Accounts indicate that about six years after becoming ruler of part of the empire, Constantine had a conversion moment and carried a Christian symbol into battle. He won the day, of course, and as he consolidated his power, set about policies to tolerate Christianity and to restore personal and corporate property seized during previous rulers' persecutions. Constantine also provided land for churches, including a Roman cathedral, and presided over the First Council of Nicaea, where the first part of the Nicene Creed was agreed upon. He's also known for sending his mother, Helena, on a Holy Land pilgrimage that yielded many relics.

Constantine's conversion rocked the world. As Catholics, we are open to those moments beyond baptism, confirmation, and the other sacraments that bring us closer to God. They may not seem big at the time, but the results of what happens when we love and serve can rock *our* world and those of people around us.

Inspiration

Peter said to them, "Repent, and be baptized every one of you in the name of Jesus Christ so that your sins may be forgiven; and you will receive the gift of the Holy Spirit." (Acts 2:38)

Challenge

The next time you receive the Eucharist, honor it as a conversion moment.

Eugène de Mazenod

August 1, 1782–May 21, 1861

We often hear the stories of women saints whose parents wanted them to make strategic marriages. But stories like Eugène's are far less common. His parents' marriage had been challenging at best—his mother's family had money, his father had a title but little else—and the French Revolution forced them to move to Italy when Eugène was eight. When he returned to France at age twenty, Eugène had put on airs, calling himself a count. His parents had separated, and his mother was determined her son would marry a rich woman. Amid all this, Eugène found solace in God, entered the seminary, and was ordained in 1811. He saw a need to evangelize among underserved Catholics in southern France, and established the Missionary Oblates of Mary Immaculate. Eugène spent the last twenty-nine years of his life as the bishop of Marseilles.

When our families are dysfunctional, it's easy to look for answers in food, alcohol, drugs, or overspending. How blessed Eugène was to learn relatively quickly that healing comes only through God.

Inspiration

Practice well among yourselves charity, charity, charity, and outside, zeal for the salvation of souls. (St. Eugène de Mazenod)

Challenge

Instead of killing emotional pain with substances, talk with a priest or other trusted spiritual adviser about ways to have permanent healing.

John Baptist Rossi

February 22, 1698–May 23, 1764

According to the practices of the time, John shouldn't have been ordained. He suffered from epileptic seizures as well as from health issues that stemmed from severe self-mortification in young adulthood. But somehow, he received a dispensation and became a priest shortly after his twenty-third birthday. John spent the rest of his life paying it forward, serving people Roman society didn't want to see: the sick, the poor, prisoners, prostitutes. He had a particular gift for ministry among homeless women, creating a haven for them.

John knew there was value within the people living on the margins, just as he knew that his physical ailments didn't mean he was worthless. Let's remember his story when we are tempted to discount or dismiss people whose abilities are different from ours—or when we regard ourselves as "less than" because of chronic illness or other challenges.

❧ Inspiration

Let the word of Christ dwell in you richly; teach and admonish one another in all wisdom; and with gratitude in your hearts sing psalms, hymns, and spiritual songs to God. (Colossians 3:16)

❧ Challenge

Pray for the grace to accept yourself as you are, ailments and all, and your role as a beloved child of God.

David I of Scotland

Circa 1084–May 24, 1153

Imagine being nine years old or so, and losing your father and mother and a brother in less than a year. That was the life of David, youngest son of St. Margaret of Scotland and King Malcolm III. As a result, David was sent to the Norman court, where his brother-in-law, Henry I, was king. David became Scotland's king in 1124. While battles ensued to determine the rightful heir to the English throne—ultimately, David's choice, his niece, lost—David is also remembered for bringing to Scotland some of the religious traditions he observed as a child. He is credited with doing much to organize Scotland's administration and for his generosity in founding monasteries and endowing churches.

Margaret of Scotland was known for her deep faith and her public and private piety. Her example, and the way people talked about their admiration of her even after her death, likely had a strong influence on David. What we do, consciously or unconsciously, has an impact on those in our lives. It's up to us what that impact is.

Inspiration

So then, brothers and sisters, stand firm and hold fast to the traditions that you were taught by us, either by word of mouth or by our letter. (2 Thessalonians 2:15)

Challenge

Set the example God desires today for a young person.

Bede the Venerable

Circa 673–May 25, 735

He never traveled more than fifty miles from the Benedictine English monastery complex where he was sent at the age of seven. He received no education or training outside the monastery. And yet, Bede for centuries has been regarded as the father of English history, in large part thanks to *Ecclesiastical History of the English People,* a five-book project that begins with Caesar's invasion and ends in 731. He produced dozens of other books as well as thirty commentaries on the books of the Bibles. In 1899, he was named the first (and, to date, still the only) English-born Doctor of the Catholic Church.

Bede embraced God's plan for him, working through the manuscripts available in the monastery library. He didn't whine about not having access to works from other countries, or about taking his turn with the other monastery tasks, such as kitchen or yardwork. His story shows us that God provides the resources we need to do his work, if not the resources we want.

Inspiration

Let each of us, in whatever vocation he is placed, strive therein to work out his own salvation. (St. Bede the Venerable)

Challenge

In your prayers today, offer gratitude for the life you have and ask for the gift of contentment.

Philip Neri

July 21, 1515–May 25, 1595

Philip was eighteen when he arrived in Rome with no money and as a result was often alone other than when he was tutoring two students. He knew no support or approval would come from his Florentine father. But Philip also knew he was where he was supposed to be; he'd had a mystical experience. After two years, he all but burst out of his attic, chatting up people on the street and encouraging them to get involved in helping those in need. People liked him; he was friendly, unassuming, even funny, and that made them more inclined to listen to him. In 1551, Philip was ordained, but continued to pursue the concept of bringing people together informally to do good. The "apostle of Rome," as he was known, and friends founded the Congregation of the Oratory, local groups of priests and brothers doing good works without taking religious vows from a centralized authority. A number of oratories exist around the world today.

Philip had a way with people. He treated them as friends and often, friendship was what he received in return. His story shows us evangelization doesn't have to involve condemnation and judgment; it can start out with a joke or a smile.

Inspiration
If you want to be obeyed, don't make commandments. (St. Philip Neri)

Challenge
Strike up a conversation with someone you don't know who always comes to Mass alone.

Gregory VII

Circa 1025–May 25, 1085

He wasn't ordained a priest until two months after he was elected pope by acclamation on April 22, 1073. But Gregory VII had served in various advisory roles under a number of popes, and had a lot of ideas on how things should run. He cracked down on nepotism, the selling of church offices, and clerical celibacy violations at the same time he issued pronouncements extending papal power, including the authority to depose emperors. Gregory's views and those of the Holy Roman emperor, Henry IV, were in conflict, and resulted in a series of threats and actions including Henry's excommunication (twice) and Gregory's forced departure from Rome. He died in Salerno within a year in what amounted to exile.

Gregory may have believed his legacy would be failure; certainly, many of the people of his time saw Henry as the victor in their disputes. But instead, Gregory is regarded as one of the greatest reformer popes. His story shows us that winners and losers aren't determined by public opinion of the day, but by God in his exquisite time.

✒ Inspiration

The Lord will rescue me from every evil attack and save me for his heavenly kingdom. To him be the glory forever and ever. Amen. (2 Timothy 4:18)

✒ Challenge

Take a stand at home or at work that will open you to ridicule or judgment but that is pleasing to the one who matters.

Bernard of Montjoux

Circa 1020–1081

Bernard had a leadership position in the Aosta diocese in the Italian Alps, and was very involved with area parishes and schools. But he worried about the French and German pilgrims who came through the area on their way to Rome. Not only were they subject to the vagaries of weather (and avalanches), they were also susceptible to robbers, in particular pagans who didn't appreciate the travelers. And so, Bernard decided to take on making that part of the journey safer. He established two welcoming places, one at eight thousand feet, to help lost and weary travelers. The breed of dogs we know as St. Bernards was developed to help in the effort, and named for this saint.

Bernard could have kept his focus on the people of his diocese; there was plenty to do there. But instead, he became a missionary right in his own backyard. We can do the same in welcoming newcomers to our family, neighborhood, workplace, and country.

Inspiration
Contribute to the needs of saints; extend hospitality to strangers. (Romans 12:13)

Challenge
Turn a stranger into a friend.

Paul VI

September 26, 1897–August 6, 1978

He will always be remembered for his 1968 *Humanae vitae* encyclical, which reaffirmed the Church's position on artificial contraception. But there are more aspects of Paul VI's papacy that were countercultural, inside and outside the Vatican. He instituted reforms of the liturgy and the Roman Curia. He built bridges with other Christian faiths. He was the first pope to leave Italy since 1809, the first to address the United Nations, and the first travel to six countries with an eye toward expanding Catholicism's reach beyond Europe. Paul also chose to simplify elements of papal vestments, eschewing tiaras.

Like Paul, we may find people lauding or criticizing in isolation the actions we take. We're too easy on our kids, we're too strict with our employees, we should spend our time on X instead of Y. While Paul had a reputation as being indecisive, he was consistent in his worldview. His example reminds us that obedience is what God desires of us.

Inspiration

The world calls for, and expects from us, simplicity of life, the spirit of prayer, charity towards all, especially towards the lowly and the poor, obedience and humility, detachment and self-sacrifice. (St. Paul VI)

Challenge

What do you feel called to do that you know will be criticized by the world? Maybe it's taking a job that will pay less but be more in line with your ethics, or moving into a smaller home so you can increase your tithing. Pray for the strength to be obedient.

Giuseppe Marello

December 26, 1844–May 30, 1895

Giuseppe's mother died when he was just four years old. Heartbroken, his father moved back to the northern Italian village where he had grown up so that his parents could help raise his two sons. Just eight years later, Giuseppe was placed in a seminary. It's perhaps no surprise that the child developed a strong devotion to the Blessed Virgin and St. Joseph (*March 19*). He was ordained a priest in 1868, and ten years later founded what is now the Oblates of Saint Joseph, a community focused on caring for people in the way that Joseph cared for Jesus. Giuseppe's initial work with the community included assistance for the elderly, orphaned boys, and those with physical disabilities. The oblates continue their work today worldwide.

Giuseppe was a lot like St. Joseph. Even though he rose to be a bishop, he loved being in the background. Let's think of the good works they both did out of the limelight the next time we crave public attention for our ministries.

✍ Inspiration

"Beware of practicing your piety before others in order to be seen by them; for then you have no reward from your Father in heaven." (Matthew 6:1)

✍ Challenge

Turn to the Gospel of Matthew's accounts of St. Joseph's dreams. How can you be more trusting of God to do his work without hoping others will notice?

Hannibal Mary Di Francia

July 5, 1851–June 1, 1927

Just months before his scheduled priestly ordination, Hannibal found himself in one of the poorest areas of the southern Italian city of Messina. His conversation with a beggar who could barely see changed his life's plan. Oh, Hannibal went ahead with his ordination on March 16, 1878, but afterward, with his bishop's approval, he didn't go the usual route of assignment to a parish. He went back to that same poverty-stricken area, and started a ministry. Hannibal and his followers provided people not only with food and the opportunity to learn skills, but also with a Christ-based family atmosphere. Out of this ministry grew two religious communities, the Daughters of Divine Zeal and the Rogationists, named for the Church's Rogation Days, when there are special prayers for crops of all sorts.

We can't live without food in our bellies. But Hannibal knew that the people of Messina's Avignone neighborhood were starving spiritually as well. His story shows us that true ministry helps with both hungers.

🐟 Inspiration

He said to them, "The harvest is plentiful, but the laborers are few; therefore ask the Lord of the harvest to send out laborers into his harvest." (Luke 10:2)

🐟 Challenge

Be a laborer. Find a field you can nourish with love and prayer.

Justin Martyr

Circa 100–165

Justin just wanted things to make sense. He had a strong grounding in Greek philosophy and other disciplines including rhetoric, but he still was not satisfied. While he was teaching at Ephesus, he struck up a conversation with an old man who convinced him that the Bible's prophets, who had been directly inspired by the Divine, had much to offer him in his quest. Justin converted and became one of the early Church's most effective apologists, explaining practices such as Mass, baptism, and the Eucharist were based in theology and were not aimed at overthrowing the secular authority. It's believed that Justin's victory in a public debate led to his beheading and that of six companions.

Who doesn't want things to make sense? Sometimes, following Christ doesn't seem to do that. We don't always have what we think we want or need, and we don't understand why bad things happen to good people, and vice versa. But we know this: nothing makes sense without God.

Inspiration

If we are punished for the sake of our Lord Jesus Christ, we hope to be saved. (St. Justin Martyr)

Challenge

Spend some time reading scriptural references to the institution of the Eucharist.

Ferdinand III of Castile

Circa 1199–May 30, 1252

It was complicated. Ferdinand's father was a king, but his parents' marriage had been annulled, though the children's rights to successions were not affected. He inherited the kingdom of Leon from one parent and Castile from another, and Castile in particular was a bit of a mess between internal dustups and invasions from the outside. Ferdinand excelled in both battle and statesmanship. He united the kingdoms and restored cathedrals at Toledo and elsewhere. In Seville, he had a mosque turned into a cathedral. He also established and endowed churches throughout his kingdom. Perhaps most meaningful to him was the ordination of a son who went on to become an archbishop of Toledo, and his daughter's discernment to become a nun.

Not all wars are executed on the battlefield. Today, we're more likely to feel challenged by our families, our jobs, even others in our parish. Sometimes, we must speak truth compassionately but forthrightly to combat the forces of evil. The prize that matters is always attainable, and the road to winning it doesn't have to be complicated.

Inspiration

He called upon the Most High, the Mighty One,
  when enemies pressed him on every side,
and the great Lord answered him
  with hailstones of mighty power. (Sirach 46:5)

Challenge

Stop avoiding that difficult conversation.

Charles Lwanga

January 1, 1860–June 3, 1886

Charles protected his friends in every way he could. The young man was promoted to oversee the pages in what is now part of Uganda after his predecessor's beheading the previous November. Charles was concerned about the pages in this world—where they faced unwelcome advances from the pedophile king—and the next. A recent convert himself—he had been baptized the night of his predecessor's death—Charles baptized four of the pages the night before they were all arrested. He and a number of others were burned alive in the following week. Twenty-two African Catholics including Charles were canonized as the Martyrs of Uganda in 1964.

Charles' story is particularly touching because he knew what was likely in store if he pursued Christianity and protected the pages. And yet, he did. May we follow his example of bravery and faith and safeguard the most vulnerable in our society, regardless of the cost.

Inspiration

"When I was with them, I protected them in your name that you have given me." (John 17:12)

Challenge

Intervene on behalf of someone who is being physically, emotionally, mentally, or spiritually abused.

Filippo Smaldone

July 27, 1848–June 4, 1923

Filippo felt their pain. The priest had been working with the deaf community in poverty-stricken areas of his hometown of Naples for years, since before he was ordained in 1871. In fact, he'd been so immersed in this ministry that his seminary tests sometimes suffered. But now, his students were frustrated with their progress, and so was he. Maybe, he thought, it was time to try missionary work in another country. But his confessor told Filippo he was needed right where he was. After prayer, Filippo recommitted himself to his ministry and expanded it, founding a school for the deaf community more than two hundred miles away in Italy's boot, as well as a congregation of women religious to support it. The ministry eventually expanded to include children who were orphaned or abandoned or visually impaired.

The day-in, day-out grind of ministry can wear us all down. There's always someone else coming through the food pantry door, someone else who needs a listening ear, someone else who needs a ride to the doctor. Filippo's rededication to his service can be an Inspiration to us. We are doing more good than we realize.

☙Inspiration

Therefore, let those suffering in accordance with God's will entrust themselves to a faithful Creator, while continuing to do good. (1 Peter 4:19)

☙Challenge

Read the Beatitudes before you engage in a ministry you're finding to be tiresome.

Boniface

Circa 675–June 5, 754

Boniface had had a good life, and many in his position (and at his age) would have been ready to rest. The English Benedictine monk had spent more than thirty years as a missionary in the Netherlands and Germany. He had had more than a little success, establishing monasteries and receiving the title of papal legate to Germany. But there were troubling reports of paganism re-emerging in the part of the Netherlands where Boniface's work had begun. So, even he was close to eighty years old, he went back. He was in a tent waiting for confirmation candidates to arrive when he and fifty or so companions were martyred.

Many of us hope for a "good death," while we're asleep in our own beds, free of pain. But a good death is more than that; it's one where we are prepared spiritually. Boniface understood that, and embarked on that final missionary trip fully ready to sacrifice himself if need be. He's a model for us as we think about how we want to meet God.

✒ Inspiration

Rejoice in the Lord; anchor your hope in God, for without delay he will render to you the reward of eternal bliss and grant you an abode with the angels in his heaven above. (St. Boniface)

✒ Challenge

Are you ready for God's welcoming embrace? If not, what do you need to do to be ready?

Norbert

Circa 1080–June 6, 1134

You might have called Norbert's faith stagnant. Or moribund. Or worse. He was in his thirties and enjoying life at the German king's court, where his responsibility was to distribute alms. Not only did he have no interest in becoming a priest, he turned down an offer to become a bishop. Then one day, Norbert was riding his horse during a horrific storm. He was thrown from his horse or hit by lightning, and a moment reminiscent of Paul's *(June 29)* conversion ensued. Norbert was ordained the same year. He would struggle for the next twenty years with a desire some considered extreme to end Church excesses. He may have been at his happiest when he was a wandering preacher in France, Germany, and Belgium, or when he was establishing his own austere order, the Canons Regular of Prémontré, which continues today in Europe, the Americas, Africa, and Australia.

Norbert's story is one of good seed that had taken root, regardless of running into rocky soil here and there. He reminds us to be patient with and pray for those we know and love who are away from faith, that we might be there to support them and gently encourage their return.

Inspiration

You will never enjoy the sweetness of a quiet prayer unless you shut your mind to all worldly desires and temporal affairs. (St. Norbert)

Challenge

Have you had a road to Damascus moment of your own, perhaps long ago? How might you share that fire with those whose faith is lukewarm?

Marcellin Champagnat

May 20, 1789–June 6, 1840

Marcellin knew how daunting a lack of knowledge could be. His formal education was spotty at best. He saw cases of bullying and corporal punishment by teachers. It's no wonder that Marcellin struggled at seminary to the point that he was sent home after the first year to think about whether he had a vocation. He returned, and was ordained in 1816. As a priest, he encountered children who knew little if anything about faith. Marcellin's own first communion had been conducted in secret, and he understood why the children's parents, who were of his generation, might not be able to provide instruction. He combined his devotion to Mary and his urge to bring Christ to young people in forming the teaching community that became the Marist Brothers.

Sometimes we try to hide what we see as our shortcomings. Marcellin used his to identify a larger societal deficit, and come up with a way to address it. He shows us that we can use those experiences to provide compassion and assistance to others.

✺ Inspiration

Oh! How unhappy would we be if we did not love God who is kindness, beauty, and goodness par excellence, the only one capable of satisfying and filling our heart which was created for the Infinite Good! (St. Marcellin Champagnat)

✺ Challenge

Is there something you're not good at because you lack experience? Ask a family member or friend to help you, then pay it forward.

Jacques Berthieu

November 27, 1838–June 8, 1896

About twenty years of this Jesuit priest's life had been dedicated to the people who lived on Madagascar or nearby islands. It was seldom easy, especially during the years of armed conflict between the indigenous people and Jacques's native France. At times, he and other religious were sent into exile; when they returned, the area for which they were responsible had grown larger due to the departure of confreres. The atmosphere grew more and more dangerous, but Jacques stayed. On the day he was martyred, his captors beat him and struck him with a machete and mocked his crucifix. They offered to spare his life and give him a position if he denounced his faith. Jacques refused, and died when he was shot at close range.

Jacques had a missionary's heart. Even as he was being marched to what would be his death, he encouraged a man to find a priest and be baptized. His story echoes Jesus carrying the cross, and reminds us that slings and arrows, verbal or physical, are temporary; what God offers is the permanent love and joy in eternal life.

✒ Inspiration

I have to pray until I die. (St. Jacques Berthieu)

✒ Challenge

When you're tempted to behave in a less than Christ-like manner today, remember you are his missionary.

Ephrem

Circa 306–373

While Ephrem was not the originator of the saying, "Singing is praying twice," it might well apply to his body of work. This man—who may have spent his life as a deacon, making him the only male Doctor of the Church not to be a priest or bishop—wrote more than five hundred poems, and his poems were meant to be sung. Is it any wonder he's known as the "Harp of the Holy Ghost"? In addition, Ephrem produced writings on nearly all of the Old Testament and a good share of the New Testament as well. For his last ten years, Ephrem did his writing from a cave.

For Ephrem, hitting the right note meant sharing his gift of praising the Lord. We all have things we're good at—writing, singing, carpentry, project management. When we do them for his glory, we too are praying twice.

❧ Inspiration

Take thou refuge in God who passes not away nor is changed. (St. Ephrem)

❧ Challenge

Think about some task around the house or the office that comes easily to you. How can you use it to help someone else get to heaven?

José of Anchieta

March 19, 1534–June 9, 1597

José, born in Spain's Canary Islands and educated in Portugal, was sent to Brazil as a Jesuit missionary before he was twenty. The hope was that change in climate would improve the young priest's health. He threw himself into his work for more than forty years, with such notable achievements as being regarded as among the founders of both São Paulo and Rio de Janeiro and developing a dictionary for the language most commonly spoken by the indigenous people. José also was known as an advocate for human rights and as a peacemaker. To help settle a dispute between two tribal factions, he served as a hostage for five months, during which time he developed and committed to memory a lengthy poem to the Blessed Virgin Mary.

Sometimes, a change of scenery—physical, mental, or emotional—is all it takes for us to grow in our relationship with God. Leaving Europe took José to the work he was meant to do. May we be just as open to invitations of change we receive from the Father.

✿ Inspiration

Now who will harm you if you are eager to do what is good? But even if you do suffer for doing what is right, you are blessed. (1 Peter 3:13-14)

✿ Challenge

Say yes to that opportunity God desires you to take that's outside your usual ministry.

Barnabas

Died circa 61

We know that Paul's *(June 29)* conversion was real, but it's easy to see why those he had persecuted were initially a bit skeptical. Barnabas vouched for Paul, and that helped with the apostles' acceptance of him. Barnabas was an easygoing, forgiving sort. He and Paul would fall out for a time over Barnabas's cousin John Mark (Mark *(April 25)*, traditionally the Gospel writer). John Mark had disappeared when the three were preaching in Turkey. It's believed the rupture eventually was healed. Tradition holds that Barnabas was later stoned to death.

Barnabas appears to have been quick to speak up for those he knew, like Paul and John Mark. His example reminds us not to join in gossip or ridicule of people, but instead to advocate for them, just as we hope the saints, canonized and otherwise, will advocate to God for us.

❧ Inspiration

There was a Levite, a native of Cyprus, Joseph, to whom the apostles gave the name Barnabas (which means "son of encouragement"). He sold a field that belonged to him, then bought the money, and laid it at the apostles' feet. (Acts 4:36–37)

❧ Challenge

Consider the translation of the nickname the apostles gave Joseph of Cyprus: "son of encouragement." What nickname would you like to be known by?

Gaspar Bertoni

October 9, 1777–June 12, 1853

This Italian priest has an impressive list of accomplishments: As a young man, caring for those injured during France's occupation of northern Italy; spiritual director for St. Magdalene of Canossa's Society of the Daughters of Charity; founder of the Sacred Stigmata of Our Lord Jesus Christ, a teaching congregation. But the way Gaspar spent his final twenty years may be the most impressive. He underwent hundreds of surgeries, most without anesthesia, for a leg wound. He was completely bedridden, unable to stand, let alone celebrate Mass, for his final ten years and was often incapacitated in the ten years before that. Still, he continued to meet with those in need of spiritual direction and advice, including the bishop of Verona, from his bed. When Gaspar was asked if he needed anything, he said, "I need to suffer."

It's shivery to think of undergoing one surgery, let alone multiple, without anesthesia. Yet Gaspar was able to embrace his pain as Christ did, confident that the hope of eternal life lay beyond his agony. His story reminds us to find good and hope in our own hurts.

✒ Inspiration
At the bottom of one's own nothingness God is found. (St. Gaspar Bertoni)

✒ Challenge
Spend an hour visiting or talking with someone who is homebound.

Anthony of Padua

August 15, 1195–June 13, 1231

The young man whose birth name Ferdinand was open to God-given redirection. He'd already begun his theological studies as an Augustinian. Then he met some Franciscan friars headed for Morocco as missionaries following the martyrdom of five of their confreres. He was on fire to do the same, and received permission to join the community, taking the name Anthony for St. Anthony of Egypt *(January 17)*. His own attempted trip to become a missionary in Morocco ended up with him in Italy instead, where he would become known as an amazing preacher, both in his words and in his ministry to the poor. Anthony was canonized less than a year after his death, and declared a Doctor of the Church in 1946, the first Franciscan to receive that honor.

We pray with Anthony for the recovery of lost keys, lost shoes, lost books. But that sells short this saint's charism. He never lost his faith, but his life plan changed frequently. Let's resolve to seek his intervention when bigger, less tangible things are absent.

☙ Inspiration

The secret of the heart is like a veil that must hang between us and our neighbor, so that he cannot look behind that veil. It should be enough to see the lamps which we carry ready in our hands and which will give him light. (St. Anthony of Padua)

☙ Challenge

Pray with St. Anthony on a faith-related matter of loss, perhaps a son or daughter's decision not to attend Mass anymore.

Benildus Romançon

June 14, 1805–August 13, 1862

Benildus did those small, everyday things that so often go unnoticed. The French De La Salle brother taught school for forty years despite his own health issues. If students were hungry, he would quietly go into the brothers' kitchen to make something. If they didn't have appropriate clothing, he would turn old robes into something they could wear. While he expected students to learn their lessons and behave, he was a patient tutor to those who needed help. All Benildus's efforts bore fruit in ways unseen and seen, including the decision by hundreds of his pupils to follow in his footsteps and join the community.

In canonizing Benildus in 1928, Pope Pius XI noted, "Sanctity does not consist of doing extraordinary things, but in doing ordinary things extraordinarily well." We can do the same if we find joy in what some consider the monotony of daily life.

☙ Inspiration

They were astounded beyond measure, saying, "He has done everything well; he even makes the deaf to hear and the mute to speak." (Mark 7:37)

☙ Challenge

Find an opportunity for grace and wonder in something you do by rote.

John of Sahagún

June 24, 1419–June 11, 1479

You might compare it to parents who do estate planning or put away money in a child's college fund. John's wealthy father tried to assure his son's financial well-being by purchasing for him church-related posts that would guarantee income. But by the time John was ordained in 1445, he had rejected all the positions other than the parish where he went to work. A Spanish bishop mentored John and gave him a position in his office, but that wasn't a good fit. Eventually, John became an Augustinian friar. He was known for calling out evil where he saw it, whether it was women spending too much money on the day's fashions or men living less than chaste lives.

We get worried when young people don't go to college or hop from job to job or volunteer in circumstances we regard as risky or dangerous. John's parents only wanted the best for him, just as we do for our children, grandchildren, and others. But it's important to remember that, like John, they may be doing exactly what God desires of them, even if we don't understand.

✒ Inspiration

For what purpose do I go up to the pulpit? To announce the truth to the listeners or to shamefully caress them with flattery? (St. John of Sahagún)

✒ Challenge

Listen to the plans of someone, old or young. Don't provide advice or your opinion unless asked.

Rainerius

Circa 1117–1160

Rainerius liked to play his lyre, have fun with his friends, and generally live a carefree life. As the only son of wealthy merchant parents, no one seemed to have a lot of problems with his choices. One day he encountered someone totally unlike him—a monk named Alberto—and started reconsidering his ways. What looked like a business trip to the Holy Land in 1146 turned into a pilgrimage. Rainerius didn't come home to Pisa until seven years later, and when he did, he looked more like Alberto than the old Rainerius. While he lived an ascetic life with a community of monks, he never formally joined them. Rainerius did gain somewhat of a reputation as a good preacher and conversationalist. His hometown, where he is the patron saint, honors him at a festival of lights that begins each year on this night.

Rainerius's conversion was sparked by someone he may have passed by dozens of times before the two of them spoke. We learn a lot about living a Christian life from those we know and love. His story shows us that people who look and live differently from us can also provide us with grace moments.

Inspiration

Do not neglect to show hospitality to strangers, for by doing that some have entertained angels without knowing it. (Hebrews 13:2)

Challenge

Take on a small project to make your home or your soul more hospitable.

Albert Chmielowski

August 20, 1845–December 25, 1916

As a teenager, this saint became involved in an uprising in Polish-held Russia, lost a leg, and had to leave his home. While he was studying business, he developed an interest in painting, and proved to be quite good at it. Albert found more and more of his paintings had religious themes, and he was spending more and more time in service to the homeless. When he was forty-two, he became a Third Order Franciscan. Shortly thereafter, he founded the Servants of the Poor, also known as the Albertines, and three years later co-founded a women's community. Brother Albert was a model for then-Father Karol Wojtyla as he discerned leaving his own interest in the arts behind. He wrote a play about Albert called "Our God's Brother." It's fitting that Pope John Paul II *(October 22)* beatified and canonized this man he so admired.

We may be good at a great many things, and enjoy them, offering our work in God's service. But as Albert discerned, God's gifts have a hierarchy. May we be as willing as he was to listen when the Father provides us with direction as to which gift to use.

✿ Inspiration

I therefore, the prisoner in the Lord, then, beg you to live a life worthy of the calling to which you have been called… (Ephesians 4:1)

✿ Challenge

If someone were to write a play about your relationship with God, what would it be titled? Think about whether your life "script" needs some refocusing.

Gregorio Barbarigo

September 16, 1625June 18, 1697

He'd checked all the boxes. Lots of connections, due to his influential Venetian noble family. Degrees in canon and civil law. Named a bishop, then a cardinal. A short-lived papal candidacy in 1689. The winner, Alexander VII, lived just twenty months thereafter, and Gregorio seemed a natural choice to many. But the conclave went on for five months, including intrigue involving Catholic monarchs, and the new pope was not Gregorio. The defeat had to sting. Still, Gregorio went back to Padua, and continued his works of charity and teaching, and living what was for a cardinal an austere life.

It's not easy, losing or never receiving a position or honor for which we've worked hard. Gregorio's example reminds us to resist bitterness, and instead focus on the essential work God has planned for us.

Inspiration

But if you have bitter envy and selfish ambition in your hearts, do not be boastful and false to the truth. (James 3:14)

Challenge

Write down a big or small defeat that still eats at you. Maybe it was not making a sports team or not winning an office. Pray that you may be released of this hurt, then burn it.

Romuald

Circa 950–1027

Romuald was twenty and living the typical life of a wealthy northern Italian—until his father killed a relative in a duel. Whether Romuald went to a Benedictine monastery to do penance at his father's request or on his own isn't clear, and isn't important. What is important is that he decided to stay, beginning a journey of more and more austerity that took him to Spain, northern and central Italy, Germany, and France. Romuald believed, after studying the lives of the desert fathers, that solitude was an essential part of salvation. Once, he was forced out as abbot because the community found him too strict. In about 1009, Romuald established a monastery in Camaldoli, a mountainous town about thirty miles from Florence, combining a monk's austerity with the solitude of a hermit.

It was a huge life change, but one that suited Romuald. We all go through them, from singlehood to marriage and back again for some, acceptance of a job thousands of miles from our support system. And with the Father's grace, we find a way to thrive regardless.

Inspiration

Better to pray one psalm with devotion and compunction than a hundred with distraction. (St Romuald)

Challenge

Look at before and after photos from a big moment in your life. What positive, lasting changes occurred?

Paulinus of Nola

355–431

The son of a high-ranking Roman official in France, Paulinus became a Christian around the time he married Therasia. Then challenges arose. Paulinus was accused in the slaying of his brother, and he and Therasia after years of being childless celebrated the birth of a son but the child died just a week later. Rather than become bitter, the grieving couple turned over much of their wealth to the Church and began living extremely simple lives. Paulinus's example drew the attention of Church authorities, who insisted on ordaining him when he was about forty, and then naming him as the bishop of Nola about 395. His gentle nature and intellect drew the likes of Sts. Augustine *(August 28)*, Jerome *(September 30)*, Ambrose *(December 7)*, and Martin of Tours *(November 11)* to him as friends or correspondents. He is considered a leading Christian Latin poet of his era.

The loss of a child and a serious, unfounded allegation could have turned Paulinus against God. Why was he being persecuted? He'd done his best! His example reminds us to cling to the only thing that is eternal and real when the world attempts to batter us.

ᴥ Inspiration

The man without Christ is dust and shadows. (St. Paulinus of Nola)

ᴥ Challenge

Reach out to someone who feels God has let him or her down. Pray for that person.

Aloysius Gonzaga

March 9, 1568–June 21, 1591

Aloysius was surrounded by a cloud of future saints, and he would need them. As the oldest son in an aristocratic Italian family, the expectation—especially of his father—was that Aloysius would become a soldier and take his rightful place in society. However, Aloysius never felt cut out for that life. Not long after his First Communion, for which he was prepared by Cardinal Charles Borromeo *(November 4)*, Aloysius determined he would become a Jesuit. Time and again in the next few years, his father refused to give his consent. Finally, he relented and in 1585 Aloysius entered the Jesuits, where Robert Bellarmine *(September 17)* became his spiritual director. Aloysius died before he could be ordained, succumbing to the plague after caring for other victims.

Aloysius's father surely had what he thought were his son's best interests in mind. But he didn't listen to his son. Aloysius was fortunate to have people like Charles Borromeo and Robert Bellarmine as spiritual mentors. While we need to provide guidance to young people, we shouldn't get in God's way.

Inspiration

"Everyone who belongs to the truth listens to my voice." (John 18:37)

Challenge

The next time someone, especially a young person, comes to you excited about a new idea, don't shoot him or her down. Listen. Ask questions. Provide guidance sparingly.

June 21

Thomas More

February 7, 1478–July 6, 1535

Were they friends? When Henry VIII was born, Thomas More was thirteen, a year from beginning his studies at Oxford. Perhaps a better way to describe the relationship would have been one-way admiration, with Henry taking note of Thomas's intellect, especially when it came to matters of faith. Their views were not always so different; in 1521 Henry wrote a defense of Catholicism against the ideas of Martin Luther.

Friends or no, Henry's spiritual views changed when they became inconvenient to him. Thomas's remained constant. When Thomas could not find any basis for Henry's naming of himself as the leader of the Church of England, he retreated rather than publicly attack the king. Ultimately, charged with treason, Thomas made his own stirring defense of the faith. We remember his testimony today—and the faith and confidence with which he faced his execution.

Inspiration

When statesmen forsake their own private consciences for the sake of their public duties, they lead their country by a short route to chaos. (St. Thomas More)

Challenge

Identify a public policy that is at odds with Catholic teachings. Write a reasoned email or letter to someone who helps set the policy expressing your views. Keep it short, so it will be read.

John Fisher

1469–June 22, 1535

John entered Cambridge at fourteen; by his early twenties, he'd earned bachelor's and master's degrees, and been ordained, something that took a special papal dispensation because he was so young. John was named a bishop at thirty-five, and Cambridge's chancellor before he was forty. He was known not only for his homilies but also for his writings opposing Martin Luther. John's faith was even stronger than his intellect. He represented Henry VIII's first wife when Henry sought to divorce her, and the king never forgave him. John also refused to take a loyalty oath to the sovereign, and was imprisoned for saying Henry couldn't be the Church of England's supreme head. The pope named John a cardinal on May 20, 1535; he was beheaded almost a month later.

When we read about the stories of John Fisher, Thomas More *(June 22)*, and our Church's other martyrs throughout the centuries, it's easy to think, "I'm glad God doesn't ask me to do that." Standing up for our beliefs in everyday conversations and activities can endanger relationships even with people we love. But remaining silent can endanger the most important relationship of them all.

Inspiration

Princes persecute me without cause,

but my heart stands in awe of your words. (Psalm 119:161)

Challenge

Plan what you will say the next time a family member, colleague or acquaintance makes a joke about a Church stance.

John the Baptist

Died circa 30

He'd been a big deal for a while. Sure, some people thought John was a little strange, what with wearing camel's hair clothing and subsisting on locust and honey. But many were moved by his message of new birth, and became avid followers. Indeed, Jesus himself went to John for baptism. But John knew when his time was done. He had heralded the coming of the Lamb of God—and seen him! Humbly, John stepped aside.

John the Baptist was only human. There had to have been at least a small part of him that was sorry to see this ministry end, even if he didn't know his own death was near. And yet, he didn't let his ego get in the way. May we do the same when our ministry is done, rather than holding on to the familiar and predictable.

✾Inspiration

"He must increase, but I must decrease." (John 3:30)

✾Challenge

Do an examen of conscience. Where do you need to decrease so that the Lord's plans may flower?

William of Vercelli

1085–1142

It was a life filled with challenges, but William kept his eyes on the promise of eternity with God. His own parents died when he was an infant, so he was raised by relatives in northern Italy. After journeying to Compostela at the tender age of fourteen, William became a hermit for two years, then started on a pilgrimage to Jerusalem. He got waylaid and beaten by robbers in southern Italy, and decided to stay there. Much of the rest of William's life followed the same pattern: find a place where he could worship privately, have others be so drawn by his charism that they wanted the same thing, build a monastery, have it fall apart. His best-known community, the hermits of Montevergine in the mountains near Naples, is now part of the Benedictine congregation.

So many times, the work William started ended in failure. But he kept on going, knowing it was God, not society or even William himself, who would determine whether he was successful. William's story is a good reminder to us to persevere when we're dealt setbacks.

✿ Inspiration

Do not fear, for you will not be ashamed;

   do not be discouraged, for you will not suffer disgrace… (Isaiah 54:4)

✿ Challenge

Pray for the grace to look forward with faith and confidence, rather than dwell on your past failures.

Josemaría Escrivá

January 9, 1902–June 26, 1975

He grew up in an ordinary Spanish household, with all the ordinary joys and tragedies. The sorrowful times included the deaths of three sisters between the time he was eight and eleven. His father's business failed, and the family had to relocate. When he was seventeen, Josemaría began studying for the priesthood, but felt God wanted something different from him. The feeling continued past his ordination in 1925. Three years later, he was on a spiritual retreat when God gave him direction: to establish Opus Dei/Work of God, a community of priests and laypeople living their professions of whatever calling in a Christian way. In 1946, Josemaría relocated to Rome, and Opus Dei received provisional papal approval the following year. Pope John Paul II *(October 22)* named Opus Dei a personal prelature, in which the movement is not tied to dioceses.

Opus Dei has its strong supporters—and strong critics. But it's hard to argue with Josemaría's advancement of the concept of a universal call to holiness; after all, it's part of the *Catechism of the Catholic Church* (2013). What can be very hard is to live that call.

❧ Inspiration

Sanctity is not for a privileged few. The Lord calls all of us. (St. Josemaría Escriva)

❧ Challenge

Are you compartmentalizing your life—one person with your family, another with your friends, a third in the workplace or service? What steps could you take to more consistently reflect Christ?

Cyril of Alexandria

Circa 376–444

Cyril is known as the Doctor of the Incarnation. It was the biggest religious argument of the day, and it came down to one word: *Thetokos,* or Mother of God. Cyril, the archbishop of Alexandria, second in size only to Rome, argued that the title was appropriate for Mary, as while Jesus had both divine and human natures, he was only one person, the second person of the Trinity. Nestorius, the archbishop of Constantinople, argued otherwise, that Jesus consisted of two persons, and Mary was the mother of only the human person, and should be called Mother of Christ. Ultimately, Cyril prevailed. He was named a Doctor of the Church in 1882.

There is much about Cyril not to admire; he was present at the synod that deposed John Chrysostom *(September 13)* for heresy, he did nothing to attempt to resolve riots between Jews and Christians in Alexandria; and his writings paint a picture of a blunt, arrogant man. But he saw himself as defending the faith, and sometimes, that makes us despised by others.

✍Inspiration
But when the Faith is attacked, we must not hesitate to sacrifice our life itself... (St. Cyril of Alexandria)

✍Challenge
Take a stand for a Church doctrine, knowing this may open you to ridicule.

Peter

Died circa 68

He believed when it was most important. Oh, sure, Peter believed there was something interesting about this Jesus his brother Andrew *(November 30)* introduced him to, but there were so many doubts or trip-ups along the way: when he told Jesus the followers had already given up everything for him; when he denied knowing Jesus not once but three times, when he failed at walking on water. But when he saw the risen Christ, Peter believed not only in the resurrection, but in the possibility of his own forgiveness and redemption. After that, there was no stopping the man on whom Jesus said he would build his Church.

We all make mistakes—and some of them grave. But we seek to make ourselves more powerful than we really are when we refuse to accept forgiveness. When we humble ourselves in this way, we open ourselves up to grace upon grace.

Inspiration

And he said to him, "Lord, you know everything; you know that I love you." Jesus said to him, "Feed my sheep." (John 21:17)

Challenge

Receive the sacrament of penance and reconciliation. Believe in forgiveness.

Paul

Died circa 64

What a life it had been! From Pharisee and witness to Stephen's *(December 26)* martyrdom to that powerful conversion on the road to Damascus. With a convert's fire, Paul had preached the Good News across the Middle East and Europe. Imprisoned in Rome for a second time, he had to be fairly certain the end of his earthly time was near. But instead of reflecting on his accomplishments or expressing regrets about what had gone undone, the focus of his final letter to Timothy *(January 26)* was aimed at encouraging his mentee to keep preaching and to carry on after him.

There's nothing wrong with remembering our glory days now and again, but dwelling on them can leave us wistful and remorseful, and open up space for evil. Paul shows us the Lord's desire that we instead do what we can to prepare and bolster those who will follow us.

☙ Inspiration

As for me, I am already being poured out as a libation, and the time of my departure has come. (2 Timothy 4:6)

☙ Challenge

Think about what your family and friends will write in your obituary. If what they will write is not exactly how you'd like to be remembered, what can you do today to begin to change that?

Theobald of Provins

1017–1066

It sounds so appealing at times: Leave everything you have behind to be in solitude with God. But then we think of how much we'd miss people and our comforts, and, well… That was not the case for Theobald. His father, a French nobleman, agreed to Theobald's plan, announced when he was eighteen, not to become a soldier, but a hermit. Theobald and a friend made a pilgrimage to Santiago de Compostela, then planned to go to the Holy Land, but the friend died when they were as far as northeast Italy. Theobald continued a solitary existence, but people in the area were drawn to his holy nature. The area bishop was so sure of Theobald's saintliness that he ordained him. Eventually, Theobald joined the hermit community at Camaldoli founded by St. Romuald *(June 19)*, and took vows shortly before his death.

Someone wise once said hermits need to learn to live with people before they can live by themselves. Theobald's life shows us that takes faith and effort. But don't discount a way of living that others say would be too hard. It may be exactly where God is leading you.

☙ Inspiration

Trust in the Lord with all your heart, and do not rely on your own insight. In all your ways acknowledge him, and he will make straight your paths. (Proverbs 3:5-6)

☙ Challenge

Talk to God about a burning in your heart that friends and family would consider outlandish.

Junípero Serra

November 24, 1713-August 28, 1784

It was a different time, and most of us would agree there were abuses of indigenous people as the Franciscans established the twenty-one missions from San Diego to San Francisco. But it is also true that Junípero, the man behind the establishment of the first nine missions, regarded this as a divine assignment. He was already thirty-five when his missionary team arrived in Mexico, and subjected himself to serious self-sacrifice—including a 250-mile walk to Mexico City. After a year of training, only half of his three hundred companions made it to San Diego with him. Junípero's successes included conversions, establishment of self-sufficient missionary communities, and a system that continued for fifty years after his death.

Junípero is not the only saint with elements of a story that are uncomfortable when we read them today. The concept of evangelizing to bring souls to Christ can make us uncomfortable too. But evangelization can take all forms, from praying the rosary in front of an abortion clinic to peaceful protest outside a munitions plant to providing a gentle witness to a suffering friend. But it's what we're called to do.

Inspiration

Keep moving forward! (St. Junípero Serra)

Challenge

Share your faith outside your comfort zone.

Oliver Plunkett

November 1, 1625–July 1, 1681

It was a predictable, comfortable life. Oliver went to Rome to study when he was twenty-two, was ordained, and became a noted theology teacher. Meanwhile, back in his native Ireland, the situation for Catholics went from bad to worse—the public practice of the faith was prohibited, and clergy were being exiled or killed. Oliver had spent half his life outside of Ireland when he was named an archbishop and sent back home in 1670. He spent a good share of the next nine years dressed as a layman so he could travel about, bringing the sacraments to his flock and confirming nearly fifty thousand people. He was arrested in 1679 for his role in what proved to be a non-existent plot to kill the English king, and ultimately was executed.

Oliver gave up his comfortable life in Rome to serve God and his people, and paid the ultimate price. Few of us living in the United States will be called to martyrdom. But we can let little pieces of ourselves—pride, fear, greed, to name a few—die in answer to God's call.

Inspiration

"Then they will hand you over to be tortured and will put you to death, and you will be hated by all nations because of my name." (Matthew 24:9)

Challenge

Do something in Jesus's name regardless of what it will cost you in pride or respect.

Thomas

Died circa 72

He doubted, and who wouldn't have in his situation? Thomas had seen Jesus arrested. He knew his friend had been flogged and crucified. Now, the rest of the group was rejoicing because Jesus had appeared to them. But Thomas would not doubt for long. He received the gift of seeing the risen Lord—and the gift of recharged faith in God. Tradition holds that Thomas's evangelization took him to India, where he was martyred.

Seeing is not always believing. Every time we go to Mass, we have the awesome ability to see, touch, and taste Christ. And yet we sometimes doubt his presence in our lives because he doesn't answer prayers exactly as we would like. Thomas's experience teaches us to have faith that God is always with us.

✐ Inspiration

Thomas answered him, "My Lord and my God!" (John 20:28)

✐ Challenge

Look for Jesus in the unexpected places today—in traffic, in the face of someone you find difficult to love, in a mundane task you dislike.

Ulrich of Augsburg

Circa 890–973

Ulrich protected his people in more ways than prayer. He became bishop of the southern German city of Augsburg in 923, and three years later, the cathedral and other churches were destroyed by Hungarian troops. Ulrich saw to it that Augsburg would be surrounded by strong city walls as rebuilding progressed, and his efforts helped to ensure final victory over the invaders in 955. He also is known for his piety—tradition is that he washed the feet of twelve poor people at the local hospital each day—and for being the subject of the first papal canonization.

It might be hard to think of your bishop being as involved with local governing as Ulrich was. But it's not unusual for bishops to participate in chambers of commerce or testify at local or state hearings. Separation of Church and state doesn't mean they can't advocate for what we as Catholics believe is right, through Sacred Tradition and doctrine.

๛Inspiration

For a bishop, as God's steward, must be blameless; he must not be arrogant or quick-tempered or addicted to wine or violent or greedy for gain; but he must be hospitable, a lover of goodness, prudent, upright, devout, and self-controlled. (Titus 1:7-8)

๛Challenge

Write a thank you card to your bishop.

Anthony Mary Zaccaria

December 8, 1502–July 5, 1539

At twenty-two, Anthony was a physician. At thirty-six, he was dead. In the intervening fourteen years, he did more work to bring Jesus to the people than some do in a lifetime. The young Italian determined his work was with people's souls, not their bodies, and was ordained in 1528. He and two noblemen founded the Clerks Regular of St. Paul *(June 29)*, with the aim of sharing St. Paul's writings and of bringing sacraments to people on a regular basis. (The community became known as the Barnabites, for the church in Milan that would serve as its headquarters.) Anthony also founded the Laity of St. Paul and a community for women religious, the Angelic Sisters of St. Paul. He may have originated, and certainly popularized, the practice of forty hours of adoration.

Anthony moved fast and confident, certain he was doing God's will. Too often, we sit back and think there's plenty of time to pray or to contribute our time, talent, and treasure to our parish or ministry. Tomorrow is not guaranteed. Let's learn from his example.

✍ Inspiration

Virtue without adversity has no consistency, or a very poor one; instead the greater the obstacles, the more precious it becomes. (St. Anthony Mary Zaccaria)

✍ Challenge

Do something for God—a morning prayer practice, signing up for an hour of adoration, service at a homeless shelter—that you've been putting off.

Goar

Circa 585–649

Goar grew up in southwest France, and was known for his preaching. But about 618, he decided to withdraw from society. He moved to Germany and became a hermit. But even hermits receive guests, especially pilgrims, and seek to make them welcome. Some of them decried Goar as a hypocrite to the bishop of Trier. Exactly what happened next isn't clear—possibly, the bishop was called out as a hypocrite himself, or a miracle made the bishop realize his mistake. In any event, the king moved to replace the bishop with Goar. Goar asked for time to think, believing he was not suited to that role. He went home and died before answering.

It would seem Goar was not a hypocrite, but hospitable. When we have guests, we spruce up the place, and maybe make a special meal. We want to be welcoming. Let's do the same to prepare our souls for a visit from God.

☙ Inspiration

So if you consider me your partner, welcome him as you would welcome me. (Philemon 1:17)

☙ Challenge

What can you do to be a more welcoming place for God?

Marcus Ji Tianxiang

Circa 1834-July 7, 1900

Once upon a time, he'd been a respected physician. But then Marcus got sick, and he did what many people in China did in the nineteenth century—he took opium for the pain. For the next thirty years, he was an addict. That addiction kept him from the Eucharist, as he kept confessing his problem to a priest, and the priest finally told him he couldn't avail himself of the sacraments anymore until he got his act together. Thirty years of daily Mass without communion. Thirty years of trying to kick his habit, without success. Then, in 1900, he and nine family members were arrested by Boxer Rebellion forces. It was clear they all would be executed. Marcus, the junkie who had refused to leave his faith behind amid judgment we know today was clearly wrong, was the last to be beheaded. He didn't want anyone else in his family to die alone.

Even with today's knowledge, loving an addict can be difficult, and sometimes is best done from a distance for our own welfare. But may we always remember that no one, regardless of how hopeless their situation seems to us, is beyond the Lord's redemption.

❧ Inspiration

"Indeed, God did not send the Son into the world to condemn the world, but in order that the world might be saved through him." (John 3:17)

❧ Challenge

Write a note of support to someone in a halfway house or in prison. You don't have to sign it.

Aquila

1st century

Acts 18 tells us that when St. Paul *(June 29)* arrived in Corinth, he met Aquila and his wife Priscilla, Jews who had been ordered out of Rome. Like him, they were tentmakers. The trio apparently got along well, as the couple went with Paul to Syria. We know they eventually returned to Rome, and that they hosted Eucharistic gatherings in their home. They left again, probably because of persecution, and spent time in Ephesus. It's believed they were martyred together in either Rome or Asia Minor.

Aquila and Priscilla are mentioned six times in the New Testament, always together. They were evenly yoked personally and spiritually, and well formed in their faith. Their example reminds us to seek out partners in life and ministry with whom we have common values. We don't have to agree on the little stuff, but mutual commitment to the big stuff makes service easier for us and more pleasing to God.

✒ Inspiration

Apollos began to speak boldly in the synagogue; but when Priscilla and Aquila heard him, they took him aside and explained the Way of God to him more accurately. (Acts 18:26)

✒ Challenge

Identify a way—a short course or retreat or book—that you and your spouse or ministry partner can grow even closer in your shared love of Christ.

Kilian

Circa 640–689

Kilian, an Irish monk, was about twenty-six years old when he felt called to take on a grand adventure: travel to southern Germany to convert pagans. He'd already traveled throughout Ireland to save souls, and saw this as the next step. He and eleven companions went to Rome to get the pope's blessing, which was readily given. Things seemed to be going all right, with many conversions, until Kilian convinced a recent convert who happened to be a duke that his marriage to his brother's widow was not pleasing to God. While the duke was convinced to make a change, his pagan wife was not, and arranged for the murders of Kilian and two of his companions.

Surely, Kilian would have been exhilarated about his new calling. But he also would have known it wouldn't be easy. Yet he said yes. His example reminds us that what God desires may stretch us past what we believe is our breaking point, but the Almighty's presence will always be with us.

Inspiration

Those who keep the commandment will live;

> those who are heedless of their ways will die. (Proverbs 19:16)

Challenge

Journal about the adventure to which God is inviting you. What will it take for you to say yes?

John Gualbert

Circa 985–1073

John was raised Catholic, but as a young man, he found plenty of diversions. That changed when his beloved older brother Hugo was slain. With their father's approval, John swore vengeance. The opportunity came on Good Friday as John was riding into town. The murderer was there, in plain sight, with no chance of escape. But before John could kill him, the other man begged for forgiveness. John found himself granting it, and calling the man his friend. The experience changed John forever. He went off to a monastery, and eventually founded a community, the Vallombrosians, which includes lay brothers, a practice that was unusual at that time. John never was ordained as a priest—he was too humble—and his community focuses on silence in prayer, poverty, and strict enclosure from the world as ways to draw closer to God.

Imagine facing the person you believe has taken a loved one away. Maybe the person was a drunken or otherwise careless driver, or a medical professional who made a mistake. Can you imagine forgiving as John did? His story shows us that when we forgive, the experience changes us as well as the other party.

✿ Inspiration

Forgive your neighbor the wrong he has done,

    and then your sins will be pardoned when you pray. (Sirach 28:2)

✿ Challenge

Forgive someone who wronged grievously someone you love.

Benedict of Nursia

Circa 480–547

We know Benedict as the father of Western monasticism. His rule provides a roadmap for monastic living, including manual labor, obedience, and community structure, and has been widely adopted and adapted. After his education in Rome—which did not include ordination, Benedict never became a priest—he left the city to find peace, including living in a cave for about three years. A group of monks was impressed by what they saw of him, and asked him to be their abbot, but his way was too restricting for them. Back to the cave he went, then established an organization of a dozen monasteries, each with its own prior. Benedict left for reasons we're not sure of—possibly a dispute with a nearby priest—and moved about seventy miles south to Montecassino in about 530. And there, the rule was developed.

Benedict persevered—and believed. His story inspires us to never give up, regardless of how burdensome our challenges may feel.

✒ Inspiration

For speaking and teaching belong to the master; the disciple's part is to be silent and to listen. And for that reason if anything has to be asked of the Superior, it should be asked with all the humility and submission inspired by reverence. (St. Benedict of Nursia)

✒ Challenge

The Rule of Benedict is available as a book or online. While much of it is specific to monastic communities, some sections also apply to laypeople's lives. Pick a section to follow for the coming week.

Louis Martin

August 22, 1823–July 29, 1894

Louis had taken up watchmaking because he couldn't learn the Latin he needed to pursue a religious vocation. He'd fallen in love with Zélie, the girl with the beautiful eyes, married her after just three months, and become the manager for her lacemaking business. Only five of their nine babies lived to their fifth birthday and now, Zélie was diagnosed with advanced breast cancer. After her death, the grief-stricken Louis sold the lace business and moved about fifty miles to Lisieux, where extended family could help him raise his daughters. A few years later, the youngest, Thérèse, just fourteen, announced she wanted to become a nun like her sisters. Rather than being bitter, Louis supported her decision. His mental and physical health went into decline shortly thereafter, and he lived another seven years, never reflecting anger, only sadness.

Like Louis, God seems so unfair to us at times. Why are those we love sometimes taken away at the very time we need them most? That's a mystery. Difficult as it is, it's best to focus on God rather than our losses. The Almighty is all we need today, and tomorrow, and the day after that.

Inspiration

I cannot say how much I loved Papa; everything in him caused me to admire him. (St. Thérèse of Lisieux)

Challenge

Rather than telling God you're angry about the state of your relationships, consider offering thanks for what you have.

Henry II, Holy Roman Emperor

May 6, 973–July 13, 1024

The man also known as Henry the Good or Henry the Exuberant collected titles the way some of us collect books or music: duke of Bavaria at twenty-two, king of Germany at twenty-nine, holy Roman emperor at thirty-nine. Consolidating his power sometimes meant conflict and revolts, in which Henry generally came out on top. But Henry also had a spiritual side; he had considered becoming a priest as a child, and some believe he mulled retiring as a monk in his final years, which were marked by illness. In addition, with his wife, Cunegund, Henry established or endowed numerous monasteries and churches, including creation of the see of Bamberg.

Henry and Cunegund worked well together in funding religious institutions under his domain, and it's also said that she took part in some of his ruling councils. Their marriage reminds us that regardless of how competent or skilled we are, we can find comfort and relief in the partners, romantic or otherwise, God gives us.

Inspiration

"But strive first for the kingdom of God and his righteousness, and all these things will be given to you as well." (Matthew 6:33)

Challenge

Talk with a spouse or trusted friend about ways you can deepen your relationship with God. Listen to what this person has to say, and act on it.

Camillus de Lellis

May 25, 1550-July 14, 1614

He was an unlikely caregiver—or priest, for that matter. Left largely to his own devices as a child, Camillus at sixteen became a soldier and joined his father in battle. The war done and having lost all his possessions to a gambling habit, Camillus took a job at a Capuchin friary. It was there his faith was rekindled. But a nagging war injury kept the Capuchins from allowing his entry into their community. Camillus's next stop was Rome, where he went to work at a hospital (and had Philip Neri *(May 26)* as his confessor). Less than impressed by the care hospital staff provided, Camillus began a ministry to fill in the gaps. Eventually, he became a priest and founded the Order of Clerics Regular, Ministers of the Infirm, better known as the Camillians.

Camillus's injury took away his livelihood as a soldier, but it made him perfect for a caregiving ministry. It's a blow when age or health keeps us from activities we once loved, but those challenges can lead us to new paths for service.

❧ Inspiration

The new moon, as its name suggests, renews itself; how marvelous it is in this change, a beacon to the hosts on high, shining in the vault of the heavens! (Sirach 43:8)

❧ Challenge

Use your knowledge of pain through a chronic illness or the aftereffects of an injury to minister to someone else. Be mindful of listening rather than engaging in one-upmanship.

Bonaventure

Circa 1221–July 15, 1274

Even the most pious and holy people on earth are human. When Bonaventure was thirty-five, he was named superior of the Franciscans. It was an honor to be sure, but not a particularly cushy position. The members were at odds over whether their rule, especially on poverty, needed to be revised, and tensions were high. Bonaventure navigated a middle path, guided by his belief that Christ is the center of all things and that nothing exists independently of our love for him. He saw faith as a continuum in which we grow as we move closer to Jesus, and expounded on the importance of contemplation regardless of our charism. In 1588, he was declared a Doctor of the Church.

As long as we're getting our way, seeing Christ in others can be easy. When the other person has a different view on a topic that we know, just know, we're right about, showing love and being respectful can get challenging. Bonaventure reminds us that if we keep Jesus at the center of our hearts and souls, we'll always stay on a right path, even when we disagree with others.

Inspiration

If your love for anything does not lead you to greater love for God, you do not yet love Him with your whole heart. (St. Bonaventure)

Challenge

Invite Jesus to mediate a dispute between your mind and your soul.

Francis Solanus

May 10, 1549–July 14, 1610

In tense situations, Francis knew just what to do. He prayed, of course. But this Franciscan friar also played the violin and sang. He knew that music is an international language, even when it's played on a two-string, homemade instrument. (His "real" violin was lost in a shipwreck when he and other missionaries were headed for Argentina from their homeland of Spain.) It's also said that Francis's aptitude for picking up languages helped South Americans warm to him and his message. And warm they did; as Francis traveled to missions and met with indigenous people and colonists, his inspiring preaching resulted in conversions by the thousands.

When we're uncomfortable, we can shut ourselves off with our body language and the words we use. Francis, on the other hand, embraced such times with love and joy, surely pleasing God and making introductions to new people.

☞ Inspiration

"Whenever you enter a town and its people welcome you, eat what is set before you; cure the sick who are there, and say to them, 'The kingdom of God has come near to you.'" (Luke 10:8-9)

☞ Challenge

Smile and say good morning, good afternoon, or good night to someone you regard as less than loveable.

Pompilio Maria Pirrotti

September 29, 1710–July 15, 1766

Was it his love for the Blessed Virgin, whom he called "Mamma bella" in his homilies? Or was it some of the dramatics he used when preaching, such as wearing a crown of thorns? Or maybe it was his leniency in the confessional, or his urging common people to receive the Eucharist as often as possible? It's not clear, but both clerical and lay leadership in Naples were so put off by Pompilio that he was banished from the city in 1759. After about four years, however, they yielded to the public outrage, and brought him back for the remaining years of his life.

It's easy to criticize priests, women religious, and others for behaviors we find annoying. Let's remember that we all have unique God-given gifts, and attempt to appreciate them, as the people of Naples did Pompilio's.

✒ Inspiration

"Do not judge, and you will not be judged; do not condemn, and you will not be condemned." (Luke 6:37)

✒ Challenge

Today, keep your negative opinions of someone else's behavior to yourself.

Simon of Lipnica

Circa 1437–July 18, 1482

It had to seem like a dream to seventeen-year-old Simon. Even though his parents were very poor, he was entering the Jagiellonian University in Kraków. It wasn't long before he attended a presentation by John Capistrano *(October 23)*, an Italian who had founded the city's first Franciscan monastery. Simon listened and determined he too was called to be a Franciscan. He was ordained about 1460, and found particular inspiration in hearing about the simple preaching style of Capistrano's friend Bernardino of Siena *(May 20)*. Simon became a noted preacher himself, emulating Bernardino's approach. Simon died of cholera, contracted while caring for others suffering from the disease.

Simon's story shows how interconnected lives are. (To take matters even further, Hedwig/Jadwiga, Poland's first female ruler and a saint herself, had directed that upon her death, her jewels should be sold to reinvigorate Jagiellonian University.) John Capistrano had no idea the impact his mission presentation would have on Simon. In the same way, when we speak God's message, we don't know what the result will be.

✒ Inspiration

"But as for that in the good soil, these are the ones who, when they hear the word, hold it fast in an honest and good heart, and bear fruit with patient endurance." (Luke 8:15)

✒ Challenge

Preach the Gospel today in your words and actions, even if you don't anticipate the words taking root.

Pambo

Died 375

When the young Pambo approached Anthony of Egypt *(January 17)* about remaining with him and the other desert fathers, he asked for guidance. Anthony advised austerity in all things, and Pambo took him at his word. It's said Pambo fasted each day until the evening, even as he threw himself into the community's physical labors. Pambo also mastered silence; when he asked one of the fathers for a lesson, the elder recited half of the first line of Psalm 39:"I said,'I will guard my ways that I may not sin with my tongue'" (NRSV). Pambo stopped him, saying he would be back for more when he had absorbed those words. Tradition indicates that took him eighteen years.

Think about Anthony's advice to Pambo: watch your tongue and your appetite, don't think too much of yourself, don't do anything you'll regret later. If we take them to heart as Pambo did, we too will be on the road to saintliness, whether or not we are ever formally canonized.

✒ Inspiration
Mercy finds confidence before God. (St. Pambo)

✒ Challenge
Use the opening words of Psalm 39 as your spiritual study today.

Barsabbas

1st century

It came down to two men to replace Judas Iscariot among the Twelve: Matthias and Joseph, called Barsabbas. We can only assume they were equally qualified, equally respected, equally devoted to evangelization. So the others did what we do in situations like that. They drew lots, and Matthias emerged as the winner. What happened to Barsabbas? We don't know, other than he's not the same man as the Barsabbas in Acts 15:22 who went to Antioch with Paul *(June 29)* and Barnabas *(June 11)*. Tradition says he went on to be the bishop of Eleutheropolis northwest of Jerusalem, and was martyred.

You've probably been in Barsabbas's shoes. You're the ideal choice for a romance or job or other position, but there's another candidate who's just as qualified, and you lose out. What's your reaction? Disappointment, yes. But it's best to shrug off the disappointment and keep your eyes forward, knowing God's plan always is in your best interest.

✒ Inspiration

For I resolved to live according to wisdom,

and I was zealous for the good,

and I shall never be disappointed. (Sirach 51:18)

✒ Challenge

Look for the growth and good, not the disappointment, in a situation where you didn't get what you wanted.

Lawrence of Brindisi

July 22, 1559–July 22, 1619

Renowned preacher. Military chaplain. Linguist. Diplomat. Capuchin leader. Writer. And, oh yes, there was that time that Lawrence marched at the head of the outnumbered Christian army in a faceoff with the Turks, bearing only a cross. (You can guess what the outcome was.) Lawrence, born in Naples, became a Capuchin friar at sixteen. He was an excellent student at the University of Padua, excelling at both ancient and modern languages, and from there, continued to roll up honors and respect, even though he was so humble that he refused a second term as the Capuchins' minister general. He also led by example by caring for plague victims. In 1959, he was named a Doctor of the Church for his sermons, letters, and other writings.

It seems about the worst thing anyone could say about Lawrence was that he was a bit thin-skinned when it came to criticism. His story is a good reminder to us to be grateful for our God-given gifts, and not listen when others make hurtful or petty remarks.

Inspiration

God is in the Church as the driver in the chariot, the sailor in the ship, the father in the home, the soul in the body, the sun in the world. (St. Lawrence of Brindisi)

Challenge

Pray for the grace to accept critical comments when they provide an opportunity to improve, and the ability to gently set them aside when they do not.

Bernardino Realino

December 1, 1530–July 2, 1616

Bernardino was on the fast track, or so it seemed. He had degrees in canon and civil law, and had held impressive government positions, including a judgeship, chief magistrate, and chief tax collector for several southern Italian cities. A beautiful woman loved him and supported his ambitions, and they may have even married. But after she died, Bernardino took a hard look at himself and his priorities, and decided to pursue a vocation as a Jesuit priest. He was thirty-seven years old when he was ordained, and spent the rest of his life in pastoral work in Italy's bootheel.

It's not that there's anything wrong with being a judge or tax collector; it just turned out that Bernardino was chasing his own dream. His story reminds us not to let our own ambitions take up more space than following God's plan.

✒ Inspiration

The plans of the mind belong to mortals,

but the answer of the tongue is from the Lord. (Proverbs 16:1)

✒ Challenge

Examine whether the way you spend your day is the way God would like you to spend it.

Declán of Ardmore

5th century

St. Patrick *(March 17)* gets the credit for bringing Christianity to Ireland, but there were four bishops intent on saving souls there before Patrick's arrival or evangelizing about the same time. Among them was Declán, born in County Waterford in north Ireland. His gifts were so evident that after studying with a local holy man as a child, he was sent on to Rome, where his learning was deepened and where he eventually was consecrated bishop of Ardmore for his home county. Declán may have gone to Rome at least once more, and possibly crossed paths with Patrick at least once.

It really doesn't matter whether Patrick's reputation overshadows that of Declán and the other three bishops. We work for God and the hope of salvation, not a place in legends and history books.

✒ Inspiration

Do not be conformed to this world, but be transformed by the renewing of your minds, so that you may discern what is the will of God—what is good and acceptable and perfect (Romans 12:2)

✒ Challenge

Don't compare your skills and accomplishments with a celebrity's, or those of someone you know and have trouble not envying.

Charbel Makhlouf

May 8, 1828–December 24, 1898

Youssef always loved his time alone with God, and he got a fair amount of it as his family's shepherd. In young adulthood, he entered the Lebanese Maronite Order and took the name Charbel for a second-century martyr. He spent sixteen years with other community members in their monastery, then in 1875 was granted permission to live in a nearby hermitage. Charbel spent the rest of his life there, but his particular charism was obvious even in his solitude, according to his confreres who would assist him at Mass. A light was seen shortly after his burial, and miracles began to be reported. It's estimated they now number in the hundreds, if not the thousands.

Charbel just wanted to be alone with God, but their love for one another was infectious and he had to share it. He shows us that evangelization is more than preaching; it's also about letting God's special light shine through our faces and hands.

✐ Inspiration

May Charbel make us understand, in a world too often fascinated by wealth and comfort, the irreplaceable value of poverty, penance, asceticism, to free the soul in its ascent to God. (Paul VI)

✐ Challenge

Be still today, even for five minutes, and know God.

James the Greater

Circa 3–44

The arrogance of James and his brother John aggravates the other apostles. Not only do they (or their mother, depending on the Gospel) ask for seats of honor in Jesus's kingdom, but they say they're ready to do whatever that involves. Likely the others were thinking that while the sons of Zebedee were among the first of the Twelve, they were also simple fishermen. But we find out in Acts 12 that indeed, James was ready. He was the first of the apostles to die a martyr's death.

He was called James the Greater because he was older or taller than the other James in the Twelve. But through his beheading, we see he was serious about backing up his words of faith in Christ by sacrificing his very life for him. It's hard to call that anything but great, and it's what we all are asked to do every day, in ways large and small.

✒ Inspiration

But Jesus said to them, "You do not know what you are asking. Are you able to drink the cup that I drink, or be baptized with the baptism that I am baptized with?" (Mark 10:38)

✒ Challenge

Read your baptismal vows out loud. Are you able to fulfill them today?

Joachim

1st century

The New Testament does not provide the names of the Blessed Virgin's parents, but tradition refers to them as Joachim and Anne, an elderly couple delighted with the prospect of finally having a child. We imagine them as kind and loving and faith-filled, providing the same sort of home for their daughter that she in turn would provide for Joseph and Jesus.

Because we have no solid information on Joachim, we turn to the examples of our own loving ancestors. And, we also have faith that the Lord would have selected carefully the parents for the woman who would bear the Son. For God, there are no throwaway babies.

Inspiration

Children, obey your parents in everything, for this is your acceptable duty in the Lord. (Colossians 3:20)

Challenge

Think about the delight you take in your children or grandchildren—or the delight your parents took in you.

Raymond of Piacenza

Circa 1139–1200

Raymond had had a busy, beautiful life: six children, a wife, a successful shoemaking business, time spent in prayer and in sharing the Gospel with others in his Italian hometown. But then five of the children died in a year, followed by his wife's death. Raymond left his remaining child with his in-laws and embarked on pilgrimage journeys, supported by begging. Then, while he was sleeping outside St. Peter's Basilica in Rome, Jesus appeared to him and told him to go back home and focus on works of mercy. And that's just what he did. Raymond's final twenty years were devoted to providing shelter for the homeless, comforting prisoners, and helping prostitutes.

Running away from pain so often seems the right thing to do, and we can empathize with Raymond's desire to leave Piacenza. But that was where the Lord wanted him, so he returned and served. In the same way, much as we might want to exit a troublesome place (physically or emotionally), it's just important to focus on where God wants us.

✿Inspiration

Remember that after this life you will not be doing the judging; instead you will be the ones being judged. (St. Raymond of Piacenza)

✿Challenge

Think about a conversation or decision you've been avoiding. Ask Jesus for help with the choice or approach so that when it's done, you will be ready to say yes to him.

Christopher

Died circa 251

We know him as Christopher, which means Christ-bearer. Tradition is that he carried the Christ child, growing ever heavier, across a river on his shoulders, not knowing the child's identity until the journey was complete. While Christopher was removed from the universal Church calendar more than fifty years ago in favor of saints whose history is more solid, parishes and other locations still are free to honor him on July 25, and he's still a go-to saint for many travelers.

Bearing Christ can get heavy, can't it? We get ridiculed and persecuted and shunned. But we soldier on, knowing that the weight of the world is even heavier without him.

✆Inspiration

"Come to me, all you that are weary and are carrying heavy burdens, and I will give you rest." (Matthew 11:28)

✆Challenge

Consider journaling or creating an image or collage about the Christ-bearers in your life.

Justin de Jacobis

October 9, 1800–July 31, 1860

Justin had been giving missions and retreats in Italy for years when his request for a posting abroad was approved by the Vincentian community leadership. He was nearly forty when he arrived in what is now Ethiopia; it's believed that at that point, there was not a single Ethiopian Roman Catholic. So, he and two other priests took what was then a somewhat novel approach. They did their best to dress and live like the Ethiopians, and to encourage vocations among the people. Justin's work was not appreciated by the Orthodox Coptic Church or the Ethiopian king. He was ordered out of the region, and died a few months later doing missionary work in what is now neighboring Eritrea.

Today we hear Justin's story, and wonder how anyone could think it was wrong to encourage vocations. But when we judge people's abilities by their gender, race, age, economic status, or physical attributes, we are doing the very same thing. Let's attempt to look at people as people, and value them for their God-given gifts, putting aside our prejudices.

Inspiration

And he said to them, "Go into all the world and proclaim the good news to the whole creation." (Mark 16:15)

Challenge

Pray for the day that it is no longer noteworthy that a woman, a man of color, or a person with a physical challenge accomplishes something the world regards as important.

Peter Chrysologus

Circa 380–450

As bishop of the northeast Italian city of Ravenna, Peter knew what the faithful wanted—and needed. And so, he gave it to them from the ambo: short, pithy homilies based on the Gospel and Church teachings, but generally with a positive note rather than one of condemnation. Small wonder the Roman empress, after hearing him, is said to have nicknamed him Chrysologus, golden-worded. Perhaps it's also no surprise that this Doctor of the Church also was successful in converting many of the remaining pagans in the area.

Being golden-worded matters beyond the ambo. The next time you start to lecture a child or someone at work, think about Peter. Keep it positive, even as you are providing needed correction.

✒ Inspiration

God seeks belief from you, not death. (St. Peter Chrysologus)

✒ Challenge

Compliment the priest who gives the homily at the next Mass you attend, even if it takes a bit of thinking to come up with sincere praise.

Ignatius of Loyola

1491–July 31, 1556

Ignatius was bored. The Spaniard was used to a life of action—as a soldier, as a gambler, as a ladies' man, and as a fighter. (He had the arrest record to prove the last.) Both his legs had been injured in battle, with one requiring resetting twice. His brother's wife gave him a book about Jesus, and the Bible and lives of the saints were also around. They weren't his usual reading material, but they were all that were available. So Ignatius read, and read, and read. He began to see a way of putting his dissolute youth behind him and using his leadership skills to serve God. After Ignatius left Loyola, he was never bored again. Through his travels, he connected with a group of young men including Francis Xavier *(December 3)* that took on the formal title of Society of Jesus in 1537. They received papal approval in 1540, and took their vows and named Ignatius their superior the following year. His spiritual exercises were first published in 1548.

Boredom is often a place that temptation and evil creep into our lives, but Ignatius had great faith resources available to combat it. Let's remember his story and turn to God, not our social media feeds or trash novels or television, when we feel at loose ends.

Inspiration
Soul of Christ, make me holy. (St. Ignatius of Loyola)

Challenge
The next time you feel bored, open your Bible to a random page and read.

Alphonsus Liguori

September 27, 1696–August 1, 1787

Alphonsus Liguori had begun practicing law when he was just nineteen years, and by the time he was twenty-seven, he had yet to lose his first case. But then it happened—a document he had reviewed several times, perhaps a bit carelessly, turned out to prove exactly the opposite of what he thought. The case was lost. Some likely thought Alphonsus was overreacting to leave the law behind and to begin studying for the priesthood, of all things. But it was there he found his true vocation. Alphonsus founded the Congregation of the Most Holy Redeemer, more commonly known as the Redemptorists, a missionary order, and to put his writing skills to work at more than one hundred books, including *Moral Theology*, perhaps his best known. He persevered despite depression and other health issues and is a Doctor of the Church.

It can be a soul-deadening experience, going through life doing what we're good at rather than what we're called to do. That lost case of Alphonsus's provided an opening for clarity. May defeats be an opportunity to examine whether we need a redirection as well.

✍ Inspiration

Our whole salvation depends on prayer…For if you pray, your salvation will be secure. (St. Alphonsus Liguori)

✍ Challenge

Think about a family member or friend who is having trouble getting over a disappointment. Gently ask questions to help the person think about the future.

Peter Julian Eymard

February 4, 1811–August 1, 1868

Peter Julian, whom John Paul II *(October 22)* called the apostle of the Eucharist, was restless. He was only fifty-seven when he died, but his journey had more twists and turns than most priests. He served as a diocesan priest for five years, then entered the Society of Mary or Marists, priests devoted to the Blessed Virgin. The community was a good fit for him, and he touched many souls through his preaching and his work with lay organizations. But in 1845, he had a spiritual experience in which he felt called to focus on the gift of the Eucharist. When the Marists determined that this singular focus was not in line with the society's charism, Peter Julian was allowed to leave and went on to found communities for male and female religious and laypeople devoted to the Eucharist.

The Marists' rejection of Peter Julian's plan wasn't necessarily wrong; his plans just were different from what they were called to do. This story reminds us that personal and professional relationships needn't end acrimoniously.

Inspiration

Live on the divine Eucharist, like the Hebrews did on the Manna. Your soul can be entirely dedicated to the divine Eucharist and very holy in the midst of your work and contacts with the world. (St. Peter Julian Eymard)

Challenge

Spend time in Adoration today, or before or after the next Mass you attend. Thank Jesus for all he has done for you.

Peter Faber

April 13, 1506–August 1, 1546

He was the son of poor Alpine shepherds with little formal education, but somehow, Peter managed to get to college in Paris. He was nineteen, as was his roommate, Francis Xavier *(December 3)*. After a time, they took on a third roommate, Ignatius of Loyola *(July 31)*. The rest is history. While Peter is not as well known as his roommates, like them he was an original member of the Society of Jesus, or the Jesuits. Peter lived out his charism as an adviser at important religious assemblies such as the Diet of Worms. One of his key assignments was working with Protestants during the Reformation. He also traveled thousands of miles in Italy, Germany, France, and Portugal on foot, preaching and offering retreats for laypeople on Ignatius's spiritual exercises.

Talk about the hand of God in roommate selection! As friends and in religious life, Peter, Francis, and Ignatius and the other founding Jesuits supported each other in prayer and camaraderie. It's a gift when we can recognize the presence of God in the people in our lives.

✈ Inspiration

It is the Lord who does all things in us, and for whom all things operate, and in whom they all exist. (St. Peter Faber)

✈ Challenge

Catch up via phone or email with a friend who bolsters your faith.

John Vianney

May 8, 1786–August 4, 1859

Life was seldom easy for John. He so wanted to be a priest, but struggled with his studies, especially Latin. There's confusion as to how he ended up drafted in France's Napoleonic Wars, but he was, and deserted. (A general amnesty a year later allowed him to return to school.) His seminary grades were such that he was dismissed. But a friendly nearby parish priest tutored John, and convinced the authorities he should be ordained anyway. John then served under this priest for two years before being named curé (pastor) of Ars, a community of about two hundred people. Many residents had fallen away from faith during the French Revolution, and didn't pay much attention to what John had to say about living in a more Godly way. He despaired to the point of leaving Ars three times to become a monk, but came back each time. Eventually, he discovered a calling in the confessional, offering the sacrament for sixteen to eighteen hours a day in his final ten years of life.

Life is seldom easy for us. Sometimes we have to work at jobs we don't enjoy so we can put bread on the table for ourselves and our families. John's story reminds us to keep one foot in front of the other, living hour by hour for Christ, regardless of how unsuccessful we feel we are.

✐ Inspiration

My God, I love you, and my only desire is to love you until the last breath of my life. (St. John Vianney)

✐ Challenge

Don't give up.

Oswald of Northumbria

Circa 605–642

They were on the run for their worldly lives—and found safety and more. Oswald was about eleven when his father, a northern England king, had been killed, and his mother took her children and a few others into exile in Scotland. Oswald and a brother were sent to the Iona monastery school, and were converted to Christianity. When the sitting pagan king died in 633, Oswald went back home, and a year later emerged as king himself after a battle. He credited his faith for his victory, and invited the Iona monks to come and convert his people. While the first monk did not do well, the second, Adrian, won so many souls for Christ that Oswald gave the monks the island of Lindisfarne for a monastery. As for Oswald, his reign was short-lived; he was killed after less than ten years of ruling.

Oswald's family was looking for a haven, and found it when they were introduced to Christianity. It's said that as Oswald was dying, he was praying for his kinsman. May we remember that if we are with Christ, we always are truly safe.

Inspiration

Listen to me your father, O children;

act accordingly, that you may be kept in safety. (Sirach 3:1)

Challenge

Bring the stresses of everyday life to Jesus. Breathe in the safety he provides.

Emygdius

279-309

When Emygdius became a Catholic at age twenty-three, he did what most converts dream of: He made a pilgrimage to Rome from his German home, possibly with three fellow Christians. Tradition has it that when he visited a pagan temple there, he destroyed an idol to the god of healing. This made him an unpopular person with the pagans, but not with the pope. The pope promptly named him a bishop and sent him to a town northeast of Rome to evangelize. It was not long before Emygdius and his three friends were beheaded in the Diocletian persecutions.

Emygdius had a convert's fire for Jesus. Many of us grow complacent in our faith, and the idea of engaging in a dialogue about faith with a non-Christian seems too risky. While we don't have to physically destroy idols, evangelizing by its very nature starts with people who disagree with us. Let's be on fire to bring those souls to Christ.

Inspiration

Proclaim the message; be persistent whether the time is favorable or unfavorable; convince, rebuke, and encourage, with the utmost patience in teaching. (2 Timothy 4:2)

Challenge

Pray for the right words to use in a conversation about Christ with someone you sense doesn't want to hear about him.

Cajetan

1480–August 7, 1547

It was a hard time to be a Catholic. Church offices and indulgences were being sold, clerical morals were seen as lax, and Martin Luther had what seemed to some to be an attractive alternative. Cajetan, an Italian nobleman by birth, believed the problems could be addressed within the Church structure. He was ordained not long before Luther published his Ninety-five Theses, and after being a part of priestly groups in a couple Italian cities was a co-founder of the Clerks Regular, or Theatines. Their members, all clergymen, vowed to preach, encourage people to avail themselves of the sacraments, and fight clerical corruption. They also agreed not to beg for alms, but to live on whatever God provided for them. Cajetan, who died a year after Luther, is known as the heart of the Catholic reformation.

Many people find it easier to "blow up" a bad relationship or situation. Cajetan inspires us to continue to look for other ways to resolve disputes, relying on God to show us the way.

✒ Inspiration

"The thief comes only to steal and kill and destroy. I came that they may have life, and have it abundantly." (John 10:10)

✒ Challenge

Ask a priest or other trusted adviser for help in discerning whether there are other approaches to address a problem than exiting a relationship.

Dominic

Circa 1170–August 6, 1221

What the world needed, Dominic decided, was a community of itinerant preachers who would go about sharing the good news as they lived simply. He came to this conclusion after seeing firsthand the failure to convert adherents of a sect in southern France, in no small part due to the relatively lavish lifestyles of the male religious who attempted to evangelize to them. The Order of Preachers, also known as the Dominicans, continues its ministry today. Dominic is also credited by some with the spread of the rosary as a prayer practice.

Think about it: Are you more likely to listen to someone who speaks simply to your heart, without a lot of physical trappings, or someone who sets himself or herself up as better than you? That's what Dominic learned when he saw the way the sect in France reacted to priests who traveled and ate better than they did. Keep it simple, as Jesus did. His message is irresistible.

✿Inspiration

"For all who exalt themselves will be humbled, and those who humble themselves will be exalted." (Luke 14:11)

✿Challenge

How can you carry Jesus's message more simply and humbly?

Albert of Trapani

Circa 1240–1307

It is not an unusual story for saints of this period. We're told that Albert's wealthy parents had waited twenty-six years for a child, and they vowed that if they were given one, they would consecrate him to God. Later, Albert's father would want to reconsider that vow and arrange a marriage for him, but Albert's mother prevailed. What might be considered a bit more unusual about this Italian Carmelite would be his passion for service. During a blockade of the city where he lived, he not only celebrated Mass in hope of an end, but also quietly arranged to have food brought in for the residents. He also was known to provide healing and assistance to Jews without requiring conversion, somewhat novel for the time. He and St. Angelus are known as the fathers of the Carmelites.

Albert didn't limit his charity or his prayers to Christians. Like him, may we show kindness and love to all we encounter, regardless of their faith or lack of one, or whether they appreciate our efforts.

Inspiration

"But love your enemies, do good, and lend, expecting nothing in return. Your reward will be great, and you will be children of the Most High; for he is kind to the ungrateful and the wicked." (Luke 6:35)

Challenge

Do a random act of kindness for someone who rejects God. Praying for that person counts!

Lawrence

Died 258

Lawrence, a deacon, was the highest-ranking Church official in Rome after the executions of his six fellow deacons and Pope Sixtus II. While he grieved their deaths, he took comfort in the pope's prediction that Lawrence would soon join them. That prediction may have provided strength when a Roman official demanded that Lawrence bring him all the Church's treasures. And so Lawrence did, presenting people with physical disabilities, people who were poverty stricken, and others he knew the official would find repugnant. Lawrence then suffered a martyr's death.

Think of the reverence we show the Eucharist. Think of the awe we feel when we see icons or paintings of holy people or scenes. May Lawrence's example teach us that treasure is also found in living, breathing people we often fail to see.

☙ Inspiration

Wealth and wages make life sweet,

but better than either is finding a treasure. (Sirach 40:18)

☙ Challenge

In service or prayer, recognize the Church's treasures.

Alexander of Comana

Died circa 275

No candidate a local council brought forth as bishop was suitable to the decision maker, the bishop of a nearby Turkish diocese. He rejected one man after another, saying each lacked the humility needed. Someone then derisively suggested Alexander, who sold coal to the townspeople and wore rags. But when he was questioned, it turned out Alexander had been a philosopher and knew the scriptures well. He got the job.

It's easy to judge people by their jobs or outer trappings. But if the philosopher dwelled inside a coal salesman, what might dwell inside your bus driver, barista, or postal carrier? God knows. Maybe it's time for you to find out.

✍ Inspiration

"Do not judge by appearances, but judge with right judgment." (John 7:24)

✍ Challenge

Say more than "hi, how are you doing?" to someone in the service industry whom you encounter regularly.

Cassian of Imola

Died 363

It was perhaps the ultimate indignity for a teacher. When Cassian refused to declare fealty to pagan gods, he was stripped naked and tied to a post. Then his persecutors set his two-hundred-plus schoolboys upon him. They used penknives, tablets, and styluses to attack and wound him. We can only imagine how long it would have taken Cassian to die. It is said that the saint encouraged them to strike him harder, saying he was ready to join the Lord.

What would have caused the boys to kill Cassian? Fear that they themselves would have been executed if they hadn't? Childish revenge on an exacting instructor? Perhaps they're not that different from us when we use our words and judgment to "kill" people society tells us are our enemies. Bad things happen when we listen to the world instead of the Lord.

☙ Inspiration
Then Jesus said, "Father, forgive them; for they do not know what they are doing." (Luke 23:34)

☙ Challenge
Be kind to someone the world ridicules.

Antonio Primaldo

Died August 14, 1480

Antonio was a simple tailor, older than many of the other eight hundred men of Otranto, Italy, who had been rounded up by Muslim soldiers. For fifteen days, the town was besieged by nearly eighteen thousand invaders. The archbishop and all the priests had been brutally murdered. All the eight hundred had to do to live was renounce Christ. But the simple tailor said no, and Antonio's rallying cry was so moving that not one man did so—although one of their executioners converted, and was promptly killed himself. When the town was liberated the following spring, the men's bodies were still there, exposed and incorrupt.

Are you ready to die for Christ, against all persecutors—those who threaten your soul as well as your body? Antonio shows us that to do that, we don't have to be learned theologians or perfect people. We just have to be willing to do what he did for us.

❧ Inspiration

Now it is time for us to fight to save our souls for the Lord. And since he died on the cross for us, it is fitting that we should die for him. (St. Antonio Primaldo)

❧ Challenge

Set an example of sacrifice for Christ that will inspire others.

Maximilian Kolbe

January 8, 1894–August 14, 1941

A choice he made early in life may have made Maximilian Kolbe's choice near the end easier. He was only twelve when the Blessed Virgin asked him to select between a white crown for purity and a red crown for martyrdom. He said he wanted both. As a Franciscan priest, Maximilian formed the Militia Immaculata, Army of Mary, to gain souls in conversion and to battle the forces that desired to destroy the Church. His activities to help refugees of the Nazi regime resulted in his arrest twice. The second time, he went to Auschwitz. And there, hearing a married man with children cry out in despair when he was selected for starvation, Maximilian made a choice: he offered to change places with the man. The request was granted; when after a few weeks he had not yet died, Maximilian was killed with a lethal injection. The man whose life he saved attended Maximilian's 1982 canonization.

We face choices every day. While they may not result in the immediate prospect of physical death, saying no to God and his people endangers our spiritual future. Maximilian's example reminds us that eternal life is the one that truly matters.

🐟 Inspiration

A single act of love makes the soul return to life. (St. Maximilian Kolbe)

🐟 Challenge

Say yes to something today that will cost you time and perhaps some ego, but which you know God desires.

Eusebius

Died August 17, 310

The question of the day in Rome was: in the aftermath of the Diocletian persecutions, what was to be done with those who had apostatized? Some thought those who committed especially grievous offenses could be pardoned by God only after they died. Others thought those who had gone away should be welcomed back, no questions asked. Pope Marcellus had taken a middle ground—welcoming returnees after penance—and had been deposed and exiled for it. Eusebius had a similar view, and was elected pope. Those who favored no penance elected an antipope, and when violence escalated on Rome's streets, the emperor banished both Eusebius and the antipope to Sicily. Eusebius died shortly thereafter, having served only four months as pope.

Maybe you're someone who never goes to confession, but receives the Eucharist each week. Or maybe you think your sins are so bad they can't be forgiven, so what's the point? Eusebius's approach is the one our Church follows today, and that's why we call it the sacrament of penance and reconciliation. Penance helps us clean our blemished hearts and souls, and celebrate our re-joining with God.

Inspiration

The sacrifice of the righteous is acceptable,
and it will never be forgotten. (Sirach 35:9)

Challenge

Go to confession. Be made clean.

Stephen of Hungary

Circa 975–August 15, 1038

Stephen was baptized when he was ten or so when his chieftain father and mother became Christians. By some accounts, he had a devotion to the Blessed Virgin Mary, and that devotion may have been his spiritual armor as he battled virtual anarchy and pagan customs (and had to defeat a relative's army) to become Hungary's first king. The battles won, Stephen and his wife Gisella, who herself has been beatified, settled into a peaceful rule that included the expansion of Christianity throughout the nation. However, that peace was marred at home by the deaths of all their children. Surely, their mutual belief in the resurrection must have comforted the couple in their sorrow.

Convert, revert, or cradle Catholic, God, our Blessed Mother, and the cloud of saints are all there to help us in the joys and tragedy that earthly live brings. All we have to do is ask.

Inspiration

…Be strong lest prosperity lift you up too much or adversity cast you down. Be humble in this life, that God may raise you up in the next (St. Stephen of Hungary)

Challenge

Talk with a friend who's a convert or revert about why he or she chose Catholicism. Or, if you are in one of those categories, journal about how Catholicism has changed you.

Hyacinth of Poland

1185–1267

Hyacinth had a good life going in southeast Poland. He'd received degrees in law and divinity, and was serving in a church position for his uncle, the bishop of Kraków. His uncle was making a trip to Rome, so Hyacinth went along. There, he met St. Dominic *(August 8)*, who had recently established the Order of Preachers, commonly known as the Dominicans. Hyacinth became one of the first men to join the congregation, and became known as the apostle of the North, due to his preaching in Poland, Germany, Lithuania, Scandinavia, and possibly beyond.

It may have been a chance meeting Hyacinth had with Dominic; what if Hyacinth and his uncle had arrived in Rome a month earlier or later? Let's use his story to remind us that God is forever putting people in our lives to help illumine his plan for us.

✒ Inspiration

Let the righteous be your dinner companions,

and let your glory be in the fear of the Lord. (Sirach 9:16)

✒ Challenge

Make a list of everyone you encountered this morning or this afternoon, real time or virtually. What did you learn from each of them?

Alberto Hurtado Cruchaga

January 22, 1901–August 18, 1952

Alberto knew what struggle was. His father died when he was just four. Paying the family's debts required his mother to sell what property she had, and so Alberto and his brother were raised by a series of Chilean relatives. When he was a little older, he worked while attending a Jesuit college to provide for his mother and brother. Alberto's journey took him to Argentina and Belgium, where he was ordained in 1933. After a few years as a university professor back in Chile, he began working with Catholic Action's youth movement. In 1944, he founded what would become Hogar de Cristo. While the ministry initially focused on providing a homelike environment for abandoned young people (Alberto made a trip to Boys Town to see what was happening in the United States), today it helps the poorest of the poor of all ages.

Alberto's childhood experiences showed him just how much one action—a warm meal, a bed, a scholarship—can mean. He paid forward those kindnesses among the forgotten Chilean children, and we can do the same.

✒ Inspiration

It is good not to do bad, but it is very bad not to do good. (St. Alberto Hurtado Cruchaga)

✒ Challenge

Write a note of thanks to someone whose help meant more to you than he or she knows. If the person is still alive, send it to him or her.

Bernardo Tolomei

May 10, 1272-August 20, 1348

Bernardo's life was one of odd turns, but filled with humility and faith. Born into a noble family, he was knighted, received an excellent education, and studied to become a lawyer. However, a progressive condition left him almost totally blind. When he was forty-one, Bernardo and two friends determined that they were called to live as hermits, and retired to land owned by Bernardo's family. Eventually they discerned that they were more suited for community life, and so received approval to found a Benedictine monastery. For a few years, Bernardo begged off becoming abbot, citing his sight issues. He finally relented in 1322 and served as the community's leader until he died of the plague.

Do you ever wish God's plan was clearer? Maybe all your friends are settled down with careers or families, and you continually find yourself on new and unfamiliar paths. As Bernardo shows us, we needn't worry if our way is not as straight as some of those we know. The hope of eternal life lies at the end for all who believe.

✒ Inspiration

I admire the humble acknowledgment of one's own sin more than any manifestation of virtue. (St. Bernardo Tolomei)

✒ Challenge

Try to go the entire day without wishing you were someone else or had something someone else does that you lack.

Bernard of Clairvaux

1090–August 20, 1153

He was the golden boy of the twelfth century. Everything seemed to come easily to Bernard: born into a noble family, a priestly discernment that resulted in him joining the Cistercians with thirty of his friends, sent to found what is now the famed Clairvaux Abbey before he was thirty. His writings, especially on Marian devotion and the Song of Songs, were praised. Bernard also was gifted at navigating Church and political waters. Small wonder that the pope called on him to rally support for the Second Crusade. And rally it he did, to the point that cloth to make crosses run short, and royalty including Eleanor of Aquitaine joined in the cause. However, victory was not to be. The crusade failed, so significantly that Bernard, always humble despite the fame and recognition that had been his all his life, felt compelled to write an apology to the pope. He died just four years later.

Bernard's example reminds us we're not always going to be successful. When we fail, the world may reject us, but God won't.

☞ Inspiration

Christian warriors, he who gave his life for you, today demands yours in return. (St. Bernard of Clairvaux)

☞ Challenge

The Lord is with us whether we're on top of the world or down in the dregs. Contemplate the ways you are being blessed.

Abraham of Smolensk

Died 1221

Maybe it was jealousy; after all, this Russian monk was very popular among laypeople for the way he ministered to the needy. And growing up in a wealthy family, Abraham had had educational opportunities that some of his confreres had not. Or maybe they disagreed with his preaching that people needed to be prepared for the Last Judgment. In any event, his abbot forbade him to preach. Abraham moved to another monastery in the area, where the same thing happened. Then things got worse: Even though Abraham was cleared of heresy and immorality charges, the bishop stripped him of his priestly functions and sent him back to the first monastery. After five years of this, a drought threatened the area and laypeople insisted that Abraham be reinstated. Finally, he was cleared. He lived out his life at a third monastery.

Abraham was trying to do the job God had given him, but others kept presenting obstacles. His story reminds us that we too face people who don't understand what we're doing or wish us ill. If we keep our eyes on God, the opinions of others don't really matter.

☞ Inspiration

A fool takes no pleasure in understanding,

but only in expressing personal opinion. (Proverbs 18:2)

☞ Challenge

Try to go through the day without contradicting anyone, even if you know he or she is wrong, or offering advice unless it's requested.

Louis IX of France

April 25, 1214-August 25, 1270

The only king of France to be canonized set a great example as both a ruler and a Christian. Louis was a model of piety; it's said that during Advent and Lent, he invited thirteen poor people into his home each evening for dinner, and often joined them. He was responsible for the construction of hospitals, monasteries, and churches, including Sainte-Chapelle, known for its beautiful stained-glass windows. As king, Louis led a crusade to the Holy Land that resulted in his capture and imprisonment. He was back in France for sixteen years before going on a second crusade, during which he contracted typhoid fever and died.

While Louis was not perfect (some of his attitudes today would be rightly recognized as discriminatory), he showed a marvelous balance, enjoying a happy life with his wife and their large family and caring for the spiritual and physical needs of his people. He reminds us that paintings and other art and meals can be evangelization tools, just as words and swords can be.

Inspiration

In prosperity give thanks to God with humility, and fear lest by pride you abuse God's benefits and so offend him by those very means by which you ought particularly improve yourself in his service. (St. Louis IX of France)

Challenge

Visit the Sainte-Chapelle website or spend some time today with your favorite religious painting or sculpture, in person or in a book or video.

Philip Benizi

August 15, 1233–August 22, 1285

Philip always seemed to underestimate his gifts. The young nobleman practiced medicine for a year in Florence before joining the Servants of Mary, or Servite, community. He found happiness as a lay brother, then became a priest at twenty-six at the urging of other members of the community. He became known as a powerful preacher; again despite his protestations, he became the Servite superior general in 1267, a post he would hold until his death nearly twenty years later. Philip didn't always yield to others' plans for him; when he learned he was being discussed as a papal candidate, he ran into a cave and hid.

It's a fine line, embracing Christ's humility in ourselves while not falling into self-hatred, the flip side of pride. Like Philip, may we carefully weigh the opinions of others as we discern what God desires of us.

Inspiration

Do not let anyone disqualify you, insisting on self-abasement and worship of angels, dwelling on visions, puffed up without cause by a human way of thinking, and not holding fast to the head, from whom the whole body, nourished and held together by its ligaments and sinews, grows with a growth that is from God. (Colossians 2:18-19)

Challenge

They say God doesn't call the qualified, but qualifies the called. Consider whether the advice of others is nudging in God's desired direction.

Bartholomew

1st century

The synoptic Gospels all refer to Bartholomew as one of the Twelve, and Acts indicates he was present when Judas's replacement was selected. Tradition tells us he evangelized in Armenia, India, and beyond, and that he met a martyr's death by being skinned alive and then beheaded.

Why don't we know more about Bartholomew? Perhaps for the same reason we likely don't know the names of all the lectors, extraordinary ministers, and ushers at our parish. Some ministries are done quietly, in the background. That makes them no less valuable to God—or to us, if we open our eyes and ears.

Inspiration

The quiet words of the wise are more to be heeded
    than the shouting of a ruler among fools. (Ecclesiastes 9:17)

Challenge

Do a kind act in secret.

Joseph Calasanz

September 11, 1557–August 25, 1648

Joseph and two other priests in 1597 opened a free school for poor children in Rome, and after just a few years, more than twelve hundred students were enrolled. In 1621, Joseph was among the founders and the first superior general for what we know today as the Order of the Pious Schools (or the Piarists or Scolopi). But as he aged, the community began to shatter from within. In 1639, an ambitious priest said Joseph's age made him no longer able to be the leader, and became superior general. Four years later, when he died, another priest, Stefano Cherubini, who was well connected in the Church hierarchy, took over. (In modern times, Cherubini has been accused of pedophilia, and Joseph accused of not reporting it.) In 1645, Joseph was restored to leadership, but the damage had been done. The pope had the Piarists report to local bishops; they were restored as a religious order twenty years after Joseph's death.

Think of all the good work Joseph did—and how people connived to bring him down for their own gain. His example reminds us there is evil in the world and that ultimately, our trust must lie in God and only God.

Inspiration

Through him you have come to trust in God, who raised him from the dead and gave him glory, so that your faith and hope are set on God. (1 Peter 1:21)

Challenge

Refrain from gossiping about or judging someone else's abilities today. Leave it to God.

Genesius of Rome

Died circa 303

Genesius really wanted his part in the play mocking Christians to be realistic. After all, Emperor Diocletian was going to be in the audience. So, the actor managed to convince a group of Christians that he was sincerely interested in joining them. Given the persecutions of the day, the believers would have been extremely wary of Genesius, but they considered his interest to be authentic. And indeed, it turned out that when Genesius acted out the sacrament of baptism, he experienced a conversion moment. He was executed shortly thereafter. Please note that while Genesius of Arles and Rome lived about the same time, one lived in Rome, the other in France.

Think about the people you know who mock you for believing Church teachings on the Eucharist or social or life issues. Sometimes, like Genesius, those who ridicule us do so because they're on the precipice of conversion. Consider answering them with love and knowledge, not defensiveness.

Inspiration

I came here today to please an earthly Emperor but what I have done is to please a heavenly King. I came here to give you laughter, but what I have done is to give joy to God and his angels. (St. Genesius of Rome)

Challenge

Pray for the conversion of a celebrity who ridicules the Catholic faith.

Pœmen

Died circa 450

Pœmen took a commonsense approach to advising the spiritual lives of others in the Egyptian desert. For example, when someone said he was prepared to do penance for three years for an offense, Pœmen suggested three days instead—but with great fervor. He also encouraged frequent Communion, and advised against excessive fasting (though his own could be extreme). His wisdom and leadership kept the monks together after numerous raids forced them to leave the Skete monastery.

Life in the desert wasn't easy, and wasn't always safe. Pœmen's sense of community helped the monks withstand adversity. When we show a cheerful face and confidence in a Spirit-filled future, we help those around us.

✒ Inspiration

Silence is not a virtue when charity calls for speech. (St. Pœmen)

✒ Challenge

Refuse to "go negative" today on the state of world, national, or local affairs. Pray for harmony.

Augustine

November 13, 354–August 28, 430

The boy was clever with a bright future. But the family's resources were limited, and raising the funds to send him to Carthage for a high-class education gave him a year to goof off. Augustine did the things many teenagers do when left to their own devices—take up with the wrong crowd, explore unhealthy relationships, and find themselves drawn to unhealthy thoughts. These activities deepened when he reached Carthage, to the despair of his Christian mother, Monica. Her entreaties played no small role in her son's eventual connection with St. Ambrose *(December 7)* that led him to baptism at the 387 Easter Vigil. Augustine was ordained four years later, and became the bishop of Hippo in 395. He was named a Doctor of the Church for his writings on theology.

Augustine's soul was never lost, really. But it took the influence of people he respected and loved to convert him. He reminds us that no one is beyond redemption, and we may have a role to play in the return of the people we privately believe are beyond hope.

✐ Inspiration

That so my mother's last request of me, may through my confessions, more than through my prayers, be, through the prayers of many, more abundantly fulfilled to her. (St. Augustine)

✐ Challenge

Call, email, or write the person, still living, who has had the greatest impact on your faith. It could be your spouse, child, parent, sibling, teacher, colleague, or friend. Say thank you.

Genesius of Arles

Died circa 303

The French notary and catechumen had had enough. A decree on persecution of Christians was being read out loud in the court where he worked. His job was not to carry it out, just record it. But Genesius refused to do that, and told the judge that what the decree would do was just wrong. He fled the courtroom, then was captured and beheaded. Please note that while Genesius of Arles and Rome lived about the same time, one lived in Rome, the other in France.

Genesius couldn't stay quiet about the injustice he was supposed to duly note. His decision stands in stark contrast to those who over the ages have stood by turning a blind eye to persecution or actively engaged in it, saying they were just following orders. Let's remember that even at the cost of a demotion or ridicule, God's rules are more important than any employer's policies.

Inspiration

"...for it is not you who speak, but the Spirit of your Father speaking through you." (Matthew 10:20)

Challenge

Speak up at work or in your family against an injustice. Don't accept wrong by another simply to keep the peace.

Raymond Nonnatus

1204-1240

As a young man, Raymond was drawn to a new Spanish religious community. The mission of the Mercedarian Order (Order of Mercy) was to free Christians held in north Africa, in the same spirit as Jesus's ransoming his people. Raymond went to Algeria and gained the freedom of some captives, then offered to be held himself in exchange for the release of others when his money ran out. The captors considered killing him, then decided he was of more value alive. After cruel torture, he was eventually released. Raymond was to be named a cardinal for his actions, but either died or was killed on the way to Rome.

Raymond's story resonates with us in the same way that the life of Maximilian Kolbe does. Few of us will be called to offer up our lives so that others may escape execution. But we are called to sacrifice in God's name so that people can eat, have shelter, and hear the Good News.

✎ Inspiration

You know that you were ransomed from the futile ways inherited from your ancestors, not with perishable things like silver or gold, but with the precious blood of Christ, like that of a lamb without defect or blemish. (1 Peter 1:18-19)

✎ Challenge

Offer yourself as virtual or spiritual ransom for an imprisoned soul.

Joseph of Arimathea

First century

Joseph loved Jesus, but he had his own standing as a member of the Sanhedrin to consider. Maybe he also had a family he felt he had to protect. So while he was considered a disciple, he kept his faith hidden during most of Jesus's public ministry. But then came the Sanhedrin council's denouncement of Jesus. Joseph didn't agree to the action. And in an extremely risky, public action, he asked Pilate for Jesus's body. Joseph bought a shroud for his friend; with the others, he lay Jesus in the tomb Joseph may have purchased for himself.

You may have a lot in common with Joseph: loving Jesus, but feeling hesitant to carry his teachings into certain venues or with certain people. Like Joseph, maybe you've had an occasion or two where you've failed to do so. His story inspires us to be more confident and fearless the next time we have the chance to be bold.

✒ Inspiration

After all these things, Joseph of Arimathea, who was a disciple of Jesus, though a secret one because of his fear of the Jews, asked Pilate to let him take away the body of Jesus. (John 19:38)

✒ Challenge

Do something risky for Christ today, whether it's inviting a family member or friend to Mass or Adoration, or engaging in a ministry that makes you uncomfortable.

Simeon Stylites

Circa 390–459

To call Simeon an ascetic would be an understatement. When he was in his teens, the shepherd's son heard the Beatitudes, and determined he was destined for a life of solitude. He entered a monastic community, but didn't find it rigorous enough. He spent three years in a hut, then in a rock crag; neither got him to the depth of spirituality he desired. Finally, Simeon came up with the idea of living atop a pillar (stylite) that had a railed living space of about eleven square feet, with no protection from the elements. He lived on pillars of varying heights for half his life. Interestingly, that did not provide the privacy he craved either. His pillar became a pilgrimage site, with people passing prayer requests and the like up the ladder he used to receive food. Stylites continued to exist in some areas into the nineteenth century.

Do you feel you have enough alone time with God? Probably none of us do, though we don't go to the extremes of Simeon. His story shows us that stripping ourselves of worldly trappings doesn't relieve us of the responsibility to serve his people.

Inspiration

"Blessed are the pure in heart for they will see God." (Matthew 5:8)

Challenge

Spend time in adoration. Afterward, come down from your "pillar" for a talk with a family member or friend.

Solomon Le Clercq

November 15, 1745–September 2, 1792

He could have left. Thousands of priests did in August 1792 under orders of the French revolutionary authorities. But Solomon chose to stay, just as he had when the new constitution gave the state control over Church property and required an oath of fealty to the government. Solomon was arrested on August 15, 1792, and taken to a Carmelite monastery. Two weeks later, a mob that had killed thirty priests on their way to prison moved on to the monastery, where another 150 priests and religious, including Solomon, were martyred with swords.

Think about Solomon's strength vs. that of Peter and the other followers of Jesus who were nowhere to be found at his trial and crucifixion. What would your response be if all Catholics were ordered out of your city or state or country?

✒ Inspiration

Let us endure with joy and thanksgiving the crosses and afflictions that he will send us. (St. Solomon Le Clercq)

✒ Challenge

Talk with a friend about what you would have done in Solomon's position.

Gregory the Great

Circa 540–604

When he was unanimously elected pope in 590, Gregory was more than reluctant. In fact, he asked the emperor not to approve him. Gregory knew about the inner workings of the Church, having served the pope for six years in Constantinople, a role at which he had excelled but one he disliked. He also knew about being an administrator; time in a Roman leadership role and in the senate had ended with him selling all his properties and becoming a monk. Ultimately, Gregory became pope only under protest, but his fourteen years were critical, re-establishing papal authority in Spain and France, dispatching missionaries to England, and working to end clerical abuses. His more than eight hundred letters and books including *Pastoral Care* (a work on the way bishops and priests should live and shepherd) resulted in his canonization by acclamation when he died. Gregory and Sts. Ambrose *(December 7)*, Augustine *(August 28)*, and Jerome *(September 30)* in 1298 were named the four Great Latin Doctors of the Church.

Gregory craved monasticism. But for most of his life, that wasn't where God called him. His story reminds us to trust and surrender when God clearly desires something of us.

☙ Inspiration

It is a less thing to renounce what one has; but it is an exceeding great thing to renounce what one is. (St. Gregory the Great)

☙ Challenge

Say yes today to something God's been nudging you to do.

Giles

Circa 640–710

Giles pursued a hermit's life in France's Provence region, possibly because his reputation for healing and service were so great that he had left Athens. But the area ruler was so impressed with his holiness that he said he would provide property for a monastery—only if Giles would be the abbot. Eventually, he agreed, and his monks provided hospitality for pilgrims to both Santiago de Compostela and the Holy Land.

Solitude and contemplation are an essential part of the Christian life. Some of us are called to it as vocation. Giles's story reminds us not to get so comfortable that we fail to listen for changes God desires.

☙ Inspiration

To make an apt answer is a joy to anyone,

and a word in season, how good it is! (Proverbs 15:23)

☙ Challenge

Be a hermit, even for thirty minutes. Get away from your life's noise and listen to God.

Bertinus

Circa 615–709

Bertinus had a desire for missionary work, but that didn't come immediately. The monk was in an abbey in central France when the call came: A new bishop to the north needed help. While the area had converted to Christianity a century earlier, the people had become indifferent or worse. Bertinus and two confreres were sent to assist in the re-evangelization. The men were successful enough that others wanted to join them, and so two monasteries were built. In 661, Bertinus became abbot of one of them, then worked with the bishop to build a church nearby.

Evangelization, especially in unfamiliar territory, can be a lonely business. Bertinus and his friends likely converted more souls because they had each other for support. We all can do more together for God than we can alone.

✣ Inspiration

Faithful friends are beyond price;

no amount can balance their worth. (Sirach 6:15)

✣ Challenge

Invite a friend to join you in a service project. Alternatively, make friends with someone who has the same passion for the project.

Lawrence Justinian

1381–January 8, 1456

Lawrence always looked to the saints—specifically, to the martyrs—for Inspiration and comfort. When he underwent a couple of painful operations, he didn't cry out, but only murmured the names of Jesus and the Blessed Mother. When observers marveled at his fortitude, he said the pain could not compare to that of martyrs burned by torches and heated irons. To emulate the martyrs, he was also known to go without fire in his rooms in the winter, and to abstain from cool drinks in the summer. His deathbed was one of straw; he said he did not need feathers since Jesus died on a cross. As the bishop of Castello (which included Venice) and later as an archbishop, Lawrence also was known for his writings, including *The Degrees of Perfection*.

Lawrence's attitudes may seem extreme to us, but there's great relevance to our lives today. We can make any small incident, like someone cutting us off in traffic or a delivery delay, into a big deal. His story helps us keep things in perspective—and to offer up our sufferings, major and minor, as an opportunity to perfect ourselves.

Inspiration

Offer right sacrifices,
    and put your trust in the Lord. (Psalm 4:5)

Challenge

Lay the day's aggravations at the altar, rather than complaining about them to your family, friends, or God.

Cloud

Circa 522–560

It's the story of a life with a very sad beginning and a happy ending. Cloud's father had murdered one cousin and then was killed by that cousin's brother. To consolidate their power, two uncles conspired to kill Cloud's brothers. Cloud, who was only about five years old, escaped and spent the next dozen or so years under the protection of first a French bishop, then a hermit. Eventually, Cloud was ordained as a priest, and reconciled with his uncles. He gave his restored wealth to the poor, and to build a monastery east of Paris that became known as Saint Cloud. Those in the surrounding area spoke of his gentleness and generosity.

One might think that Cloud would have taken on the family feud; after all, he had lost people who were dear to him. Perhaps it was the time in solitude and with religious communities that allowed him to forgive his uncles. It's a good reminder to be merciful, even with those who don't ask for mercy from us.

Inspiration

"Blessed are the merciful, for they will receive mercy." (Matthew 5:7)

Challenge

Pray for the conversion of someone who has wronged you.

Ciarán of Clonmacnoise

Circa 516-549

Ciarán, one of a group of monastic saints known as the Twelve Apostles of Ireland, spent most of his brief life around some of the best-known religious names in his country. He studied first under St. Finnian of Clonard, then under St. Enda of Inishmore, who ordained him and counseled him to erect a monastery. Ciarán and a group of companions did just that, founding Clonmacnoise monastery in central Ireland in about 548. While Ciarán was selected as the first abbot, he died of the plague not long thereafter. The monastery continued to function for a thousand years, and the ruins still can be visited today.

Ciarán likely didn't stop to think how long Clonmacnoise would stand; he was simply being obedient to the message God had given him through St. Finnian, which was to build it. The saint wasn't around to enjoy the monastery for more than three years at most. His story shows us that our role is to do what God asks, not to daydream about our earthly legacy.

Inspiration

Like good stewards of the manifold grace of God, serve one another with whatever gift each of you has received. (1 Peter 4:10)

Challenge

As you scan your to-do list today, consider which of those items is on God's list for you. Rewrite as necessary.

Peter Claver

June 26, 1580–September 8, 1654

Every year, ten thousand enslaved Africans would arrive on ships in the Colombian port of Cartagena, sick, scared, and starved. And those were the "lucky" ones who hadn't died on the month-plus voyage. Whenever possible for nearly forty years, Peter, a Spanish-born Jesuit priest, was there to meet them. He provided them with food, medicine, and comfort as best he could, and offered the sacrament of baptism and the hope of Christ. Peter also ministered to those who put the enslaved people to work in their mines and plantations and to the Spanish colonists. But he never got used to the awful way he saw the African people treated, and called himself their slave.

Despair is an instrument of the evil one. He tells us there's no point in saying a rosary in front of an abortion clinic, because abortions will never be eradicated. He tells us there's no point in battling unjust imprisonments, because they will always exist. Peter's story reminds us that it's not for us to stop just because we think our efforts on the Lord's behalf are futile. We never know the full extent of the help we may provide.

✎ Inspiration

We must speak to them with our hands before we try to speak to them with our lips. (St. Peter Claver)

✎ Challenge

Think of a hopeless situation in your community, such as homelessness or hunger. Then do something—volunteer, write an email, make a phone call—anyway.

Nicholas of Tolentino

Circa 1246–September 10, 1305

Nicholas was known for his austerities, but this particular fast of his apparently went on longer than some others. The Italian Augustinian priest felt weak. Then he had a vision—accounts vary as to whether it was Jesus, the Blessed Virgin, St. Augustine *(August 28)*, or St. Monica— to incorporate bread marked with a cross and soaked in water into what he was eating. Nicholas did so, and his health was restored. Thus began the Augustinian tradition of blessing and distributing St. Nicholas bread. Nicholas was so passionate about distributing bread at the monastery gates to the poor and sick that he was sometimes criticized by the community's leaders.

Nicholas did exactly what God calls us to do when we receive a blessing: He shared it. Let's do the same with the gifts we receive, tangible and intangible.

☙ Inspiration

I do it all for the sake of the gospel, so that I may share in its blessings. (1 Corinthians 9:23)

☙ Challenge

Pay forward a blessing you've received in the past week.

John Gabriel Perboyre

January 6, 1802–September 11, 1840

John Gabriel was fifteen when he accompanied his brother Louis to a Vincentian seminary about seventy-five miles away from their French home. John Gabriel found an interest, and his uncle, a priest who had founded the seminary, received permission for John Gabriel to stay. Later, Louis was tapped to be a missionary to China, but died en route. John Gabriel, who had always had an interest in missionary work but had been assigned as assistant novitiate director, pressed his case anew. His request was granted, but after less than three years in China he had to go into hiding and a student was forced to disclose his location. John Gabriel was imprisoned and tortured for a year, but still refused to provide the names or locations of the other missionaries. He was strangled with a rope while hanging on a cross.

It makes you wonder: If Louis had made it to China, would John Gabriel have been allowed to follow? But what would have happened to those souls who met Christ due to John Gabriel's presence, and his example of faith during his torture? Perhaps his story shows that if we feel strongly about a call to service, we must be fearless and faithful in our obedience in spite of the possible consequences.

Inspiration

If we have to suffer martyrdom it would be a great grace given to us by God; it's something to be desired, not feared. (St. John Gabriel Perboyre)

Challenge

Speak up for Christ today, even if it's likely to cost you a friend or result in ridicule.

Guy of Anderlecht

Died circa 1012

Guy was a simple man and, it turned out, easily duped. The son of peasants, he found a calling as the sacristan, janitor, and all-around helper at a parish near Brussels. A local merchant took advantage of Guy's desire to raise some money for the poor and as a result, the gullible man lost all his funds. He spent the next seven years on a series of pilgrimages, all on foot, that took him as far away as Rome and Jerusalem. When he returned home, he was sick, and died soon afterward.

Guy's life may sound no more special than your own. And yet, miracles were reported at his gravesite, and many consider his simple way to be an Inspiration. It's a good reminder that we don't have to be martyrs or theologians to touch the lives of others.

☙ Inspiration

The law of the Lord is perfect,
    reviving the soul;
the decrees of the Lord are sure,
    making wise the simple (Psalm 19:7)

☙ Challenge

Consider the charism of someone in your parish who does something that others consider menial or unimportant.

John Chrysostom

Circa 347–407

They called him Chrysostom, or golden-mouthed, for his eloquent speaking. But not everyone liked the words that came out of the reluctant archbishop of Constantinople's mouth. John called for clergy and rulers alike to live simple lives and help the poor, and while that was popular with the people, it grated on the Eastern Roman emperor's wife and the archbishop of Alexandria, who had wanted John's position. They engineered his indictment by a synod of bishops, mostly on trumped-up charges, and sent him into exile.

Jesus didn't say we'd be popular if we spoke his truth. Yet, like John, we are called to carry the Gospel message. Whether others chose to listen or to persecute us is beside the point.

Inspiration

Christ has clothed us with weapons which are of greater splendor than gold, more resistant than steel, which burn better than any flame, and are more slight than a puff of breath. (St. John Chrysostom)

Challenge

Don't worry about how golden-mouthed you sound. Speak up today for your beliefs.

Lambert of Maastricht

Circa 636–705

Lambert became a bishop when he was thirty-five or so when his uncle was murdered. Political unrest in what is today the Netherlands led to his expulsion a few years later, and Lambert then spent seven years as a monk. The political winds changed again, and in 681 he was reinstated by the local ruler, Pepin of Heristal. The two men initially had a good relationship but when Pepin's affair with his sister-in-law came to light, Lambert denounced Pepin. There may have been further intrigue associated with their break, but in any event, the bishop was murdered, possibly by relatives of Pepin's sister-in-law, and is considered a martyr.

Pepin's affair was the tipping point for Lambert; he could not accept this open violation of the sanctity of marriage. We all have those times when God calls us to step forth and carry a holy message of correction. And carry it we must, even when that means permanent rupture of relationships or other losses.

☞Inspiration

All scripture is inspired by God and is useful for teaching, for reproof, for correction, and for training in righteousness, so that everyone who belongs to God may be proficient, equipped for every good work. (2 Timothy 3:16-17)

☞Challenge

Spend time with scripture to find the words to use in a conversation with a friend or family member whose behavior has reached your tipping point.

Francesco Maria da Camporosso

December 27, 1804–September 17, 1866

He was great at begging—really great, it appears. This Capuchin friar began his religious life in other roles, but when he became a country beggar assistant in Genoa's environs, his charism became apparent. Three years later, he was named the Capuchins' city beggar; six years later, he took over responsibility for all begging. Francesco also was a giver; he was beloved in the city for his healings and compassion for all those he encountered, rich or poor. He died from cholera, which he contracted while caring for people during an epidemic.

Sometimes, all people need is an invitation to do good. Francesco's friendly manner and "ask" for donations to help the poor attracted others to show their better angels. Let's remember that as we put aside our dislike of the word *no* and start offering our own invitations.

☙ Inspiration

An hour of suffering is worth more than a hundred years of delights. (St. Francesco Maria da Camporosso)

☙ Challenge

Ask family members and friends to contribute some time and talent to your favorite ministry. Don't sulk if they say no; delight when they say yes.

Stanislaus Papczyński

May 18, 1631–September 17, 1701

This Polish saint's initial venture into religious life did not go well. He was ordained in the Piarists, a teaching order, just before he turned thirty. The fit was less than easy; Stanislaus thought his brethren were not rigid enough. Things got worse; he ended up spending about three months in two different monastery prisons! He was released from the order nine months later. Stanislaus then discerned he was to form a community devoted to the Blessed Mother and to praying for the souls in purgatory. Stanislaus received diocesan approval for the Congregation of Marian Clerks of the Immaculate Conception nine years later. While it began as a community of hermits, it expanded to include active ministry. Stanislaus died three months after formal approval was received from Rome.

Stanislaus thought he was following God's will, and yet his brethren kept isolating him. Still, his trust in the Lord helped him to his true vocation. His story reminds us never to give up hope in God.

Inspiration

And not only that, but we also boast in our sufferings, knowing that suffering produces endurance, and endurance produces character and character produces hope… (Romans 5:3-4)

Challenge

Do you have a bad fit in ministry or at work? Pray for the wisdom to endure—or to discern the next step.

Robert Bellarmine

October 4, 1542–September 17, 1621

He was short, wore glasses, and was all but deaf in one ear. He played the violin and other instruments well. He was friendly and engaging, but not the world's best orator or preacher. His cardinal's ring and other worldly goods were often in the pawnshop so that the funds he received could be used to help the needy. On the surface, there was nothing that would make one think that Robert would be regarded as one of the effective Catholic Reformation writers and spokespeople. His writings, including his views on papal authority, resulted in his naming as a Doctor of the Church in 1931, a year after his canonization.

The old saying goes that you can't judge a book by its cover, and that's certainly true in Robert's case. The most intellectually gifted among us aren't always brooding and introverted, and those to whom charity comes most naturally aren't always wealthy extroverts. Let's stop judging people by our preconceived notions, and be open to receiving whatever gift they have to share.

Inspiration

A humble recognition of our need is often more eloquent to the ears of God than many prayers. (St. Robert Bellarmine)

Challenge

Write an email or note of appreciation to someone whose gifts you have recently recognized.

Joseph of Cupertino

June 17, 1603–September 18, 1663

Joseph had trouble with his studies, and his lack of education caused the Conventual Franciscans to refuse to accept him. He went to the Capuchins, and was dismissed after less than a year because he couldn't do anything right. Joseph ended up back with Conventual Franciscans as a stable boy; though his intellectual capacity didn't improve, he managed to be ordained as a priest at twenty-five. But while he wasn't gifted in the classroom, Joseph stood out in another way: He levitated, as many as seventy times in just seventeen years. This caused him to be a public spectacle despite his own and his community's efforts. For example, he couldn't eat with the rest of his community or celebrate Mass publicly during his priesthood, and he was called up before an inquisition (and cleared). It's said his last levitation was just before he died.

Joseph spent most of his life being mocked, ridiculed, or judged. Yet he kept his faith in God and kept putting one foot in front of the other. His example shows us that it's not about whether people understand or appreciate us—the Almighty always does, and that grace is sufficient.

⟡ Inspiration

Those who mock the poor insult their Maker;

those who are glad at calamity will not go unpunished.

(Proverbs 17:5)

⟡ Challenge

Pray for the wisdom to see what God sees in someone with whom you are impatient.

Juan Macias

March 2, 1585–September 16, 1645

It's perhaps not a surprise that Juan, orphaned by the time he was four and raised by an uncle, felt a special connection to the Blessed Mother and St. John the Apostle *(December 27)*. When Juan considered a vocation with the Dominicans, St. John told him it would not happen in his native Spain but thousands of miles away in Peru. Juan waited patiently. Then, when he was in his early thirties, he had a business opportunity to go to South America. Eventually, Juan made his way to Lima, where he became a Dominican. He was known for his service to the poor—including sending his donkey out to collect alms—and his gentle welcome as an assistant porter for more than twenty years.

Waiting is hard, especially when we're certain of God's message but not of God's timing. Juan must have wondered why he wasn't to become a Dominican in his homeland. But he waited for the path to be made clear. Juan's story reminds us to be as patient, trusting that God is with us.

✒ Inspiration

But if we hope for what we do not see, we wait for it with patience. (Romans 8:25)

✒ Challenge

Pray for the gift of patience—with yourself, with someone else, and with God.

Paul Chŏng Ha-sang

Circa 1795-September 22, 1839

Paul knew that being public with his Catholic faith was dangerous. His father, one of Korea's first Catholic converts, and his older brother had both been martyred when Paul was seven. But Paul was a believer to the bone. He used his position working for a government interpreter to lobby the Beijing bishop and the pope to establish a diocese in Korea. When Catholics were persecuted, Paul was among the faithful who held the community together, providing comfort and encouragement. He had entered the seminary to become a priest himself at the time of his martyrdom. His mother also was killed for the faith the same year.

Would it give you pause about living your faith openly if people in your family had been persecuted and killed, or would it make you all the more determined that evil would not prevail? Paul knew his own death was a likely outcome if he said yes. What would your answer be?

✒ Inspiration

"I am the living bread that came down from heaven. Whoever eats of this bread will live forever; and the bread that I will give for the life of the world is my flesh." (John 6:51)

✒ Challenge

Live your faith openly today in a challenging situation.

José María de Yermo y Parres

November 10, 1851–September 20, 1904

José's uncle was a bishop in Mexico and as one might expect, he tapped the young priest for some duties in his chancery. It was in administration, people seemed to agree, that José would live his vocation. Except when the uncle died and the new bishop came in, he was not nearly as fond of José and his work, and assigned him to two rundown chapels. It was a definite demotion. Then came the day that José was going to one of his chapels and saw a horrific sight: pigs eating two newborns. From then on, his passion was service to the poor and abandoned. It was not long thereafter that he founded what would become the Servants of the Sacred Heart of Jesus and the Poor.

Like José, we all see horrific sights—people who need food, shelter, medical assistance—all too often. His example encourages us not to turn away in disgust, but to see what we can do to alleviate suffering in a small or large way.

Inspiration

I am your friend, Lord, and with your grace I will be a faithful friend forever. (St. José María de Yermo y Parres)

Challenge

Be a friend to someone in whom you struggle to see God's love.

Gaetano Catanoso

February 14, 1879–April 4, 1963

He was a parish priest—from the time he was ordained in 1902 until his death about sixty years later. Gaetano never became a bishop, didn't steadily advance up the ladder of more and more important parishes. He spent all those years at just two Italian parishes. That is not to say, however, that Gaetano did not make a difference in people's lives. He went on foot or on mule to visit his parishioners in the remote mountain areas. He opened an orphanage to help care for children left without parents due to World War II. He encouraged devotions to the Eucharist, the Blessed Mother, and the Holy Face of Jesus. You know, all the things that seem small, but matter so much.

Gaetano bloomed where he was planted. And we can do the same. God's work for us can be found wherever we are—in small towns, big cities, beach houses, ranches—anywhere.

Inspiration

However that may be, let each of you lead the life that the Lord has assigned, to which God has called you. (1 Corinthians 7:17)

Challenge

Do something counterculturally Christian, unnoticed, for a friend or coworker.

Zechariah

Died 1st century

It's both ironic and fitting that while Zechariah was serving as priest, offering incense in the sanctuary, that God sent an angel to tell the old man of the important role in salvation that he and his wife would play. But instead of giving praise, Zechariah asked questions in disbelief. As a result, he could not speak until the baby was born. When their friends and relatives challenged Elizabeth on naming the boy John rather than after his father, Zechariah showed how much his faith had strengthened. After he wrote "His name is John" on a tablet, his speech was restored.

How often are we like Zechariah? Maybe every day of our lives. Instead of accepting wondrous and unusual things God gives us, large and small, we question and question and question. May we, like him, place our earthly questions at the altar, and trust.

✒ Inspiration

Immediately his mouth was opened and his tongue freed, and he began to speak, praising God. (Luke 1:64)

✒ Challenge

Attempt to go the entire day without a question for God.

Zygmunt Szczęsny Feliński

November 1, 1822–September 17, 1895

Zygmunt became archbishop of Warsaw in 1862, but his selection wasn't met with joy. People were concerned because the Russian government had approved him, and while his first acts included reopening the churches with forty hours of adoration, many Catholics didn't like that he wouldn't let parishes be used for political purposes, and banned hymns of patriotism. Apparently, they didn't know or chose to ignore the fact that his own mother had been exiled to Siberia for several years. The year after he became archbishop, Zygmunt resigned from the local Council of State after a failed Polish uprising, and wrote the Russian tsar condemning the actions taken. The tsar's response was to exile Zygmunt in a town northeast of Moscow for twenty years, with no contact with Warsaw. When he was released in 1883, he finished out his life in semi-exile in Ukraine.

People—from his flock to the tsar of Russia—didn't always agree with Zygmunt's words and actions. But his focus was on God, not on politics. It's a good reminder to us not to get too caught up in world events at the expense of living our faith.

✏ Inspiration

Inner peace is the most expensive treasure on earth and the only gift the Savior promises his disciples on earth. (St. Zygmunt Szczęsny Feliński)

✏ Challenge

Don't take in any news today, fake or otherwise. Use the time you would have spent watching or reading in prayer instead.

Thomas of Villanova

1488–September 8, 1555

For more than twenty years, Thomas had been an Augustinian friar. But his "no" to become archbishop of Valencia wasn't accepted, and so he began the seventy-five-mile journey to his new home: on foot. Wearing the same monastic habit he'd been wearing for years. He'd continue to wear it for some time to come. That budget to improve the archbishop's residence? Thomas redirected it to a hospital. In the eleven years before he died, Thomas would again and again defy people's preconceived notions about how archbishops dressed, lived, and ate. For him, his position was all about the authority it offered to improve the welfare of those living on society's margins.

People were confounded by Thomas. He didn't disrespect his office or God, but he cared more for his duty to his flock than whether his outer garments were of the finest brocade. His example reminds us to resist the temptations and trappings of the outside world so we can improve what's inside our souls.

✒ Inspiration

Do you not know that I shall be called to account by God if I dare to deprive the poor of what belongs to them? (St. Thomas of Villanova)

✒ Challenge

"Deprive" yourself of one small luxury—a doughnut or gourmet coffee, perhaps, or an hour of texting or social media. How can you give the savings to someone in need?

Wenceslaus

Circa 907–September 28, 935

Today's political intrigues look tame compared with the story of Wenceslaus. His paternal grandmother, Ludmila of Bohemia, was in charge of his spiritual and cultural education. While his mother had been baptized at her marriage, there was little devotion in her heart and soul to Christianity or her son. Wenceslaus's father died in battle, and his grandmother was named regent. This did not sit well with the mother, who had Ludmila (also a saint) killed. Wenceslaus had his mother exiled when he ascended to the throne, but her evil ways had already corrupted his younger brother Boleslaus. The brother was among those who objected to some of Wenceslaus's peacemaking plans and his devotion to Christ. Legend has it that Wenceslaus was headed for Mass when his brother waylaid him and killed him.

Perhaps the most positive takeaway from Wenceslaus's story is the relationship he had with his grandmother. The seeds Ludmila planted took root and sustained Wenceslaus to his death. The way we live our faith may be doing the same in ways we don't even realize.

✒ Inspiration

But the steadfast love of the Lord is from everlasting to everlasting
    on those who fear him,
    and his righteousness to children's children… (Psalm 103:17)

✒ Challenge

Pray today with a memory, tangible or intangible, of a grandparent.

Vincent de Paul

1581–September 27, 1660

Vincent knew the needs of peasant families like the one in which he had grown up. He'd also rubbed shoulders with the rich, serving at the French court and in the households of nobility. Why not put together a group of wealthy laywomen to help with his ministry to the sick and poor? The women were willing to provide money, but often would send their servants to do the actual work. Because they were untrained, the upper-class women and their servants often did more harm than good. Enter Louise de Marillac, a widow who had moved in wealthy circles and who was one of Vincent's spiritual directees. Together, they founded what is now known as the Daughters of Charity of St. Vincent de Paul,. The congregation was novel at the time, women religious moving about in prisons, hospitals, and orphanages rather than remaining enclosed.

Vincent had a great idea. But he wasn't successful in executing it until he teamed with Louise,. Their example shows us that collaboration can be a critical piece of bringing comfort to the world, and souls to the kingdom.

✒ Inspiration

It is not enough for me to love God if my neighbor does not love him as well. (St. Vincent de Paul)

✒ Challenge

Ask someone to help you with something you believe you are perfectly capable of doing alone.

Lorenzo Ruiz

November 28, 1594–September 29, 1637

Lorenzo's life was unremarkable: altar boy, church clerk, happily married, father of three. But things changed drastically when the Filipino was accused of murder when he was forty-two. To escape, he accompanied four priests and another man who were leaving for Japan. Their boat was blown off course, and they made land in an area unfriendly to Christians. The six were arrested and tortured, suffering martyrs' deaths. In 1987, they and ten other people were canonized by Pope John Paul II *(October 22)*.

Our lives can change in an instant. Maybe it's losing a loved one or a job, or a negative diagnosis of our own health. The ensuing hours and days and months and years can be physical, emotional, and spiritual torture. Like Lorenzo, we learn that the only form of solace that is always available is our faith. May we cling to it.

☞ Inspiration

Had I many thousands of lives I would offer them all for him. (St. Lorenzo Ruiz)

☞ Challenge

Read the biblical story of Job, and think about the parallels in your life or the life of someone you love.

Gregory the Illuminator

Died circa 331

During his thirteen years in an Armenian prison that amounted to little more than a pit, Gregory may have questioned his decision to leave his wife and two sons to pursue the monastic life. Relief would come in a most unusual way about 300. The king who had condemned him became extremely ill, and the king's sister was convinced that Gregory and only Gregory could save him. So he was brought forth—and the king recovered. The king converted, and became the first monarch to make Christianity the state religion. Gregory, known as the apostle of Armenia, in his later years retired to a small monastic community.

Gregory's belief in God was so strong that he put aside any ill will he might have had for the king in hopes of healing and evangelizing. It's important to remember that one interaction with our persecutors may be the moment that begins their conversion journey.

Inspiration

For neither herb nor poultice cured them,

but it was your word, O Lord, that heals all people. (Wisdom 16:12)

Challenge

Do a kindness for someone who has wronged you.

Jerome

Circa 342–420

Few saints have been involved in as many public controversies as Jerome, and his quick wit and sharp tongue, not to mention his ability to hold a grudge, would indicate the fault did not always lie exclusively with his enemies. For example, when Jerome took on the teachings of a theologian from more than one hundred years earlier, a breach with his longtime friend Rufinus ensued, replete with personal insults. When he became spiritual director to a group of widows and their daughters, first in Rome and then in Bethlehem, there were whispers about improper relations. Despite these difficulties, Jerome is remembered as an astute scholar, especially for his translation of most of the Bible into Latin, and is recognized as a Doctor of the Church.

Let's be honest: Sometimes, people are not very nice. Sometimes, *we're* not very nice. Jerome's story shows us that even the greatest thinkers can struggle in relating to other people. May we share in such encounters some of the infinite patience God shows us.

Inspiration

The signs of a true apostle were performed among you with utmost patience, signs and wonders and mighty works. (2 Corinthians 12:12)

Challenge

Be patient with someone who works your last nerve. Remember God's patience with you.

Romanus the Melodist

Circa 490–556

Tradition tells us that Romanus was woefully unprepared for Christmas, and here it was Christmas Eve. He was responsible for the music, and he had no lyrics and no tunes. The Blessed Virgin appeared and gave him a scroll, instructing him to eat it. When the time came, Romanus began, seemingly extemporaneously, singing what today we know as the Nativity Kontakion, the most famous of his thousand hymns. Sixty to eighty of them, on feast days, saints, Bible lessons, and other topics, survive today.

Some might call this Syrian composer a procrastinator, and perhaps he was. (And who among us today is ever completely ready for Christmas?) Or, maybe Romanus was dissatisfied with his own initial efforts and was being obedient in waiting for heavenly assistance. May we have his faith and confidence in God's timing.

Inspiration

Sing to the Lord, bless his name;

tell of his salvation from day to day. (Psalm 96:2)

Challenge

Try singing a hymn today to praise God.

Bavo of Ghent

622-circa 655

Exactly what it was that Bavo, a Belgian nobleman, did in his youth and young adulthood, we do not know. Various sources call his youth undisciplined, irregular, and disorderly. (Whatever his behavior, it likely met with family concern; his mother, Itta, and sisters Begga and Gertrude of Nivelles also are Catholic saints.) After Bavo's wife died, he heard a homily about how unfulfilling earthly goods are, and it spoke deeply to him. Bavo reformed and became a monk. Atonement for his past sins may have including going on missionary trips himself to warn others against the way in which he had lived. He may have briefly lived in a tree trunk, and finished out his days as a recluse in woods near a monastery.

One sermon. That was all it took for Bavo. We never know what will spark a return or deepening of our love for God. We do know we'll miss it if we don't keep our eyes, ears, and souls open to the possibility.

☙ Inspiration

Now the Lord came and stood there, calling as before, "Samuel! Samuel!" And Samuel said, "Speak, for your servant is listening." (1 Samuel 3:10)

☙ Challenge

The next time you are at Mass, really listen to the homily and its lesson. Don't work on your mental to-do list.

André de Soveral

1572–July 16, 1645

It started out like any other Sunday in northeast Brazil for André. For more than a decade, the Portuguese and Dutch had struggled for control in the region. But this Sunday, as he was celebrating Mass for his parish of mostly sugar cane workers, Dutch soldiers and a band of indigenous people burst into the church and killed André and a parishioner. Three months later at a parish twelve miles away, the pastor and twenty-seven others met a similar fate. The thirty were canonized in 2017 as the Martyrs of Natal.

André likely went about his usual Sunday routine that morning, dressing, praying, perhaps talking with a few parishioners. But his usual routine prepared him to meet God any day, at any time. Like him, may we be prepared for death each and every day, for few of us will know when it is coming.

Inspiration

"Therefore you must also be ready, for the Son of Man is coming at an unexpected hour." (Matthew 24:44)

Challenge

Make a short list of what you need to do to prepare yourself spiritually to meet Jesus. Some items might include making a full, heartfelt confession or setting aside quiet time each morning or evening for prayer. Then take that short list and start doing the items on it.

Francis of Assisi

Circa 1181–October 3, 1226

Francis was a literalist—and an obedient listener. When he was told in a dream to "follow the master rather than the man," he gave up his plan to join the papal army in favor of the pursuit of a simple life of charity and prayer. When Jesus asked him to rebuild the Lord's church, he started doing so physically—eventually realizing that Jesus was talking about spiritual decay as well. When he heard Jesus's advice in the Gospel of Matthew to sell one's possessions and deny himself or herself, he simplified his life even further. Francis's acceptance of God's word at face value has drawn millions of people to name their children after him, take his name at confirmation, and attempt to walk in his footsteps as laypeople or male and female religious.

Jesus distilled all of the commandments and law into two: love God and love your neighbor as yourself. Francis's story shows us it can be done, literally. The choice is ours.

⮞ Inspiration

Pure holy simplicity confounds all the wisdom of this world and the wisdom of the flesh. (St. Francis of Assisi)

⮞ Challenge

If your dream is eternal salvation, what tangible steps in the manner of Francis will you take today to achieve it?

Simón de Rojas

October 28, 1552-September 29, 1624

It was this simple: Simón loved the Blessed Virgin. He loved her for her fiat, for her total trust in God. And while this Spanish Trinitarian priest spent most of his adult life as a monastery superior, his worldview was so based in Marian devotion that his nickname was "Father Ave Maria." He did not limit his work to his confreres; Simón also founded a lay organization, the Congregation of the Slaves of the Most Sweet Name of Mary, to minister in her name to those in need.

It's easy to understand why Simón was so inspired by Mary's obedience to God and acceptance of his will. Simón's devotion reminds us that while we do not worship Mary as we do the Trinity, growing in love for her leads us to growing in love for her son.

Inspiration

By her complete adherence to the Father's will, to his Son's redemptive work, and to every prompting of the Holy Spirit, the Virgin Mary is the Church's model of faith and charity. (*Catechism of the Catholic Church*, 967)

Challenge

Say a Hail May, pausing to ponder in your heart each word in the prayer.

Bruno

Circa 1032–October 6, 1101

After about twenty years at the cathedral school where he had studied, most of it as the director, Bruno was named chancellor of the Rheims, France, diocese. But the archbishop proved so odious that Bruno and some other priests complained about him to the pope. In response, the archbishop destroyed their homes and may have even excommunicated them, causing the priests to flee. A few years later, after the archbishop was temporarily removed, some thought Bruno should take the position, but he had other plans. He became a hermit under Robert of Molesme *(January 25),* then after a few years moved on with six others to a remote Alpine region called La Grande Chartreuse, which was the beginning of the Carthusians. Inspired by the desert fathers, the monks live in almost complete solitude, gathering only for their main meal and two prayers of the Divine Office.

It wasn't that Bruno was running away from the world as much as he was running toward God, as the saying goes. While we may not be called to the solitude of the Carthusians, withdrawing ourselves from the noise of life from time to time strengthens our spiritual armor immensely.

✿ Inspiration

Indeed, what other good is there besides God? (St. Bruno)

✿ Challenge

Spend a morning or afternoon in silence. Afterward, journal about the experience.

Denis

3rd century

Denis was so successful at his work that it cost him his life. The Italian-born bishop and six others were sent to bring Christianity to France, and Denis was named the first bishop of Paris. Many conversions resulted from their efforts, which did not please the authorities. As a result, Denis and two of his companions were beheaded and their bodies thrown into the Seine River. The site where the bodies were buried after being recovered is now home to a basilica named for Denis.

Evangelization is risky business. But that didn't stop Denis and the others. May we show the same faith and confidence in doing what God desires of us.

✒ Inspiration

"Those who try to make their life secure will lose it, but those who lose their life will keep it." (Luke 17:33)

✒ Challenge

Do something for God that may cost you personally.

Louis Bertrand

January 1, 1526–October 9, 1581

Often, Louis wasn't about doing the comfortable thing. His father was convinced that Louis wasn't healthy enough or smart enough to join the Dominicans. Louis didn't have the voice or the style that typically makes a good preacher, but when he set his mind to it, he began to draw crowds. When others shied away from helping plague victims, Louis put himself front and center to help them. Louis also provided spiritual counsel to St. Teresa of Ávila, who was pretty good herself at making people uncomfortable. When he was thirty-six, he realized his dream of becoming a missionary to the Americas and converted thousands. After seven years, Louis came back home to Spain, where he continued to advocate for the indigenous people he had served.

We hear the phrase "speak truth to power" a lot these days, and Louis wasn't reluctant to do that. He knew God was the power driving him, regardless of how good his voice or his health was, or what people thought of him. He reminds us that God is the ultimate truth and power.

✒Inspiration

Now may our Lord Jesus Christ himself and God our Father, who loved us and through grace gave us eternal comfort and hope, comfort your hearts and strengthen them in every good work and word. (2 Thessalonians 2:16-17)

✒Challenge

Make yourself uncomfortable today in a way that provides solace to someone else.

John Henry Newman

February 21, 1801–August 11, 1890

His first conversion occurred when he was just fifteen, going all in to evangelical Calvinism and criticizing the Catholic Church at seemingly every turn. John became an Anglican priest in 1824, and gained a reputation as a theologian and preacher. As time went on—some credit his first trip to Rome, others the sorrow of a sister's death—John began to find more and more truth in Catholic teachings, and was involved in a movement aimed at reincorporating some Catholic practices into his church. Finally, he realized he was in fact Catholic. John came into the Church in 1845, prompting much dismay among friends and family, and became a Catholic priest two years later. He was named a cardinal in 1879.

Have you ever noticed the things we most battle against are often the things we later embrace? John reminds us that it's our soul, not our brilliant or not-so-brilliant brains, the Lord desires. Let's not let the latter get in the way of the former.

✹ Inspiration

God has created me to do Him some definite service. He has committed some work to me which He has not committed to another. I have my mission. I may never know it in this life, but I shall be told it in the next. (St. John Henry Newman)

✹ Challenge

Have a conversation with a friend of a different faith. Explore not only the differences in your beliefs, but also the similarities.

Francis Borgia

October 28, 1510–September 30, 1572

Francis's faith had always been strong, but as part of a wealthy, politically connected family, it had never been seriously tested. Then, when he was twenty-eight, he was called upon to formally identify the unenbalmed corpse of the Empress Isabella. As he looked at the ruler's decaying face, he was struck by just how impermanent earthly life is. Seven years later, his beloved wife, Eleanor, died, leaving Francis to start the next stage of his journey. And what a stage it was! He became a priest, rising to father general of the Society of Jesus, and by some is regarded as the second most important Jesuit ever, after only St. Ignatius of Loyola *(July 31).* He is known for growing the community's missionary work and founding what is now the Gregorian University and a number of other colleges.

Francis is also known for his extreme humility and willingness to do without complaint work that others regarded as menial. His example reminds us to do the same, regardless of how many degrees and awards we receive.

✿ Inspiration

Enlighten my blindness, O my Lord, that by knowing what I am, I may know what Thou art. (St. Francis Borgia)

✿ Challenge

Journal about a time when your life took a significant turn, good or bad, after a loss and how you found (or are still struggling to find) healing.

John XXIII

November 25, 1881–June 3, 1963

Angelo Giuseppe Roncalli never left his roots as a northern Italian farmer's son; it's just that the places where he planted and sowed changed. He began studying for the priesthood before his teen years, and was ordained at twenty-two. As a priest, he saw the world through a variety of lenses: as a canon law student in Rome; as a stretcher bearer for the Italian army in World War II; as a diplomat who helped numerous Jews escape Europe by issuing transit visas. His grandest sowing opportunity came when he was nearly seventy-eight years old, and was elected pope. As John XXIII, he brought a sort of gentle, jolly acceptability to the papacy and convened Vatican II, the first ecumenical council in nearly one hundred years.

John XXXII is remembered for poking fun at himself and at overformality. He reminds us that while we need to take our faith seriously, God is pleased when we come as little children, with hands, hearts, and souls open. We should be impressed with God, not with ourselves.

☞ Inspiration

Man has the right to live. He has the right to bodily integrity and to the means necessary for the proper development of life, particularly food, clothing, shelter, medical care, rest, and, finally, the necessary social services. (St. John XXIII)

☞ Challenge

Laugh at one of your shortcomings today, then pray for the strength to use that shortcoming as God desires.

John of Dukla

1414–1484

John was no longer young. The Franciscan priest had carried the good news to people in his native Poland, Belarus, and Ukraine, where he spent most of his life. Now he was blind. Some people would have seen that as a reason to retire or go back to his early days as a hermit. But instead, John used a novice to help him prepare his sermons. He also continued to hear confessions after losing his sight.

John refused to let what some viewed as a disability slow him down. He simply adjusted by bringing in the novice. In the same way, our own frailties needn't end our service to God; we just might have to change things up a bit.

Inspiration

Likewise the Spirit helps us in our weakness; for we do not know how to pray as we ought, but that very Spirit intercedes with sighs too deep for words. (Romans 8:26)

Challenge

Is there a service you've given up or decided not to pursue because it would be too demanding? How could someone help you so you can say yes to God?

Edward the Confessor

1003–1066

Call it palace intrigue, call it family intrigue. Edward's life was filled with alliances and misalliances. His father, King Ethelred II, died when Edward was thirteen or so, and he and his mother went into exile until he was in his late thirties. A nobleman helped Edward gain the throne when his half-brother died, and Edward then married the nobleman's daughter. But not all was well; hard feelings caused Edward to banish his father-in-law after a time, and the father-in-law prepared to overthrow Edward. Instead, the men were able to meet and resolve their differences for the most part. After that time, Edward became more focused on his faith ("confessor" refers to his piety, not that he was ordained).

It's the rare family that hasn't had some drama—someone who won't speak to a sibling over a long-ago hurt, children estranged from their parents after a divorce. Edward's example shows us that while relationships may never be restored to what they once were, with God's help, respect and civility can be restored.

Inspiration

"For if you love those who love you, what reward do you have? Do not even the tax collectors do the same? And if you greet only your brothers and sisters, what more are you doing than others?" (Matthew 5:46-47)

Challenge

Humble yourself. Take the first step to repair a relationship.

Callistus I

Died circa 223

The early details of this pope's life are in question, given that much of what we are told came from an enemy, antipope Hippolytus. We're told Callistus, a young Christian slave, in some way lost his master's funds and served time as a mine worker as a result. After his release, he became a deacon by the pope and was responsible for Rome's public Christian burial ground. Upon his patron's death, Callistus was selected as pope and served for about five years. During that time, he was roundly criticized and undercut by Hippolytus for his liberal policies, including sharing the Eucharist with people who had atoned for mortal sins.

Imagine having your enemy's version of your story be the generally accepted one! But then, Jesus had the same experience before the Resurrection, didn't he? Callistus's mercy despite the criticism of Hippolytus and others reminds us that God's judgment is the only one that matters.

✒ Inspiration

Then the high priest tore his clothes and said, "He has blasphemed! Why do we still need witnesses? You have now heard his blasphemy. What is your verdict?" They answered, "He deserves death." (Matthew 26:65–66)

✒ Challenge

Think about what you have said about people you know (or know of) whom you find difficult to love. How can your future comments reflect mercy?

Ignatius of Antioch

Circa 35–107

There is a legend that Ignatius may have been the child mentioned in Mark 9:36-37. If that's the case, the man the child grew up to be certainly welcomed God into his heart and soul. Ignatius, likely born to Syrian parents who were pagans, may have been a follower of St. John the Apostle *(December 27)*. Ignatius was the first writer to use the term Catholic Church to refer to the Christian community, leaving behind seven letters on topics from the Trinity to the Eucharist as he was being taken to Rome, where he was thrown to the lions.

People—especially children—can be noisy and disruptive to our plans for the day. But when we turn them away, we also turn away the opportunity to welcome the Almighty.

Inspiration

Then he took a little child and put it among them; and taking it in his arms, he said to them, "Whoever welcomes one such child in my name welcomes me, and whoever welcomes me welcomes not me but the one who sent me." (Mark 9:36-37)

Challenge

Welcome a child today.

Gerard Majella

April 6, 1726–October 16, 1755

Gerard believed he had found his vocation as a lay Redemptorist, throwing himself into whatever task the community assigned him: sacristan, gardener, carpenter, and of course tailor, which had been the young man's training. But that life was endangered when a woman he had helped secure a dowry left the convent and accused him of sexual impropriety with a young girl. Gerard remained silent, and as a result was denied communion and kept under surveillance by the Redemptorists. Eventually, the accuser recanted. When asked about his silence, Gerard said he thought it best to be patient and trust. He died of tuberculosis the following year.

When someone makes malicious, untrue statements about us, we want to defend ourselves. That's human nature. But it's important to remember that unfounded allegations will never change the Lord's love for us. There's something to be learned from Gerard about not overly prizing the world's perception.

✎ Inspiration

Then Pilate said to him, "Do you not hear how many accusations they make against you?" But he gave him no answer, not even to a single charge, so that the governor was greatly amazed. (Matthew 27:13-14)

✎ Challenge

Offer a smile instead of a defense, excuse, or rebuttal the next time someone falsely accuses you.

Philip Howard

June 28, 1557–October 19, 1595

Philip was on top of his game, professionally, anyway. He was a favorite at the court of England's Queen Elizabeth I. His political ambitions didn't leave him much time for his wife, and while he was nominally a Church of England member, he didn't have much time for God either. That began to change in 1581 when he attended a dispute or debate about the differences between Catholics and Anglicans. After time of struggle and discernment, Philip converted in 1584. He wrote the queen to explain how important Catholic teachings were to him and fled the country, but was captured. Imprisoned for high treason, Philip spent the rest of his life in prison, much of it in prayer. He is among the forty people canonized as Martyrs of England and Wales.

We all know people who seem to sleepwalk through life, oblivious to God. We never know what's going to spark their conversion moment. It just might be a word from us.

Inspiration

The more affliction we endure for Christ in this world, the more glory we shall obtain with Christ in the next. (St. Philip Howard)

Challenge

Invite a friend who doesn't have a religious practice to an event at your parish. The worst he or she can do is say no.

Luke

1st century

Luke gives us the story—and then the rest of the story. The writer, who we know as a disciple of St. Paul *(June 29),* drew on St. Mark's *(April 25)* Gospel for his own version of the story of Jesus' life on earth. Luke was not among the original disciples. But he gives us an in-depth picture in Acts of how the early Church carried out Christ's ministry. Luke is called a physician in Colossians 4:14 and is regarded as a thorough, careful researcher and historian.

We would be poorer without Luke's moving version of the parable of the prodigal son and his version of Jesus's infancy narrative. Luke knew that sharing Jesus's stories and those of his followers was an important piece of evangelization. We do the same when we pass on our own traditions and stories to our children and grandchildren.

Inspiration

Since many have undertaken to set down an orderly account of the events that have been fulfilled among us, just as they were handed on to us by those who from the beginning were eyewitnesses and servants of the word, I too decided, after investigating everything carefully from the very first, to write an orderly account for you, most excellent Theophilus… (Luke 1:1-3)

Challenge

Find photos from one of your sacramental moments. Share your story with a loved one, or capture it for future generations in a brief note.

Isaac Jogues

January 10, 1607–October 18, 1646

Isaac had been beaten, burned, starved, and bitten. His left thumb had been cut off. A confrere had been killed. Now, after a year of captivity among the indigenous people, he was finally free, back in France. But the Jesuit priest did not feel his work was complete. After a year and a half, Isaac returned to missionary work in North America. He was tomahawked less than a year later. He is one of eight Jesuit priests and lay brothers honored as the North American martyrs.

Isaac's first-person account of his torture is sickening. It is difficult to think of how he willingly went back—in fact, volunteered—to return to the place that had brought him so much physical pain. Few of us ever will be asked to suffer for God as he and the others did. But their example reminds us to have the faith to complete our journey, no matter what lies ahead, with the hope of eternal life.

Inspiration

"Then they will hand you over to be tortured and will put you to death, and you will be hated by all nations because of my name." (Matthew 24:9)

Challenge

Do something for God that you know will cost you greatly in pride.

Paul of the Cross

January 3, 1694–October 18, 1775

A brief stint in the Venetian army hadn't worked out well for Paul. As one of sixteen children, his formal education was extremely limited. He was in his mid-twenties when he saw a vision of a habit—black, with an emblem of Jesus and the cross in white—that would be used in a new congregation he was to found. To Paul, the Passion showed Jesus's extreme love for us, a message he felt called to carry to those away from the Church as well as the sick and dying. With his brother John, he established the Congregation of the Passion, or the Passionists.

When we think of the time from Jesus's agony in the garden to his death, his pain and suffering usually are our focus. Paul also saw the awesomeness of Jesus's willingness to offer his life to redeem us, and took that message to the masses. Let's do the same.

Inspiration

The holy sufferings of Jesus is a sea of sorrows, but it is also a sea of love. (St. Paul of the Cross)

Challenge

Spend some time with the Stations of the Cross, and say thank you to Jesus for what he did for us.

Hilarion

Circa 291–371

Hilarion converted to Christianity in his mid-teens, but traditional Church practices didn't speak to his soul. Then he heard about St. Anthony of Egypt's *(January 17)* life in the desert. He spent two months with the desert father, and knew he wanted to praise God in a similar way—minus the great number of visitors Anthony had. Hilarion returned home to Gaza, where he dissolved the family estate and became a hermit. Ironically, he would find the same challenge as Anthony: So many people admired Hilarion's holiness that it became harder and harder for him to find solitude. He spent the last few years of his life in a cave in Cyprus.

Consider Hilarion's struggle: if Anthony hadn't spent time with him, Hilarion might not have found his vocation. And yet, to practice it, he had to say no to those he in turn inspired. Perhaps the lesson is to carefully discern God's desires for us, and not give in to the temptation to please people first.

Inspiration

Cursed be he who looks for the refreshment of the body before that of the soul. (St. Hilarion)

Challenge

Spend an hour in silence with God in the coming week, even if it means disappointing someone.

John Paul II

May 18, 1920–April 2, 2005

It was a young adulthood that promised little on the surface. Karol Wojtyła was working in a quarry. His father, who been the last remaining member of his immediate family, had recently died, and the Nazis had closed the university where Karol had studied. It was during this time that Karol met a fellow parishioner, Jan Tyranowski. While Karol originally was put off by the tailor's mystic spirituality, a friendship developed and Jan became his mentor. Jan's influence was a factor in Karol's discernment of his vocation, a journey that would lead him to become second-longest serving pope in history and one of the most important men of the twentieth century.

Sometimes, young people are suspicious of those who have an intense relationship with God. But if we live our faith authentically and openly with words and actions, we may plant some amazing seeds.

✍ Inspiration

Dear young people, let yourselves be taken over by the light of Christ, and spread that light wherever you are. (St. John Paul II)

✍ Challenge

Talk with a young adult about a service opportunity you can do together—volunteer at a food pantry, circulate a petition, participate in a walk or march. Ask about his or her dreams and goals.

John of Capistrano

June 24, 1386–October 23, 1456

John's life seemed to be off to a good start: law degree, newlywed, and governor of Perugia, Italy, by the time he was thirty. But when he was sent to broker peace between his city and a neighbor, he was imprisoned, and started rethinking his focus. After he was released, his marriage was annulled and he became a Franciscan and was ordained in 1420. He was friends with St. Bernardino of Siena *(May 20),* and advocated for his canonization. John had his failures too, including efforts to reunify two Franciscan factions. Further, his anti-Semitic public pronouncements resulted in the deaths of many Jews in southern Germany.

John's good works, including personally leading an army unit to successfully defend the city of Belgrade, are overshadowed by his powerful preaching against Jews. Let's remember that God and the world will judge us for the totality of our actions, not just the positive ones.

✸ Inspiration

The Lord who made the beginning, will take care of the finish. (St. John of Capistrano)

✸ Challenge

Consult with a priest about ways you might make amends for your hurtful words and actions.

Anthony Mary Claret

December 23, 1807-October 24, 1870

Maybe it was envy. Maybe it was fear. Maybe it was jealousy of his strong faith and the beauty with which he expressed it in his writing, preaching, and service. Regardless, Anthony found himself among enemies throughout his life. Ordained in his native Spain, he spent time in Rome, then in the Canary Islands and later as the archbishop of Santiago, Cuba. In that role, numerous assassinations attempts were made against him, including one that resulted in injury. People gossiped about him. And yet, thousands of ordinations and baptisms occurred where he went, due in no small part to his preaching process. He reluctantly returned to Spain to be the queen regent's confessor, then when the royal family was dethroned, relocated to France with them. Despite all this, the founder of the Missionary Sons of the Immaculate Heart of Mary, or Claretians, left behind a strong example of evangelization in his more than 25,000 homilies and 144 books.

There are some people we will never please. But as we attempt to love and accept them, may we remember, as Anthony did, that it is the Almighty alone whose opinion of us matters.

❧ Inspiration

My God, you have been so good to me! I have been very late in understanding the many great graces you have given me. … But Lord, I give you my word that I will work. (St. Anthony Mary Claret)

❧ Challenge

Be generous to someone whom you find difficult to satisfy.

Luigi Guanella

December 19, 1842-October 24, 1915

In the summer of 1865, the year before his ordination, Luigi decided to visit Turin, about a hundred miles from his home in northern Italy. There, he first met St. John Bosco *(January 31)*. The men would be connected for years to come. After ordination, Luigi served as a parish priest for nine years, then rejoined Bosco and took temporary vows as a Salesian. After three years, he was called back to his diocese. But his time with the Salesians and their ministry to at-risk young men likely informed Luigi's passion the rest of his life: to serve those with physical and mental disabilities. He founded the Servants of Charity, also known as the Guanellas, as well as a community for women religious, the Daughters of Saint Mary of Providence. After visiting the United States in 1912, Luigi sent women religious to Chicago to help with the burgeoning Italian immigrant population there.

So many of our saints' lives were touched by the lives of other saints, such as in the case of Luigi and John Bosco. It's a good reminder that we may never know the spark our charity and compassion may strike in others.

Inspiration

Our union in heaven will depend upon our communion with God on earth. (St. Luigi Guanella)

Challenge

Check in with someone who considers you a role model, whether you feel like one or not.

Gaetano Errico

October 19, 1791–October 29, 1860

Fulfilling God's desire seems to come easily for some people. Gaetano was not among them. He knew by the time he was fourteen that he was called to the religious life, but two communities in southern Italy rejected him because he was too young. Gaetano trusted, and became a parish priest in 1815. Three years later while he was on a retreat, St. Alphonsus Liguori (*August 1*) appeared to him in a vision, saying Gaetano would build a church honoring the Blessed Mother and establish a congregation. It took twelve years for him to get the financial and community support to open Our Lady of Sorrows north of Naples, and another six years to receive local approval be for what would become the Missionaries of the Sacred Hearts of Jesus and Mary.

There had to have been times Gaetano wondered if he truly understood what God wanted of him. His patience reminds us to surrender our will to God's timetable.

✒ Inspiration

But if we hope for what we do not see, we wait for it with patience. (Romans 8:25)

✒ Challenge

Surrender your own expectations to God and be patient.

Simon the Zealot

1st century

There are apostles we know so much about: Peter. James. John. Even Thomas, Philip, and Andrew get brief moments in the sun. But not Simon the Zealot, as he is called in the Gospel of Luke and Acts, or Simon the Cananaean, as he is referred to in Mathew and Mark. For centuries, people have theorized about his zealotry: about Judaism, that then transferred to following Christ? About overthrowing the Roman power structure? We just don't know. Tradition tells us Simon went on to evangelize in Egypt and Iran, and was martyred.

Who doesn't like a mystery? But for all we might speculate about Simon, this is certain: Jesus selected him as one of the Twelve, and Simon stayed with the community after the Ascension. And really, what else do we need to know?

Inspiration
"Be still, and know that I am God!

I am exalted among the nations,

I am exalted in the earth." (Psalm 46:10)

Challenge
Still waters run deep. Observe the way a quiet person in your parish or neighborhood lives his or her devotion to Christ.

Jude

1st century

We know little about Jude's life, other than that he was one of the Twelve and possibly one of Jesus's relatives; that he suffered a martyr's death; and that his remains were moved to St. Peter's Basilica. But he has a prominent patronage: the saint for hopeless causes. Praying with Jude when all else had failed appears to have begun in France and Germany in the late eighteenth century, and people continue to ask for his intervention today.

It's perhaps fitting that in Hebrew, Jude's name means "praise," for praise to God is an essential element of any intercessory prayer. While we have an idea of how we would like the earthly situation—hopeless or otherwise—to resolve, we also trust that God's "solution" will always be best.

Inspiration

Immediately (the blind man) regained his sight and followed him, glorifying God; and all the people, when they saw it, praised God. (Luke 18:43)

Challenge

Do or say something that will ease a relative or friend's despair in a seemingly hopeless situation.

Narcissus of Jerusalem

Died circa 215

Narcissus may have been in his eighties when he was named bishop of Jerusalem, and he wasn't universally popular. Some people thought he was too strict; others disagreed with his support of a move to adopt Roman church customs, including putting the Easter celebration permanently on Sundays. The result was a spurious, unspecified criminal allegation. Narcissus just disappeared—for years. Other bishops of Jerusalem came and went. People assumed he had died. Then one day, he came back, and resumed the bishopric. The priest named as in effect his bishop-in-waiting wrote that Narcissus was 116 years old in 212.

Sometimes, the best way to deal with contentious situations is to leave, as Narcissus's story shows us. That doesn't mean we should be passive in our faith or our relationships, but extricating ourselves from unhealthy situations isn't necessarily a bad thing.

Inspiration

"If any place will not welcome you and they refuse to hear you, as you leave, shake off the dust that is on your foot as a testimony against them." (Mark 6:11)

Challenge

Stop defending yourself against a baseless rumor or allegation. Trust God will set things aright eventually.

Angelo of Acri

October 19, 1669–October 30, 1739

Luca Antonio Falcone was scared. He'd been admitted to the Capuchins, but found monastery life too difficult. Besides, the nineteen-year-old missed his mother, and maybe God wanted him to fall in love and get married. He went back to the monastery about a year later to the same result. The third time proved to be the charm: he made it through his novitiate, took the name Angelo, and was ordained a few months after his twentieth birthday. As a priest, he experienced the same fits and starts, including three straight nights when he couldn't remember what he was going to preach. Finally, he let the Holy Spirit lead him, and people marveled at what he had to say. Angelo spent much of his remaining years preaching in southern Italy, or listening to confessions with a gentle, kind ear.

People laughed at Angelo when he forgot his homilies, and they probably laughed at his indecisiveness when it came to the religious life. But he didn't let them discourage him too much; he listened to God instead. We can do the same, not letting our pride or self-doubt get in the way of our faith and hope and trust.

✒ Inspiration

"Do not fear them, for it is the Lord your God who fights for you." (Deuteronomy 3:22)

✒ Challenge

Write down five self-doubts or fears and put them in an envelope. Then tear it up and throw it away.

Alphonsus Rodriguez

July 25, 1532–October 31, 1617

God was all thirty-eight-year-old Alphonsus Rodriguez had left. His father had died when he was a teenager, forcing Alphonsus to stop his priestly studies to help his mother and siblings. And now, within just six years of his wedding, he had lost his mother, wife, and young children. God, it turned out, was all he needed. Alphonsus became a lay brother after six months of study at a Jesuit school on the island of Majorca and stayed there the rest of his life, working as a doorkeeper. He welcomed all visitors with warmth and kindness, and he became so well known that people would journey from mainland Spain, an hour's ferry ride today, to see him. Among the souls he touched was that of St. Peter Claver *(September 9)*, whom Alphonsus encouraged to become a missionary.

The love Alphonsus had had for his family was magnified as he poured it out in his doorway ministry. That's the funny thing about love and hospitality; when we offer freely, with no expectation of a return, grace tends to happen.

Inspiration

"Whoever welcomes you welcomes me, and whoever welcomes me welcomes the one who sent me." (Matthew 10:40)

Challenge

After leaving your home, say hello today to the first five people you see.

Hubert

Circa 656-May 30, 727

Hubert was at court in Paris at a relatively young age, and things seemed to be going just the way he could have hoped, with faith an afterthought at most. Perhaps best of all—other than perhaps finding a beautiful wife—the environs of Paris allowed him to indulge his very favorite pastime, hunting. Now, one might think that Good Friday would not be an appropriate time to hunt, but Hubert was not to be stopped. It was on that day he encountered a stag with an image of the crucified Jesus in its antlers, and was told he was on the way to hell. Hubert was taken aback, and became serious about God that day. (If his wife had not already died in childbirth, she did so soon after this revelation.) In later life, he served as the bishop of Maastricht, Netherlands, succeeding his spiritual mentor, St. Lambert *(September 14).*

Hubert turned his passion for hunting animals to a passion for hunting souls to bring to Christ. While we likely won't receive a nudge quite as unmistakable as his, Hubert's story shows us that God won't be afraid to warn us when our priorities are out of whack.

Inspiration

For the Lord your God is a devouring fire, a jealous God. (Deuteronomy 4:24)

Challenge

Are you setting up your family, your job, or your ministry as a false idol? What can you do to put God first, where he rightfully should be?

Joannicius

754–846

Joannicius knew all about the importance of keeping things in order. He was a swineherd as a child and young man in Turkey, then turned to soldiering as a profession for twenty years. Joannicius initially embraced iconoclasm, that is, the destruction and banning of religious images. It was not an unpopular view of his time; some people believed the icons violated the commandment against graven images. His beliefs had changed by the time he left the military and became first a hermit, and later a monk. At that stage of his life, Joannicius urged understanding and respect between the two different views on religious images.

Having been both an iconoclast and a man who revered icons, Joannicius was in a perfect position to attempt to bridge the chasm. Converts and reverts in particular may find Inspiration in his story as they attempt to explain why they believe what they believe—and how that changed for them.

Inspiration

My hope is the Father, my refuge is the Son, my shelter is the Holy Spirit, O Holy Trinity, glory to you. (St. Joannicius)

Challenge

Identify another faith tradition followed by a friend or acquaintance. Have a conversation about the roots of that person's belief. Establish upfront that your goal is dialogue, not an argument.

Martin de Porres

December 11, 1579–November 3, 1639

Martin's life can be summed up in a single word: healing. Suffering was something he knew well as the son of a Spanish nobleman who was not married to Martin's mother, an African/indigenous woman. Martin's father ignored Martin after he was two years old. The boy had two years of schooling, then trained in what were considered the medical arts by a barber-surgeon when he was twelve. His ethnicity prevented him from formally entering a religious community, so he became a jack-of-all-trades at a Dominican convent when he was fifteen, doing everything from barbering to cleaning. Eventually, the head of the community disregarded the law and Martin became a full member, something that was not universally welcomed by the others. He then took charge of the pharmacy, where he became known for his loving care and respect for all lives, from rats to Lima's poor and disenfranchised to his confreres.

Consider how easy it would have been for Martin to be resentful and bitter about the hand life had dealt him. Instead, he found healing in caring for others—and in his faith. Healing brought him joy—and the charism of sharing both.

Inspiration

Does anyone harbor anger against another,
   and expect healing from the Lord? (Sirach 28:3)

Challenge

Talk with a priest or other spiritual adviser about how you might be healed of a longstanding hurt, and find joy.

Charles Borromeo

October 2, 1538–November 3, 1584

Charles, born into an Italian noble family, had money. He had connections—he served in positions including secretary of state to his uncle Pope Pius IV. He was well educated, with doctorates in both civil and canon law. But it may have been his older brother's death in 1562 that took the way Charles lived his faith in a different direction. Charles was ordained in 1563, and shortly thereafter became a bishop. He would become the first archbishop of Milan to actually live in the city in eighty years, and set a breathtaking example for clergy and laity alike, giving away his income, feeding people during a famine, and nursing people during a plague. His Church reform activities were so vigorous that he was the subject of an unsuccessful assassination attempt. Charles is regarded as a key figure in the Catholic Reformation and one of the leading bishops in Church history.

Charles could have lived a very holy life in privilege and comfort. But instead, he tended directly to his flock and sought to curb Church excesses. May we have the courage to experience a little discomfort in our vocations.

Inspiration

Be sure that you first preach by the way you live. (St. Charles Borromeo)

Challenge

Crises can bring out the best or the worst in people. Journal about what you will do to ease suffering the next time your community faces a natural or manmade disaster or challenge.

Guido Maria Conforti

March 30, 1865–November 5, 1931

The life of St. Francis Xavier *(December 3)* inspired the young Italian, and he believed missionary work was in his future. But Guido's health was never good, which may be why the Jesuits and Salesians both rejected him. So he was ordained a diocesan priest in 1888, and less than ten years later had established what would become the Xaverian Missionary Fathers. Guido also served as the bishop of Ravenna, then as bishop of his hometown diocese in Parma. While he never became an overseas missionary himself, Guido visited members of his community in China three years before his death, and came home even more on fire to share the good news abroad as well as at home.

Guido learned that his vocation beyond his diocese was to prepare others to be missionaries, not to be one himself. It's a good reminder to us that teaching and training people is just what Jesus did with the apostles and others, and is a special gift.

☞ Inspiration

Every one of us should be intimately persuaded that the vocation to which we have been called could not be greater or more noble; it draws us close to Christ, the author and consummation of our faith... (St. Guido Conforti)

☞ Challenge

Do something today, small or large, to strengthen someone's desire to know and serve Christ.

Théophane Vénard

November 21, 1829-February 2, 1861

Théophane wasn't even ten years old when news came of the 1837 martyrdom in Vietnam of Father Jean-Charles Cornay. Like Jean-Charles, he became a member of the Society of Foreign Missions when he was ordained at twenty-four. Théophane initially was stationed in Hong Kong, then was sent to Vietnam. He preached publicly and in secret for eight years before he was captured. When he refused to apostatize, Théophane was kept in a small cage for weeks, then beheaded. In 1988, Théophane and Jean-Charles were both among those canonized by John Paul II *(October 22)* as martyrs of Vietnam. In turn, Théophane's story would inspire Thérèse of Lisieux to consider becoming a Carmelite missionary, though her health ultimately precluded it.

Théophane didn't know Jean-Charles, but his story inspired Théophane to become a missionary and give up his own life. In the same way, we are inspired not only by our family and friends, but by those in the Church today whose work endangers their lives or whose truth speaking holds them up to public ridicule and persecution. We don't have to know our role models personally for them to help us.

✏ Inspiration

If you see that God is calling you, and I have no doubt that you do, don't hesitate to obey! (St. Théophane Vénard)

✏ Challenge

Write a note of thanks to someone whose service encourages you to pick up your cross.

Willibrord

658-739

It would have been easy to have given up. Willibrord, born in England and educated there and in Ireland, had been leading missionary work in what is now the Netherlands for twenty-five years. But then a pagan duke conquered the area, destroying churches and generally undoing the missionaries' efforts. When the duke died three years later, Willibrord returned and redoubled his evangelization, assisted for three years by St. Boniface *(June 5)*. Willibrord is perhaps best known for the abbey he established in Echternach, Luxembourg, where he died. A "dancing saints" procession is held there each spring.

Imagine how Willibrord must have felt, leaving the Netherlands and knowing much of what he had done would be destroyed. But he knew the church is more than buildings; it is what's in people's hearts and souls, and that knowledge carried him as he undid the damage. Like Willibrord, may hope and faith triumph over despair in our lives.

Inspiration

We are afflicted in every way, but not crushed; perplexed, but not driven to despair; persecuted, but not forsaken; struck down, but not destroyed... (2 Corinthians 4:8-9)

Challenge

Believe in the joy and healing that will follow a rough spot you're going through.

Sergius of Radonezh

1314-September 25, 1392

Before Sergius came on the scene, monastic community life had not existed in Russia for nearly one hundred years due to the Tatar invasions. Sergius joined his brother, who was already a monk, in the forests not far from their home after their parents died. A few years later, he built a wooden chapel, now known as Trinity Lavra of St. Sergius, northeast of Moscow. As time went on, more and more men found the community's concept appealing; a few years later, a rule was adopted. Sergius founded a total of forty monasteries, and it is said his peacemaking abilities prevented several wars between Russian princes. The monk regarded as the St. Francis of Assisi *(October 4)* of Russia and possibly the greatest Russian saint always retained his humility; at one point, he rejected the offer of an important Church position in Moscow.

It's tempting to sigh and complain about what we don't have. Sergius's story shows us that if no formal structure exists to praise and serve God in the way we want, maybe it's time for us to do something about that.

Inspiration

Therefore prepare your minds for action; discipline yourselves; set all your hope on the grace that Jesus Christ will bring you when he is revealed. (1 Peter 1:13)

Challenge

Refrain from making "I wish" or "if only" statements today. Instead, think about "How can I?" or "what would I need to do?"

Diego of Alcalá

Circa 1400–November 12, 1463

It started out as what should have been a trip of joy and devotion. Diego, a Spanish Franciscan lay brother, was among those dispatched to Rome for the 1450 canonization of St. Bernardino of Siena *(May 20)*. Diego had recently spent four years of missionary work in the Canary Islands, and likely was looking forward to the journey for many reasons. His focus changed, however, while in Rome; a number of his confreres and others became ill and so Diego took charge of an infirmary to help nurse them back to health. After three months, he returned to Spain, and spent his remaining years in the contemplative life he so loved.

It's funny, the way we think God has placed us on a path for one reason, only to find out the purpose was something else entirely. Diego's work in the Canary Islands made him the ideal person to organize care in the emergency situation in Rome. Let's keep our eyes and hearts open to what seem to be redirections in our lives.

Inspiration

Commit your work to the Lord,

and your plans will be established. (Proverbs 16:3)

Challenge

Be open to plans B, C, and D today. After all, any one of them may be God's Plan A for you.

Leo the Great

Circa 400–November 10, 461

To Leo, unity strengthened faith. It was that simple—and that challenging. He was the first pope to call himself St. Peter's *(June 28)* heir, not his successor, and to advance the pope's authority over bishops and others. Leo, named a Doctor of the Church, also advanced doctrine including Christ's divine and human natures coexisting in one divine person. Deep thinking and administrative skills would be impressive enough charisms, but Leo also is remembered as a loving, caring shepherd to his flock; his surviving ninety-plus sermons are filled with calls for charity.

Leo's efforts to forge unity were conducted in an environment in which heresies such as Manichaeism were threatening the Church and her people. Today, unity is threatened by the temptations and judgments of the secular world. Leo's example helps us to resist the heresies that threaten to creep into our lives.

Inspiration

For no one's income is small whose heart is big, and the measure of one's mercy and goodness does not depend on the size of one's means. (St. Leo the Great)

Challenge

Examine what you are most tempted to believe because of worldly pressures that run counter to Church teachings. Some aspect of life issues might be a good place to start.

Martin of Tours

Circa 316–November 8, 397

Martin's choices in life had been limited. His parents were pagans, and his father was a Roman army officer, so of course that was the plan the family insisted he pursue. Martin had begun studying to become a Catholic but had not yet been baptized when he saw a shivering beggar. Martin ran his sword through his cloak, and gave the beggar half. A mystical experience resulted, hastening Martin's conversion. He was imprisoned for his refusal to fight; after his release, he eventually made his way to Hilary of Poitiers *(January 13)*, who ordained him and provided him with land for a hermitage. Martin continued to live as a monk throughout his twenty-five years as bishop of Tours. He is believed to be the first non-martyr the Church considers to be a saint.

Becoming a Christian freed Martin from a need to live up to the expectations of his parents or his military commanders. His story reminds us that even if people have financial control over us, it is God, not them, who we serve and who we must put first.

🐟 Inspiration

I propose to go wherever the Lord calls me. (St. Martin of Tours)

🐟 Challenge

Invite God to help you make the decision with which you've been wrestling.

Josaphat

Circa 1580–November 12, 1623

It was a time of "either/or," and Josaphat was more of a "both/and" person. Born in what is now Ukraine, this monk supported the reunion of part of the Orthodox Church with the Latin rite. However, he also stood strong in his support for acceptance of traditions in the Eastern church. Small wonder then that he encountered resistance nearly everywhere he turned. A mob supporting one of his rivals broke into the house where Josaphat was staying and shot him.

Sometimes, a willingness to hear out the other side and compromise where possible gets you in trouble, as Josaphat learned. But like him, may we hold fast to our beliefs and trust in God, regardless of pressure on us.

☙ Inspiration

Do not answer before you listen,

   and do not interrupt when another is speaking. (Sirach 11:8)

☙ Challenge

Instead of anticipating the next comment of someone with whom you disagree, listen to what the person has to say. There may be more common ground than you realize.

Homobonus

Circa 1130–1197

That his name means "good man" in Latin tells you all you need to know about this saint, who was canonized a year after his death. His death, by the way, occurred as he was prostrated in the form of a cross while he was at Mass. Homobonus was a successful cloth merchant and tailor who lavished his love and money on abandoned children, as he and his wife had none of their own. He also was known to provide wise counsel to families in trouble.

Being a "good person" means more than going to Mass. Homobonus knew that he could be helpful even in situations where he didn't have any experience, such as with children. Like him, if we reflect love and concern in such cases, the Lord will do the rest.

Inspiration

In all toil there is profit,
   but mere talk leads only to poverty. (Proverbs 14:23)

Challenge

Be a good person today. Your other "commitments" will keep. Spend fifteen minutes listening to a friend or family member's concerns.

Stanislaus Kostka

October 28, 1550–August 15, 1568

Visions associated with a serious illness convinced young Stanislaus that he was called to join the Jesuits like those who were his instructors in Vienna. Given his age and the antipathy of his politically connected Polish father, the Jesuits rejected him. Not to be deterred, Stanislaus and two companions walked hundreds of miles to Rome. After that act, the Jesuit general, Francis Borgia *(October 10)* could hardly refuse him. Stanislaus was accepted into the Society of Jesus on his seventeenth birthday, but died nine months later.

It's easy to understand Stanislaus's father's reluctance to say yes to his son's plan. He was, after all, just fourteen years old. But Stanislaus's story shows us that young people are sometimes more in tune to what God wants from them than adults might be.

☞ Inspiration

I find a heaven in the midst of saucepans and brooms. (St. Stanislaus Kostka)

☞ Challenge

Listen encouragingly to someone whose words you might typically consider with some skepticism because of their youth, their age, their education, or some other factor.

Albert the Great

Circa 1206–1280

Albert was curious, and you know what curious people do: They ask questions. They do research. And, often, they love teaching as a means of sharing what they've learned. Albert's curiosity is breathtaking. He conducted research into virtually every known natural science, outdoors and in the laboratory, and took the same considered approach to questions about the life of the Blessed Virgin, to whom he was devoted. The Dominican was a respected instructor at numerous European colleges, and one of his students, Thomas Aquinas *(January 28),* would become a close friend. Like Thomas Aquinas, Albert is a Doctor of the Church. As happens far too often, Albert's intellect failed him in his later years; he may have suffered from Alzheimer's disease.

Curiosity isn't a bad thing. Albert used his own wisely, and carefully noted what he had and had not been unable to prove. Asking questions often can lead us to a deeper understanding, not a rejection, of our faith.

✒Inspiration

It is by the path of love, which is charity that God draws close to man and man to God, but where charity is not found God cannot dwell. (St. Albert the Great)

✒Challenge

Delve into reputable videos, books, and other writings to find answers to something you don't understand about Catholicism.

Giuseppe Moscati

July 25, 1880–April 12, 1927

Perhaps it was seeing the care his beloved older brother received for serious head trauma, and the comfort that faith brought the family, that sparked Giuseppe's interest in uniting his knowledge and devotion. Giuseppe's gifts as a physician, researcher, and hospital administrator were such that the Italian army rejected his effort to enlist in World War I; the thought was that he was of much more value as a practicing doctor. He was known for his tender care, especially for those who could not afford medical assistance as well as research that helped lead to the use of insulin in treating diabetes.

The army said no to Giuseppe because his gifts were better used elsewhere. Let's remember that when our own volunteer efforts are rejected; it very well may be because God is seeking to direct our energies in other ways.

Inspiration

Remember that life is mission, it is duty, it is suffering! Every one of us must have his battle station. (St. Giuseppe Moscati)

Challenge

Pray for assistance in staffing your own "battle station" as God desires.

Hugh of Lincoln

1135–November 16, 1200

The first canonized Carthusian had an impact on the world beyond the walls of France's Grande Chartreuse monastery where he was ordained. Hugh ended up in England in 1175 to serve as abbot of England's first Carthusian monastery. Henry II had agreed to establish the monastery as part of his atonement for Thomas Becket's *(December 29)* murder, but when Hugh arrived, building had yet to begin. Hugh made a practice of building and rebuilding, whether it was the Carthusian monastery or re-establishment of discipline when he was named bishop of Lincoln, a position that had been vacant for nearly twenty years. Hugh also is remembered for denouncing the persecution of Jews in England.

As a Carthusian, Hugh's spiritual practice would have included much time for contemplation. Perhaps that time with God provided him with the words he needed to navigate conversations with Henry II and his successors.

Inspiration

When words are many, transgression is not lacking,

but the prudent are restrained in speech. (Proverbs 10:19)

Challenge

Be restrained, not reactive, in situations that are ripe for verbal confrontation.

Joseph Pignatelli

December 27, 1737–November 15, 1811

He's likely the most important Jesuit you've never heard of. Joseph faced a choice in 1767: He'd been a priest for less than five years, but for a variety of reasons, all five thousand Jesuits were being expelled from his native Spain. He and his brother could have stayed in the country—their family there was well respected—but instead chose to leave with the others. In 1773, the pope completely suppressed the society, leaving more than twenty thousand men no longer under vows. Joseph eventually ended up in Russia, which refused to enforce the suppression, and renewed his vows. Several years later, Pope Pius VII welcomed Joseph and others to Rome, where they had a teaching presence in six diocesan seminaries within six months. The Society of Jesus was fully restored three years after Joseph's death but had he not persevered between 1767 and 1811, there may have been little or nothing to restore.

During his thirty-plus years of hard work and prayer to keep the Jesuits alive, Joseph likely didn't spend much time thinking about his place in history. It's a good reminder to us to focus on the work at hand to serve God, not how others will judge or remember us.

Inspiration

The Lord's gift remains with the devout,
> and his favor brings lasting success. (Sirach 11:17)

Challenge

In your interactions with family, friends, co-workers, and others, don't think about whether your words and actions will bear fruit.

Raphael Kalinkowski

September 1, 1835–November 15, 1907

Raphael always had a strong sense of God's presence, but his road to becoming a Discalced Carmelite friar took more than forty years. Born in what is now Lithuania, he studied engineering in St. Petersburg, and rose through the ranks of the Russian army to captain. Raphael did not expect a January 1863 Polish uprising to succeed, but he resigned his army post to serve as a war minister for the effort. After it failed, he spent ten years in a Siberian labor camp, where he provided support and hope to his fellow prisoners. After his release, Raphael was prohibited from returning home and went first to Paris, then to Warsaw, then to Austria, where he was admitted to a Carmelite priory and ordained. He was known as a sensitive, devoted confessor and spiritual director.

Sometimes, we wonder about the twists and turns our lives took before we found our vocation, and worry about the time lost. Raphael's story—from engineer to military officer to prisoner—show us no time and no experience is ever wasted. Even when we get off-track, God will guide us back.

✒ Inspiration

Your way was through the sea,

    your path, through the mighty waters;

    yet your footprints were unseen. (Psalm 77:19)

✒ Challenge

Give thought to some of your biggest mistakes. How has God worked to turn them into good?

Leopold of Austria

1073–1136

It's easy to imagine a lot of joy in the home of this Austrian saint, known as Leopold the Good. He became the country's military governor at twenty-three, a post he held for forty years. He turned down an opportunity to be the Holy Roman emperor. He was the father of at least eighteen children, eleven of whom lived into adulthood. Leopold also had a strong spiritual side, endowing a number of churches and charitable causes and founding Cistercian, Augustinian, and Benedictine monasteries that exist to this day.

Leopold was a wise leader, caring for his people's spiritual and physical needs. While he supported the First Crusade, his time as ruler saw few other armed conflicts. Perhaps it's a lesson to us, that when people are respected, confrontations may be reduced or even disappear.

Inspiration

If it is possible, so far as it depends on you, live peaceably with all. (Romans 12:18)

Challenge

Make this a day of no drama. Pray for God's help in defusing the tensions in your life.

Gregory of Tours

538–594

It was fitting Gregory would spend two decades as bishop of Tours; it was a visit to St. Martin of Tours' *(November 11)* tomb that he believed cured him of an illness and set him on a path toward the religious life. His relationships with the area's rulers were not always optimal, and perhaps that's why rather than political alliances, Gregory is best known for his writings, including a biography of St. Martin and the *History of the Franks,* a well-regarded ten-volume work about France from creation to Gregory's time.

Gregory is more remembered for his books than for any accomplishments as a bishop. It's a good lesson for us, to take stock of what God's priority for us is. For example, it could be that the day job pays our bills, but our most important accomplishment is raising our family.

✒ Inspiration

Try to find out what is pleasing to the Lord. (Ephesians 5:10)

✒ Challenge

Think about your priorities for the day. Are they in harmony with God's?

Columban

Circa 543–615

In addition to a gift for evangelization, Columban had a way of getting under people's skin. Maybe the two were related. After many years as a monk, the Irishman and twelve companions in about 590 embarked to revitalize the Church in Gaul (modern-day France and parts of Belgium, Germany, and Italy). As time went on, Columban ran into trouble with the area's rulers, in part because the missionaries wouldn't recognize the local bishops' authority over them. (There were also Columban's pronouncements against the king of Burgundy's lifestyle.) The missionaries moved elsewhere, but things didn't go well there either. A few years before his death, Columban walked across the Alps to northern Italy, and was given land to establish a community at Bobbio, which still exists today.

Columban often was in conflict with secular authorities for speaking unvarnished truth to them. His life reminds us that we may be persecuted and ridiculed in Jesus's name, but that cannot prevent us from sharing his message of good news.

❧ Inspiration

For it is God's will that by doing right you should silence the ignorance of the foolish. (1 Peter 2:15)

❧ Challenge

Say something today that needs to be said.

Clement of Rome

Died circa 100

Tradition has it that Clement was baptized or ordained by St. Peter *(June 28)* himself, and was pope the final eight or so years of his life. Clement's letter to the Corinthians is regarded as one of the oldest Church documents beyond the New Testament Gospels and letters, and sets forth early papal authority to resolve disputes among local Christian communities. By legend, he was exiled to Crimea and evangelized so persuasively among fellow prisoners that he was martyred by being thrown into the sea, anchor tied around his neck.

When we follow in the footsteps in people we admire greatly—raising our children with the example of our own wonderful parents before us, or succeeding a successful boss—it can be tempting to do exactly what they did. While Clement certainly honored and abided by the apostles' teachings, with thought he also advanced the pope's role in line with those teachings. Let's remember that honoring those who taught us also can mean expanding through the Holy Spirit on what we learned.

Inspiration

Boldness, and arrogance, and confidence belong to them who are accursed of God; but moderation, humility, and meekness to those who are blessed by him. (St. Clement of Rome)

Challenge

Think about something you do in your personal or professional relationships that you learned from someone you love and respect. How can you take what you do a step further?

Andrew Dũng-Lạc

1795–December 21, 1839

Twice, Andrew had been taken into custody by the Vietnamese government and ransomed by his parishioners. The priest had even changed his name in hopes that his vocation could be lived without drawing the authorities' attention. When he was arrested a third time with another priest, he advised the faithful not to pay for his freedom. The two were beheaded, and are among the 117 clergy and laypeople martyred in Vietnam between 1625 and 1886 and canonized in 1988.

Andrew showed bravery and faith in refusing a third opportunity for freedom, knowing perhaps the weight it put on the laity and the likelihood he would only be arrested again. It's reminiscent of Jesus's surrender to the Roman soldiers who came for him. May we show the same trust in the daily sacrifices, large and small, that we face as Christians.

❧ Inspiration

O Lord, you will hear the desire of the meek;
  you will strengthen their heart, you will incline your ear
to do justice for the orphan and the oppressed,
  so that those from earth may strike terror no more. (Psalm 10:17–18)

❧ Challenge

Find the courage to surrender and be meek today.

Leonard of Port Maurice

December 20, 1676–November 26, 1751

Like so many young men, Leonard believed his vocation would lead him to China as a missionary. But after his ordination as a Franciscan priest, he developed a bleeding ulcer. His recovery took four years. It was not long after that that Leonard embarked on what would be his true calling: preaching missions throughout Italy. For forty years, laity, clergy and even popes gathered to hear his words. His missions were so popular that they sometimes lasted two weeks. But Leonard was about more than words: He also believed that exposure to the Stations of the Cross was a powerful conversion and reversion element. During his travels, he set up more than five hundred Stations across Italy, including one in Rome's Colosseum.

Leonard found his own backyard—his homeland—was fertile ground for missionary work; he didn't need to go to China. May we never forget that evangelization begins with our families and friends.

Inspiration

As for ourselves, do not let us fail to be true to God, trying to grow more and more perfect. (St. Leonard of Port Maurice)

Challenge

It's not just for Lent! Pray the Stations of the Cross today.

Humilis of Bisignano

August 26, 1582–November 26, 1637

This lay Franciscan brother had little opportunity for formal education as a child in southern Italy. But he loved attending Mass, receiving the Eucharist, and contemplating the Virgin Mary. Apparently, great devotion yielded great intellect; theologians were amazed at his deep understanding of scripture and Church doctrine, to the point that he was called upon to counsel two popes. His request to become a missionary in his late forties was denied, perhaps because his superiors knew his gifts were better used at home.

The "smartest" person in the room isn't necessarily the one with the most advanced degrees or highest IQ. Often, it's the person who listens the most, especially to God. Rocket scientists don't have any advantages over humblest of us when it comes to adoring the Father.

❧ Inspiration

"Should the wise answer with windy knowledge,
    and fill themselves with the east wind?" (Job 15:2)

❧ Challenge

Listen to what someone with less formal education has to teach you.

John Berchmans

March 13, 1599–August 13, 1621

John, the oldest of five children in a Belgian family, loved being an altar server. In fact, it wasn't unusual for him to serve at more than one Mass in a day. It probably was not a surprise that he was among the first students to enroll in a new Jesuit school. When he wrote his parents to say he wanted to become part of that community, his father encouraged him to become a Franciscan instead. Nonetheless, John became a Jesuit novice when he was seventeen. He was in Rome studying philosophy when he was struck down by a high fever and dysentery.

In some aspects, John's spirituality was similar to that of Thérèse of Lisieux, focused on finding holiness in life's small things. Both of them also heard the call to a vocation when they were young, and did not let others' efforts to dissuade them drown out God's voice. May we do the same when what God wants doesn't dovetail with what loved ones see as what is best for us.

✒ Inspiration

If I do not become a saint when I am young, I shall never become one. (St. John Berchmans)

✒ Challenge

Find holiness in the words of a young person you know.

Sylvester Gozzolini

1177–November 26, 1267

It had to come as a shock to the fifty-year-old Italian priest. Sylvester had been most respectful in his remarks about the bishop's less than Christ-like lifestyle. Respectful or not, the bishop was not pleased, to put it mildly; he threatened to revoke Sylvester's faculties. Sylvester chose instead to become a hermit; a vision of St. Benedict *(July 11)* led him to establish the Sylvestrine, or Blue, Benedictines. He led the community for the rest of his life, by some accounts building more than two dozen monasteries.

When we lose a loved one, find out we have a serious illness, become unemployed, or encounter some other challenge, it just doesn't seem right or fair. Sylvester's story reminds us depending on God rather than falling into despair and bitterness is the best way to get through the shock and sorrow.

Inspiration

"Yet God prolongs the life of the mighty by his power;
   they rise up when they despair of life." (Job 24:22)

Challenge

Just for today, don't ask God "why" about a disappointment you've recently had. Instead, pray that you will be shown how to endure it.

Stephen the Younger

Circa 714–764

Stephen had lived as a Turkish monk, including twelve years as an abbot, and then as a hermit. One might not think this would have made him of particular interest to the emperor, Constantine V, but it did. Stephen was also vocal in his opposition to the iconoclast movement of the time, and in his support of the value of the monastic life. Constantine objected to both of these views—after all, more monks meant fewer tax funds in his coffers—and imprisoned Stephen for two years. Tradition says that when he was released, Stephen compared disrespect for religious images to disrespect for coins carrying Constantine's image. For this, he died a martyr's death.

As Christians, our beliefs will be inconvenient at time to the secular world. But like Stephen, we must hold fast to what we know is true.

❧ Inspiration

"…and you will know the truth, and the truth will make you free." (John 8:32)

❧ Challenge

Pray for the strength to discern how to speak God's truth in a challenging situation.

Andrew the Apostle

First century

He was among the first to be drawn to the young rabbi. Andrew and another of John the Baptist's *(June 24)* disciples heard John refer to Jesus as "the Lamb of God," and began following him. At the end of a day with Jesus, Andrew did what many of us do when we make an amazing discovery. He went to his beloved brother to share the news of the Messiah. Andrew is regarded as part of the inner circle of apostles. It's believed that after the Resurrection, he preached in Eurasia until his own crucifixion.

Based on Biblical accounts, Andrew doesn't seem to have been concerned about his place in the pecking order of Apostles. He just loved Jesus and wanted others to meet him. We can learn from that example of putting our own interests aside so that we may grow in grace.

❧ Inspiration

One of the two who heard John speak and followed him was Andrew, Simon Peter's brother. He first found his brother Simon and said to him, "We have found the Messiah." (John 1:40-41)

❧ Challenge

Spend some time today with a sibling, blood or of the heart, talking about how you can help each other on your spiritual journeys.

Edmund Campion

January 25, 1540–December 1, 1581

Edmund addressed both Mary I of England and her half-sister, Elizabeth I. He was thirteen and a schoolboy and gave a greeting in Latin when Mary returned to London in 1553; a decade later, when Elizabeth visited Oxford, he was selected to welcome her. Initially, he embraced the Church of England, becoming a deacon and taking the oath of supremacy. But his doubts grew. Eventually, he left England and became a Jesuit priest. He and another Jesuit returned in London in June 1580. Edmund made persuasive pro-Catholic arguments in publications including *Ten Reasons* and used disguises to move about and minister to prisoners and other laity. He was arrested after about a year, and refused entreaties to denounce his faith, even amid horrific torture. He is among those canonized as the Forty Martyrs of England and Wales.

Edmund's oratory skills and personality would have meant a bright future for him as a member of the clergy in most faiths. But the more he discerned, the more Catholicism spoke to him. Let's remember his story and guard against becoming lukewarm Catholics.

✒Inspiration

The expense is reckoned, the enterprise is begun; it is of God, it cannot be withstood. So the faith was planted: so must it be restored. (St. Edmund Campion)

✒Challenge

Use your gift—speaking, listening, writing, sculpting, painting—to God's glory today.

Eligius

Circa 590–660

Eligius could see beauty in the rough. His father was a metalsmith, and recognized early on his son's gift in the same trade. Eligius would become King Clotaire II's master of the mint in Paris, where he was known for his honesty as well as his skill, once making two ornate thrones from the materials ordered for one. Upon the king's death, his son Dagobert I named Eligius his chief counselor. Eligius's fame and wealth grew, and he used much of it to ransom slaves, aid the poor, and found monasteries. After Dagobert's death, Eligius was ordained and served as the bishop of Noyon-Tournai the final twenty years of his life.

Eligius was more than a talented metalsmith. He was also good with people, and at seeing the potential in them. His story inspires us to look at others not through our own preconceptions, but through God's eyes.

✒ Inspiration

On that day the Lord their God will save them
for they are the flock of his people;
for like the jewels of a crown
they shall shine on his land. (Zechariah 9:16)

✒ Challenge

Pray for the vision to see the beauty in someone who seems to have some rough edges.

Francis Xavier

April 7, 1506–December 2, 1552

Just a week in age separated Francis and his Paris college roommate, Peter Faber *(August 3)*. Then Ignatius of Loyola *(July 31)* joined them. Ignatius was fifteen years older, and intense about living a simple life for Christ. It took Francis a while to buy into Ignatius's vision, but he eventually did, and all three were among the first seven men to take vows in the Society of Jesus, or the Jesuits. Francis's vocation as a missionary would take him thousands of miles to the Far East, evangelizing in India, Sri Lanka, Japan, and beyond. Conservatively, the work of one of the Church's greatest missionaries resulted in thirty thousand conversions. Francis became ill en route to his dream of bringing Jesus to China, and died on an island in sight of the mainland.

Perhaps Francis was an effective missionary because he had in essence been "converted" by Ignatius into an active faith life. His inner fire was just waiting for a spark. May we find a way, whether it's at home or thousands of miles away, to spark faith in others.

Inspiration

May God our Lord grant us in time the gift to perceive his holy will. (St. Francis Xavier)

Challenge

Pray for the person who put your faith life into full bloom. If that hasn't happened yet, pray for the person who will.

John Damascene

Circa 676–749

To John, religious images and icons were meant to be venerated, appreciated for the way in which their beauty might draw the viewer closer to God, who alone is worthy of worship. Just as those who couldn't read learned about God by hearing scripture and other teachings read aloud, so did images serve as a formation aid. The Syrian-born priest, who spent most of his life in a monastery near Jerusalem, was the leading force against the iconoclasm (destruction of icons) of his time, writing three discourses to explain his position. John, who is a Doctor of the Church, is also regarded as the Doctor of Christian art. In addition to his writings on icons and theological issues, including the Blessed Virgin's Assumption, John wrote hymns and poetry.

Imagine a world without Michelangelo's Sistine Chapel, without Raphael's Madonnas. John's strong, reasoned explanations were key to iconoclasm's ultimate defeat. Let's keep the struggle in mind as we savor the experience of God through the arts.

Inspiration

The one who seeks God continually will find him, for God is in everything. (St. John Damascene)

Challenge

Find God today in an art form—music, sculpture, painting, literature.

Giovanni Calabria

October 8, 1873–December 4, 1954

Giovanni, an Italian seminarian, had finished calls at the local hospital when he saw the child on his doorstep. The little boy said he had run away after being physically abused. Perhaps something about the boy reminded Giovanni of himself; the youngest of seven children, he had had little formal schooling after losing his father. Giovanni's response wasn't to find a few coins for the boy, but to welcome him in. He spent the rest of his life welcoming in people—in his own home or in the homes and hospitals established by the congregations he founded, the Congregation of the Poor Servants of Divine Providence and a like community for women. Giovanni also is known for the letters, written in Latin, that he and C.S. Lewis exchanged on Christian unity in the final seven years of Giovanni's life.

It may be that our hearts and souls open just a bit more widely for those who are going through something we have—divorce, cancer, perhaps the loss of a child. Like Giovanni, let's provide more than funding for ministries that strike a chord with our own stories.

❧ Inspiration

"Whoever welcomes one such child in my name welcomes me." (Matthew 18:5)

❧ Challenge

Pray for a way to help someone who's navigating a situation you've lived through.

Nicholas of Myra

Died circa 350

Nicholas, the bishop of Myra, Turkey, gave gifts that were more lasting than the kind we find under the Christmas tree. He gave two years of his life for his faith during the Diocletian persecutions. He gave his voice at the Council of Nicaea in decrying Arianism, which challenged Jesus's codivinity with God the Father. While tradition tells us he was also a charitable, pious man, the gift-giving traditions around Nicholas's name did not begin until several hundred years after his death.

Who doesn't like the idea of jolly old St. Nicholas, the plump man with white hair wearing a red suit? But our appreciation for him deepens when we consider the facts of his life, just as our faith deepens when we explore the mystery of God the Father as something beyond an old man with white hair in the clouds.

Inspiration

"God is spirit, and those who worship him must worship in spirit and truth." (John 4:24)

Challenge

Consider sharing Nicholas's true gifts this Advent.

Ambrose

Circa 340–April 4, 397

Conflict was boiling over in Milan between the orthodox Christians and the Arians, who held that Jesus, while great, was not equal to God the Father. The sitting bishop, who was an Arian, had died, and those on both sides wanted the next bishop to reflect their beliefs. Enter Ambrose, the provincial governor, who tried to calm the crowds. Instead, this man, trained as an attorney who considered himself Christian but as yet hadn't been baptized, became bishop, almost by public acclamation! Ambrose was reluctant to say yes, but when he did, he was all in. He gave away his wealth, and proceeded to preach and write about the Church's supremacy over the state in religious matters and its responsibility for morality. Some—but far from all—of Ambrose's writings, especially those regarding Jews, remain controversial today. Besides his writings, which resulted in his declaration as a Doctor of the Church, he is best known as the priest involved in St. Augustine's conversion and who baptized Augustine.

We've all ended up with responsibilities we didn't ask for and perhaps didn't want. But as Ambrose found, God has a way of sustaining and inspiring us in those cases where we feel woefully ill equipped to do what's needed.

Inspiration

The earth belongs to all, not to the rich only. (St. Ambrose)

Challenge

Say yes to God in a situation where you know you are unqualified.

Abraham of Kratia

Circa 474–558

Some saints offered up their worldly freedom through imprisonment. Abraham offered his up in being with people. Raiding nomads meant an end to this Syrian monk's first community. He and another monk relocated to the Constantinople (now Istanbul) area, and there Abraham became in essence the finance manager for a monastery. Just a few years later, he became abbot of a community on Turkey's Black Sea coast. Ten years was enough for Abraham, and he went back into solitude. However, his bishop located him and made him come back—and then Abraham found himself as bishop shortly thereafter! He carried out the post's responsibilities faithfully for thirteen years, then in about 525, finally was able to regain the solitude he craved.

Especially at this time of year, we can sympathize with Abraham. People want so much of our time and attention. That can be invigorating—but it's also draining. Let's remember that pleasing God is more important than pleasing people, even those we love dearly.

Inspiration

For God alone my soul waits in silence,

for my hope is from him. (Psalm 62:5)

Challenge

Resolve to say no to one party or other invitation between now and Christmas—and to spend that time in silence.

Juan Diego

1474–1548

Juan Diego was running late for Mass on December 9. But as he approached Guadalupe's Tepeyac hill, he heard sweet music, then a voice calling his name, then a beautiful woman he recognized as the Blessed Virgin. She asked him to have a chapel built for her. His bishop was skeptical. When Juan saw Mary again the next day, she said she would provide the bishop with proof. But Juan was unable to come on that day; his uncle, who was like a father to him, was seriously ill. When he returned on December 12, Mary said she would heal his uncle, and told him to pick flowers from the hill—typically, an impossibility in the arid area in December—to take to the bishop. When Juan reached the bishop, the cloak in which he carried the flowers showed an imprint of Mary's face. The church was built within a year.

The Americas' first canonized indigenous saint recognized that listening to the lady was even more important than Mass. He reminds us to keep our ears attuned to God rather than keeping our eyes on the clock.

✒ Inspiration

"Much deeper than the 'exterior grace' of having been 'chosen' as Our Lady's 'messenger,' Juan Diego received the grace of interior enlightenment and from that moment, he began a life dedicated to prayer and the practice of virtue and boundless love of God and neighbor." (Vatican biography)

✒ Challenge

Take off your watch and turn off your phone as you pray today. The Lord will let you know when that time together is finished.

Peter Fourier

November 30, 1565–December 9, 1640

The thirty-two-year-old Augustinian had his choice of three assignments. Two of them offered some familiarity; either family members or mentors were nearby. The third was in Mattaincourt, a hilly area of northeast France where Calvinists were gaining ground. Peter chose Mattaincourt, and would stay there for thirty years. He brought free education to the region's poor children and with (Blessed) Alix LeClerc, established an institute of women religious now known as the community of Notre Dame Sisters.

Peter knew going to Mattaincourt would be more challenging that either of the other clerical opportunities he had. But the easy way out is seldom what God desires for us.

✒ Inspiration

Those who trust in him will understand truth, and the faithful will abide with him in love, because grace and mercy are upon his only ones, and he watches over his elect. (Wisdom 3:9)

✒ Challenge

Don't rush to make a decision that your head says is a no-brainer, but doesn't sit right with your soul. Pray for guidance.

Gregory III

Died November 28, 741

The burning issue of the day was religious icons, paintings, and other images. Iconoclasts, including Emperor Leo III, advocated destroying them. The Church—including the new pope, Gregory III—saw them as a means of drawing closer to God. The issue was so important that Gregory convened a synod on the topic just months after he became pope. To make his position even clearer, Gregory did more than talk and negotiate. He added a wall of icons and paintings at St. Peter's Basilica along with new statues. Besides his strong stand against iconoclasm, Gregory is remembered as the last non-European pope before Pope Francis.

Actions speak louder than words. If people wondered how serious Gregory was about fighting iconoclasm, all they had to do was go to St. Peter's. It's a good reminder to show our faith in the way we interact with others, not only by what we say.

Inspiration

"Take action, for it is your duty, and we are with you; be strong, and do it." (Ezra 10:4)

Challenge

Show your faith today. Some ways might include being patient or non-judgmental. If you're looking for something more tangible, wear a crucifix necklace, a rosary bracelet, or a scapular.

Finnian of Clonard

Circa 470–549

Finnian started out life in Ireland's County Carlow, but his studies took him far, possibly including France, England, and Wales. He had considered a trip to Rome as well before his twenty years of travel ended, but instead ended up back in Ireland. Finnian began establishing monasteries and schools, most notably Clonard in County Meath—just two counties away from where he grew up. At Clonard monastery, thousands of students were prepared for evangelization, including the group referred to as the Twelve Apostles of Ireland.

Finnian logged thousands of miles to prepare himself as a teacher. It's somehow fitting that his students also traveled many miles, most of them to bring Christ to their native Ireland. Never discount the value of catechesis, especially in your own backyard.

Inspiration

"A disciple is not above the teacher, nor a slave above the master; it is enough for the disciple to be like the teacher, and the slave like the master." (Matthew 10:24-25)

Challenge

Teach people about Jesus today in your conversations. Refrain from gossiping and complaining.

Nimatullah Kassab

1808–December 14, 1858

Nimatullah knew what he was good at—and what he was not. The Lebanese Marionite monk was a skilled bookbinder for his community, a craft he had learned from his own father. He was a valued instructor whose students included St. Charbel Makhlouf *(July 24)*. He was noted for his piety, in particular his devotion to the Blessed Virgin and the Eucharist. But Nimatullah knew he was not an administrator. When his name was floated as a candidate for general of his order—he had served three terms as assistant general—he said death would be preferable. His community got the message, and selected someone else.

Nimatullah was humble but confident about his gifts, and knew his shortcomings. It wasn't false humility that caused him to make that statement about becoming the order's leader. We've all been in organizations where others have decided it's our turn to lead, and we know in our souls it's not where we're called. It takes courage to say no.

✒ Inspiration

When pride comes, then comes disgrace;

but wisdom is with the humble. (Proverbs 11:2)

✒ Challenge

Compliment someone who excels at something that is not your gift. Don't make the compliment about your own inadequacies.

John of the Cross

June 24, 1542–December 14, 1591

John was good at caring for the sick. He'd been such a gentle nurse's assistant that the hospital director encouraged him to study to become a chaplain. John chose instead to become a Carmelite priest, but almost as soon as he was ordained, he began thinking that life with the Carthusians would be better for him. Enter Teresa of Ávila, who was embarking on her own effort to reform the Carmelites and take them back to their roots. She invited John to join her in the effort. It was not long thereafter that he and four others opened a Discalced Carmelite community for men; a few years later, he became the spiritual director for Teresa's Convent of the Incarnation. When John refused to abandon the reformation efforts, he was imprisoned for nine months, during which time he wrote *Dark Night of the Soul*. For this book and his other writings, John was named a Doctor of the Church in 1926.

John healed with his hands, his words, and his faith-filled courage. Dark nights will come to us all; patience and trust, as John articulated so beautifully, will carry us forward.

✍ Inspiration

God leads into the dark night those whom He desires to purify from all these imperfections so that He may bring them farther onward. (St. John of the Cross)

✍ Challenge

If you're going through a dark night, consider reading John's masterpiece. If you're not, pray for those who are.

Paul of Latros

Died circa 956

Paul's mother had recently died, and it seems not unusual that his older brother Basil wanted Paul to join him in a monastery. Their father, a military officer, had been killed in battle some time earlier. However, the Turkish villagers would have none of that. Was it because they didn't think Paul was cut out for a monk's life, or because he was such a good swineherd? We don't know. But finally, after three attempts, Paul was able to leave town and join Basil. Paul spent the rest of his life as either a monk or a hermit; his holiness was so apparent that even when he retreated to a cave, a community grew around him.

As far as we know, the villagers had no real power over Paul's comings and goings, just strong opinions. Some of the people in our lives have strong opinions about what we should be doing as well. While we should listen respectfully, it never works out when we listen to others more than God.

Inspiration

Commit your work to the Lord,

and your plans will be established. (Proverbs 16:3)

Challenge

Pray for ways to stand strong against those who want to take over directing your life.

John of Matha

June 23, 1160–December 17, 1213

Any priest's first Mass is special, but John's changed his life. He had received his vocation relatively late and was ordained at age thirty-seven. As he celebrated in the Paris bishop's chapel, he saw an angel touch the heads of two enslaved people. John knew God was calling him to ransom Christians. The practice of enslaving Christians during raids in North Africa, Sicily, southern France, and parts of Spain was not unusual at that time. Through his Order of the Most Holy Trinity, or Trinitarians, hundreds of Christians were freed during John's lifetime.

Few of us will ever have the opportunity to free enslaved people with money. But we can secure the freedom of the evil's captives with prayer and other interventions. Remember, the chains of slavery are not always visible.

Inspiration

"So if the Son makes you free, you will be free indeed." (John 8:36)

Challenge

Pray for someone you know who needs to be freed of the chains of evil.

Lazarus of Bethany

1st century

Jesus loved Lazarus. We know that, because the Gospel tells us. They were good enough friends that he dined with Lazarus and his sisters— and Jesus's most jaw-dropping miracle while on earth involved raising his friend from the dead after four days. What happened to Lazarus after he was raised to life is not known; tradition tells us he may have been martyred, served as a bishop, or gone to Syria.

The raising of Lazarus may have been the last straw for the religious authorities; more miracles like that would destroy the delicate political balance in the region, they believed. They failed to recognize the Messiah in their midst. Let's not make the same mistake.

Inspiration

So the sisters sent a message to Jesus, "Lord, he whom you love is ill." But when Jesus heard it, he said, "This illness does not lead to death; rather it is for God's glory so that the Son of God may be glorified through it." (John 11:3-4)

Challenge

If you're grieving, take a moment to offer up your pain. If you're not, pray for faith for someone who is.

Winebald

Died December 18, 761

An invitation changed Winebald's life. He, his father, and brother Willibald were on pilgrimage to Rome and the Holy Land when the father died. The brothers got to Rome, then Winebald's precarious health meant Willibald went on by himself. Rome suited Winebald; he studied for seven years and became a monk at the nearby Montecassino Benedictine abbey. But in about 737, St. Boniface *(June 5)*, a relative, convinced Winebald and Willibald to join a group of English missionaries he was putting together to evangelize Germany. Winebald's accomplishments there included establishment of a double monastery at Heidenheim, where he served as abbot and his sister (St.) Walburga as abbess.

Winebald might have lived a very happy life if he had stayed at the Rome abbey. Saying yes to Boniface and God meant uprooting himself from a comfortable situation to bring Jesus to people who hadn't heard of him. Let's remember his story when God's call puts us out of our comfort zone.

❧ Inspiration

Every generous act of giving, with every perfect gift, is from above, coming down from the Father of lights, with whom there is no variation or shadow due to change. (James 1:17)

❧ Challenge

Pray for the faith to embrace what you see as a big change.

José Manyanet i Vives

January 7, 1833-December 17, 1901

José had experienced family tragedy—but also gritty family strength. He was the ninth child born to his Spanish parents, and his father died before José was two years old. Rather than send any of the children to live with relatives, his mother carefully managed what she had, selling and selling farmland so her family could stay together. She died two years before José's ordination in 1859. After serving for twelve years as his bishop's private secretary and other administrative roles, José received permission to found the Sons of the Holy Family Jesus, Mary, and Joseph and later a similar community for women religious. Both communities continue to work today to enhance the Christian formation of families.

Families were under attack in José's time by war and sectarianism. They are under attack today as well. Whether our family consists of blood relatives or a group of friends brought together as a family by choice, we know that the family is at the center of our faith life and must be preserved.

✐ Inspiration

"The Christian family constitutes a specific revelation and realization of ecclesial communion, and for this reason it can and should be called a *domestic church.*" (*Catechism of the Catholic Church*, 2204)

✐ Challenge

Pray for (and if possible, with) your family.

Dominic of Silos

1000–December 20, 1073

St. Sebastian of Silos monastery in northern Spain had seen better days. It was in physical and spiritual disrepair when Dominic and two companions arrived in 1041. Only six other monks remained. They had to make the best of the situation, having been exiled from their previous home a hundred miles away over a land dispute. And make the best of it they did; St. Sebastian became one of the most famous monasteries in the country. It was so famous that long after Dominic of Silos's death, St. Joan of Aza made a pilgrimage to seek his intervention in having a second son. When he arrived, she named him Dominic *(August 8).*

Dominic of Silos must have been a visionary or extremely confident in God, given the speed with which he brought the monastery back to life. His story reminds us that with God's help, anything is possible.

Inspiration

But Jesus looked at them and said, "For mortals it is impossible, but for God all things are possible." (Matthew 19:26)

Challenge

Undertake that home improvement or personal improvement project you've been putting off; pray first.

Peter Canisius

May 8, 1521–December 21, 1597

It started with an Ignatian retreat—given by Peter Faber *(August 3),* one of the Society of Jesus founders. Peter Canisius, a Dutch aristocrat, had already earned a master's degree and was studying canon law. What he learned through the spiritual exercises resonated deeply with him, and in September 1549, he professed as a Jesuit. Peter would spend most of the next thirty years in Germany, a leading voice for Catholicism (indeed, he's been called the second apostle of Germany, after Boniface *(June 5)).* His final seventeen years were spent in Switzerland, where he founded Fribourg University. Peter, a Doctor of the Church, is known for his prolific writing, including lives of saints; scriptural discourses; and a catechism, translated into fifteen languages, that had two hundred editions and was used for more than three hundred years.

Retreats are wonderful things, virtual or in-person. They deepen our relationship with God by taking us out of the day to day and into holy space. Let's follow Peter's example and make time for a spiritual getaway.

Inspiration

My people will abide in a peaceful habitation,

in secure dwellings, and in quiet resting places. (Isaiah 32:18)

Challenge

Pledge to give yourself the gift of a retreat, do-it-yourself or guided, next year.

Dagobert II

Circa 650–679

The intrigue in what was called Austrasia—parts of what today is France, Germany, the Netherlands, and Luxembourg—was thick. Dagobert fled to Ireland and later England when his father died; his guardian decided to put his own son on the throne. The exiled ruler seemed to settle into his new life well; he married and had children, and developed a friendship with the bishop of York. However, Dagobert was recalled to Austrasia after the sitting king died; Dagobert himself died while hunting four years later. Despite the murkiness of the situation, he is regarded as a martyr.

Dagobert's established life in England sounds pretty good, but his demise is a reminder that the desire for power is a temptation of the devil. Let's be happy with what God provides.

ᕲ Inspiration

Your throne, O God, endures forever and ever. (Psalm 45:6)

ᕲ Challenge

Give thanks for all God has given you. Don't ask for another thing, tangible or intangible, today.

John of Kanty

June 23, 1390–December 24, 1473

John's rise had been impressive. His scholarship at his Polish college had been so obvious that he became a lecturer on scripture soon after his graduation and ordination. His preaching also drew rave reviews. Everything changed when John was forty-one, and some jealous colleagues manufactured a path to have him ousted. Suddenly, he found himself assigned to a small parish thirty miles away. But John didn't turn bitter or wrathful. Instead, he treated this new assignment with the same humility as he had handled his university role. It was only a few years before he was back at the university in Kraków as the theology chair.

John's grace in accepting his temporary reassignment inspires us to show the same humility when people start spurious rumors about us. Even if we are never vindicated here on earth, God knows the truth.

✎ Inspiration

Fight all error, but do it with good humor, patience, kindness, and love. Harshness will damage your own soul and spoil the best cause. (St. John of Kanty)

✎ Challenge

Pray intentionally for the private intentions of someone who has wronged you intentionally.

Thorlak

1133–December 23, 1193

Today we hear about "best practices" for just about everything business-related. You might say Thorlak was invested in finding best practices for Catholics in his native Iceland. He became a deacon at fifteen, and was ordained three years later. But instead of taking on a parish immediately, he went for further studies in France and England. When he returned home in his early thirties, he founded a monastery and became its abbot. At forty-three, he became one of his country's two bishops, and rattled a few cages by insisting on financial independence for churches and battling lax clerical discipline.

Some of the changes Thorlak advocated didn't sit well with people. But his reforms were based on those he had seen in place during his studies. His example shows us that faith isn't a popularity contest; it's about pleasing God.

☙ Inspiration

So whether we are at home or away, we make it our aim to please him. (2 Corinthians 5:9)

☙ Challenge

Think about your personal faith "best practices." Is it time for a refresher course?

Peter Nolasco

Circa 1189–1256

On the day that Jesus was born to ransom us, it's fitting to consider a saint who spent his life ransoming Christians. Peter came of age during a time when Muslims were in control of much of Spain, and some found it profitable to conduct sea raids and capture and imprison Christians in north Africa and Grenada. He was exposed to this activity on business trips, and quickly spent his inheritance ransoming Christians. Peter founded in 1218 the Order of the Blessed Virgin Mary of Mercy, or Mercedians. In addition to traditional vows, Mercedians agree to give up their lives if necessary to save souls. About 2,700 prisoners were ransomed during his life; today, the Mercedians continue his work among imprisoned souls such as people who are drug addicts or incarcerated.

Jesus was on a mission like no other. But the stories of Peter and other saints remind us there is still plenty for us to do to bring him to the world, especially among those who lack faith and hope.

✒ Inspiration

But the angel said to them, "Do not be afraid; for see—I am bringing you good news of great joy for all the people; to you is born this day in the city of David a Saviour, who is the Messiah, the Lord." (Luke 2:10-11)

✒ Challenge

Rejoice in the birth of him who brought freedom to the world.

Stephen

Died circa 34

Stephen knew how the crowd wanted it to end—with his anguished cries and sobbing and moaning. They weren't believers in Jesus, and they certainly hadn't appreciated his criticism of them. He knew they were going to take some cold satisfaction in watching him suffer in the thirty minutes or more that stonings took. But he didn't care. The Lord had given him words, and he had said them. Leave it to God to cheat those who hated Stephen by showing his faithful servant a glimpse of the glory to come—and take Stephen's spirit before the stoning began.

Some people call them Godwinks, some call them Godincidences. Our glimpses may not be as dramatic as Stephen's or the visions that some have received throughout the ages. But if we keep our eyes on God, he will show us comfort in the most difficult of circumstances.

Inspiration

"Look," he said, "I see the heavens opened and the Son of Man standing at the right hand of God!" (Acts 7:56)

Challenge

Keep your eyes open today for God's special signs of love.

John the Apostle

Circa 6–100

John was the youngest of the apostles, most likely younger than Jesus was when his public ministry began. But at the crucifixion, the older men, including Peter *(June 28)* and John's brother James *(July 25)*, were nowhere to be found. Near death, Jesus showed his confidence in John, turning over care of his grieving mother to her. Tradition has it that John cared for Mary until her assumption, and is the only one of the twelve to die of natural causes.

John may have been young, but his faith and trust continue to inspire us two thousand years later. His strength in staying with Jesus even when more cautious people fled, fearful for their own safety, serves as an example to us in a world where we are ridiculed for being followers of Christ.

Inspiration

Then he said to the disciple, "Here is your mother." And from that hour the disciple took her into his own home. (John 19:27)

Challenge

Do something dangerous for Jesus today. Offer to pray for a nonbeliever, or stand up for Church teachings in a conversation about a hot-button issue such as immigration, abortion, or capital punishment.

Gaspar del Bufalo

January 6, 1786–December 28, 1837

Gaspar knew what it was like to feel lonely and like an outcast. This Italian priest, ordained in 1808, like others was asked to take an oath of fidelity to Napoleon, and refused, as per the pope. Gaspar spent four years in prison or in exile as a result of his faith-filled obedience. It was during this time that devotion to the Precious Blood of Jesus, sustained him. After Napoleon was out of power, Gaspar returned to Rome. He considered becoming a Jesuit, but instead became the founder of the Missionaries of the Precious Blood, who continue today to provide healing in situations of disharmony in homes, workplaces, and beyond.

It's not really surprising that Gaspar was called to form this community, given how much of a comfort the Precious Blood provided for him in times of distress. Novenas, adoration, scapulars, and praying with the saints are all practices that can help us deepen our faith.

✒ Inspiration

Then he took a cup, and after giving thanks he gave it to them, saying, "Drink from it, all of you; for this is my blood of the covenant, which is poured out for many for the forgiveness of sins." (Matthew 26:27-29)

✒ Challenge

Explore a devotion that hasn't been a mainstay for you to date.

Thomas Becket

Circa 1119–December 29, 1170

Thomas managed to work himself up from being a clerk to a position in the archbishop of Canterbury's household, to archdeacon, to lord chancellor for England's Henry II. He warned Henry not to name him as the archbishop of Canterbury. But Henry did anyway, likely assuming Thomas would yield to his authority. Thomas was ordained a priest one day and consecrated as archbishop the next. And his prediction proved true, and fatal. Thomas refused to go along with plans to give the state some clerical authorities. When three other bishops crowned Henry's son as "junior king," Thomas excommunicated the trio. After Henry expressed frustration, a group of knights brutally murdered Thomas. He was canonized by Pope Alexander III less than two years later.

Regardless of how long we've settled for going through the motions of faith, it is never too late to open our souls and hearts to God. It's much easier to live as a sycophant or wily politician, but the ultimate reward is worth the price.

✒ Inspiration

All saints give testimony to the truth that without real effort, no one ever wins the crown. (St. Thomas Becket)

✒ Challenge

Take a look at the people outside your family with whom you spend time. Identify those who expect you to go along with them without questioning. Prune where needed.

Egwin

Died December 30, 717

Egwin had become a monk as a youth and then after several years, served as an adviser to a central England ruler. That may have paved the way for his consecration as the bishop of Worcester about 692. Egwin apparently was surprised by the lack of discipline among the clergy, and a priest complained to the archbishop of Canterbury about his severity. (Priestly celibacy and marriage seem to have been among the issues.) He went to Rome and successfully defended himself. When he returned, he had a vision of Mary that led him to found the Evesham monastery, where he returned to his religious roots and became abbot.

It's a tough situation, when you believe you're doing the right thing, as Egwin did, and you don't get support from your boss or your family or friends. Constructive criticism can help us identify ways to handle situations better, but it's important not to become a people-pleaser at the expense of being a God-pleaser.

Inspiration

" and you will be hated by all because of my name. But the one who endures to the end will be saved." (Matthew 10:22)

Challenge

The next time someone tells you you're too strict or too lax, too judgey or too lenient, take it to prayer for the Almighty's opinion.

Sylvester I

Died 335

Sylvester I was one of the longest-serving popes—twenty-one years—and yet we know little about his accomplishments or failures. Perhaps it's because he grew up in Rome during severe persecution of Christians; it was not until the year before he became pope that there was agreement to tolerate religion in the empire. Sylvester's life experience may have been behind what appears to have been a willingness to let Constantine drive such memorable events as the first ecumenical council at Nicaea.

Sylvester's papacy appears to have been passive, other than the construction of many churches including St. Peter and St. John Lateran. But perhaps his approach was correct for the time. When God directs us to be cautious and move slowly amid change, we do well to listen.

Inspiration

"Listen carefully to my words,

and let this be your consolation." (Job 21:2)

Challenge

Today's the day many people make resolutions for the coming year. Consider including fewer snap judgments and more compassion in yours.

Franciscan Media is a nonprofit ministry of the Franciscan Friars of St. John the Baptist Province. Through the publication of spiritual books, *St. Anthony Messenger* magazine, and online media properties such as *Saint of the Day, Minute Meditations,* and *Faith & Family,* Franciscan Media seeks to share God's love in the spirit of St. Francis of Assisi. For more information, to support us, and to purchase our products, visit franciscanmedia.org.

Live in love. Grow in faith.

ABOUT THE AUTHOR

Melanie Rigney loves almost nothing better than listening to the saints and sharing their stories. In addition to *Brotherhood of Saints* (and *Sisterhood of Saints*), her books include *Radical Saints: 21 Women for the 21st Century* and *Blessed Are You: Finding Inspiration from Our Sisters in Faith* (both Franciscan Media). She also writes for *Living Faith*, CatholicMom, and other Catholic blogs and publications. Learn more about Melanie at www.rejoicebeglad.com.